Debbie Mumm's
Quick Country
QUILTS
FOR EVERY ROOM

Wall Quilts, Bed Quilts, and Coordinating
Accessories Using Easy, Timesaving Techniques

Rodale Press, Inc.
Emmaus, Pennsylvania

OUR PURPOSE

"We inspire and enable people to improve their lives and the world around them."

©1998 by Debbie Mumm

Step-by-Step and Technique Illustrations ©1998 by Sandy Freeman
Photographs ©1998 by Barros & Barros

Printed in the United States of America on acid-free ∞, recycled ♻ paper.

We're always happy to hear from you. For questions or comments concerning the editorial content of this book, please write to:

Rodale Press, Inc.
Book Readers' Service
33 East Minor Street
Emmaus, PA 18098

Look for other Rodale books wherever books are sold. Or call us at (800) 848-4735.
For more information about Rodale Press and the books and magazines we publish, visit our World Wide Web site at: **http://www.rodalepress.com**

Cover Quilts and Projects: On the table is the Apple Table Quilt (page 56). The Apple Valance (page 71) is hanging in the window. Below the window are the Piney Woods Quilt (page 119), the Four-Apple Quilt (page 63), and the Watering Can Wallhanging (page 101). Draped from the basket is the Cabin-in-the-Pines Quilt (page 130).

Editor: Ellen Pahl
Interior Designer: Carol Angstadt
Assistant Designer: Nancy Smola Biltcliff
Cover Designers: Carol Angstadt and Nancy Smola Biltcliff
Watercolor Illustrations and Box Logos: Debbie Mumm
Interior Illustrator: Sandy Freeman
Cover and Interior Photographer: Barros & Barros
Interior Photo Art Directors and Stylists: Debbie Mumm and Marcia Smith
Cover Photo Stylist: Lois Hansen
Photography Editor: James A. Gallucci
Layout Designer: Dale Mack
Copy Editors: Patricia A. Sinnott and Jennifer Hornsby
Manufacturing Coordinator: Patrick T. Smith
Indexer: Nanette Bendyna
Editorial Assistance: Jodi Guiducci

Rodale Home and Garden Books
Vice President and Editorial Director: Margaret J. Lydic
Managing Editor, Quilt Books: Suzanne Nelson
Director of Design and Production: Michael Ward
Associate Art Director: Carol Angstadt
Studio Manager: Leslie M. Keefe
Copy Director: Dolores Plikaitis
Book Manufacturing Director: Helen Clogston
Office Manager: Karen Earl-Braymer

Mumm's The Word Staff
Project Directions: Kelly Fisher, Jodi Gosse, and Geri Zimmer
Seamstress: Candy Huddleston
Art Director: Marcia Smith
Art Studio Assistant: Jackie Saling
Artist: Lou McKee

Library of Congress Cataloging-in-Publication Data

Mumm, Debbie.
    Debbie Mumm's quick country quilts for every room : wall quilts, bed quilts, and dozens of coordinating accessories for you to make / by Debbie Mumm.
        p.   cm.
    Includes bibliographical references and index.
    ISBN 0–87596–775–2   (hardcover)
    1. Patchwork.   2. Appliqué.   3. Quilts.
4. Quilted goods.   I. Title.   II. Title: Quick country quilts for every room
TT835.M825   1998
746.46″041—ddc21   98–8914

Distributed in the book trade by St. Martin's Press

2 4 6 8 10 9 7 5 3   hardcover

In loving memory
of my father,
Richard L. E. Kvare

CONTENTS

INTRODUCTION

I am stating the obvious when I say that I love decorating with quilts! Doing this book has been a wonderful experience—I have enjoyed creating the room settings to go along with the quilt projects that I designed. This really shows off how beautiful the projects can look in your home.

I enjoy many different styles of decorating, and I love themes. It was fun to pick themes that would match up well with a room and inspire a variety of project ideas. Of course, there were always many more project ideas than we could fit in the book! By redecorating and showcasing some of the rooms in my own home, I was able to have free reign to take a theme as far as I wanted.

A definite highlight was designing the romantic renaissance environment in my bedroom—a fun departure from my typical country style. The process was certainly challenging, but the results were stunning. I love to see the astonished looks on the faces of friends when I show them the room. They feel as if they have walked into another world. It was also satisfying to use my home-decorator fabrics to create this fusion of classic and country looks.

Another high point of the book was planning, sketching, and painting the pages for "Country Decorating with Debbie Mumm." This special section is a visual interpretation of favorite decorating ideas culled from a notebook that I kept for more than a year. As I planned how to translate my notes and inspirations into watercolor illustrations, I always kept in mind that I wanted this section to be visually fun while providing useful tips and ideas to spark your imagination. This entire process involved a great deal of planning and coordination, but ultimately, it became what I had envisioned. I am very pleased with the results, and I hope you enjoy looking at the pages as much as I enjoyed painting them.

The process of doing this book has given me plenty of insights into decorating and redecorating. Here are my tips.

Debbie's Decorating Checklist

✓ Pick a room. Focus on one room at a time.

✓ Scour decorating books and magazines for inspiration. Start a scrapbook for all your clippings, notes, and thoughts.

✓ Choose a theme and a color scheme.

✓ Do a brainstorming of ideas. Rally your creative friends for ideas and help.

✓ Estimate the costs and develop a budget.

✓ Hold a yard sale to get rid of the old and raise money for the new.

✓ Look for refurbishing possibilities—chairs and sofas to be reupholstered, furniture to be painted.

✓ Start the hunt for accessories to carry out your theme. Hit the flea markets and thrift stores first for frugal finds. Then move on to antique stores, catalogs, craft shows, gift shops, and interior design stores.

✓ Decide on wall treatments. Some options include fresh paint, faux or sponge texturing, wallpaper, and stenciled borders.

✓ Consider your floors. Look for a new area rug or a painted floor cloth. Maybe the hardwood floors are ready for refinishing.

✓ Select three or four fabrics in a variety of scales and textures for window treatments and room accessories.

✓ Choose a design or pattern for a quilt to hang or drape.

✓ Come up with a schedule and get started. Do the walls first, floors next, and then furniture, windows, and accessories.

Remember that it usually takes a little longer and costs a little more than you plan on. Ouch!

Whatever you choose to do, have fun and try not to get stressed out about the process!

I designed the quilts and projects in this book around room themes, but most of them can be mixed and matched or used in other rooms. This is the first time that I have included bed quilts, and that was a welcome change of pace for me. Now you can get a total look for a room all in one book. To get inspiration, study the photos. There are plenty of accessories and ideas that you can apply to decorating your own home.

As you thumb through the book, you'll see a "Weekender" stamp on some of the project photos. These are especially suited to start and finish in a weekend. You'll also notice I've scattered tips of all kinds throughout the pages. Be sure to look for these box logos.

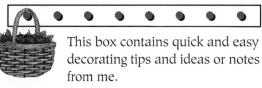

This box contains quick and easy decorating tips and ideas or notes from me.

Look for creative options and suggestions for varying the basic projects in these boxes.

This is the cue that you'll find an important helpful hint for making the project here.

I hope you have fun making the quilts and displaying them in your home. Happy Quilting and Happy Decorating!

Debbie Mumm

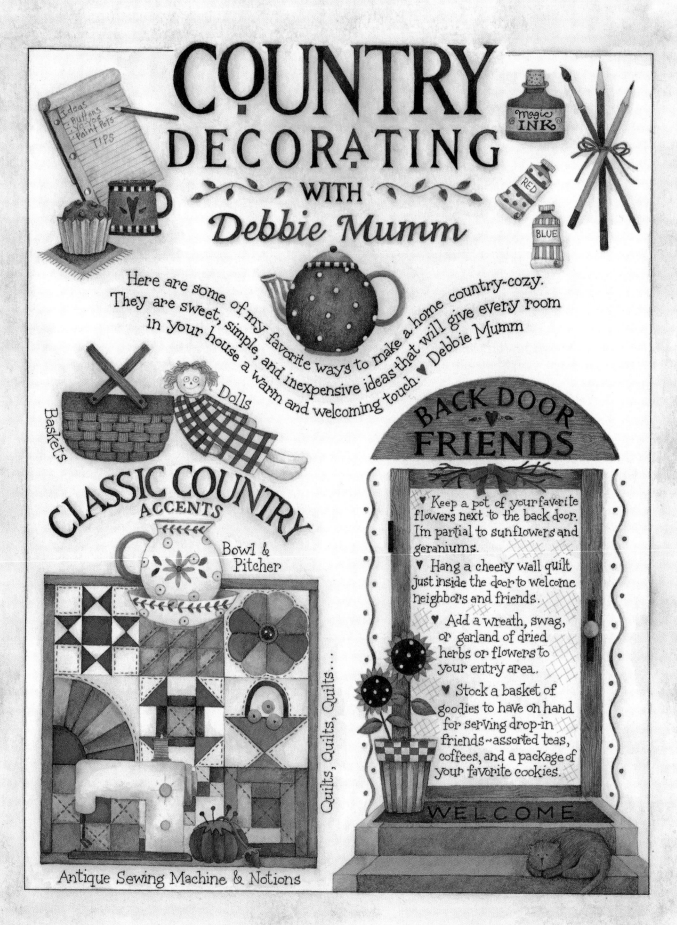

COUNTRY DECORATING
WITH
Debbie Mumm

Here are some of my favorite ways to make a home country-cozy. They are sweet, simple, and inexpensive ideas that will give every room in your house a warm and welcoming touch. ♥ Debbie Mumm

Baskets

Dolls

CLASSIC COUNTRY ACCENTS

Bowl & Pitcher

Quilts, Quilts, Quilts....

Antique Sewing Machine & Notions

magic INK

RED

BLUE

BACK DOOR FRIENDS

♥ Keep a pot of your favorite flowers next to the back door. I'm partial to sunflowers and geraniums.

♥ Hang a cheery wall quilt just inside the door to welcome neighbors and friends.

♥ Add a wreath, swag, or garland of dried herbs or flowers to your entry area.

♥ Stock a basket of goodies to have on hand for serving drop-in friends~assorted teas, coffees, and a package of your favorite cookies.

WELCOME

Stack up comfy pillows and tie them with a pretty ribbon.

HOMESPUN TOUCHES

ABUNDANCE OF BUTTONS

FRAME 'EM & HANG 'EM

Hang framed quilt blocks with other prints and pictures on a decorative drapery rod. Interesting finials add a fun touch.

Fill baskets, mason jars, pots, tins or well-worn wooden drawers with buttons. Sew them on your quilts~to the corners, around the borders, and to the blocks. Decorate pillows, fragrant sachets, lampshades, and pots. Buttons add dimension and charm to everyday items.

QUILTS MAKE IT FEEL LIKE HOME

PILLOWS WITH PIZZAZZ

Stitch yo-yos, buttons, tassels or appliqué designs to a plain, purchased pillow to create a unique, one-of-a-kind accent.

COZY COMFORTS

Blanket stitch fabric or felt motifs and simple appliqué shapes to a plain, purchased knit or fleece throw.

SOFT LIGHTS

Decoupage lamp shades with fabric shapes, buttons, stickers, gift wrap, greeting cards, sports cards, yo-yos, and quilt block designs cut from colored paper.

GREAT SPOTS FOR QUILTS

Hanging from the mantel, draping out of a basket, folded and stacked in a hutch on an end table or dining table, draped over the back of a sofa or chair, over the stair railing.

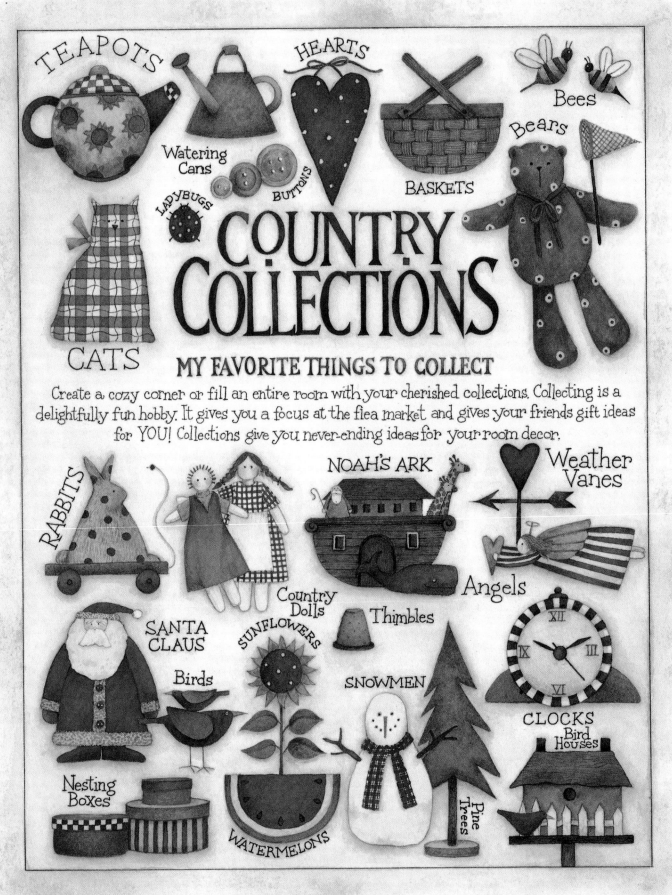

TEAPOTS

HEARTS

Bees

Bears

Watering Cans

BASKETS

BUTTONS

LADYBUGS

COUNTRY COLLECTIONS

CATS

MY FAVORITE THINGS TO COLLECT

Create a cozy corner or fill an entire room with your cherished collections. Collecting is a delightfully fun hobby. It gives you a focus at the flea market and gives your friends gift ideas for YOU! Collections give you never-ending ideas for your room decor.

RABBITS

NOAH'S ARK

Weather Vanes

Angels

Country Dolls

Thimbles

SANTA CLAUS

SUNFLOWERS

SNOWMEN

Birds

CLOCKS
Bird Houses

Nesting Boxes

Pine Trees

WATERMELONS

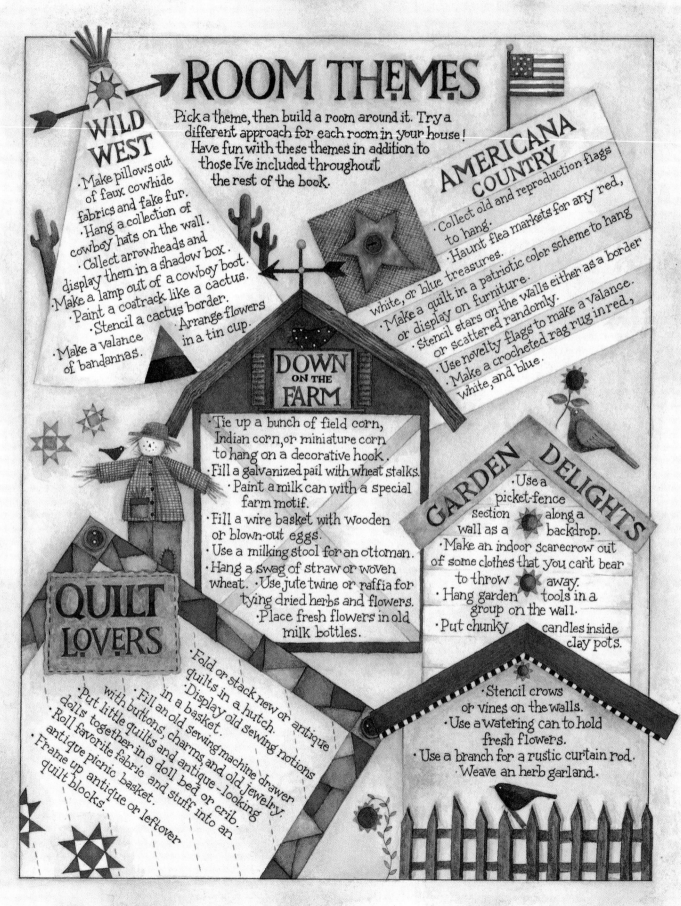

ROOM THEMES

Pick a theme, then build a room around it. Try a different approach for each room in your house! Have fun with these themes in addition to those I've included throughout the rest of the book.

WILD WEST

· Make pillows out of faux cowhide fabrics and fake fur.
· Hang a collection of cowboy hats on the wall.
· Collect arrowheads and display them in a shadow box.
· Make a lamp out of a cowboy boot.
· Paint a coatrack like a cactus.
· Stencil a cactus border.
· Arrange flowers in a tin cup.
· Make a valance of bandannas.

AMERICANA COUNTRY

· Collect old and reproduction flags to hang.
· Haunt flea markets for any red, white, or blue treasures.
· Make a quilt in a patriotic color scheme to hang or display on furniture.
· Stencil stars on the walls either as a border or scattered randomly.
· Use novelty flags to make a valance.
· Make a crocheted rag rug in red, white, and blue.

DOWN ON THE FARM

· Tie up a bunch of field corn, Indian corn, or miniature corn to hang on a decorative hook.
· Fill a galvanized pail with wheat stalks.
· Paint a milk can with a special farm motif.
· Fill a wire basket with wooden or blown-out eggs.
· Use a milking stool for an ottoman.
· Hang a swag of straw or woven wheat.
· Use jute twine or raffia for tying dried herbs and flowers.
· Place fresh flowers in old milk bottles.

GARDEN DELIGHTS

· Use a picket-fence section along a wall as a backdrop.
· Make an indoor scarecrow out of some clothes that you can't bear to throw away.
· Hang garden tools in a group on the wall.
· Put chunky candles inside clay pots.
· Stencil crows or vines on the walls.
· Use a watering can to hold fresh flowers.
· Use a branch for a rustic curtain rod.
· Weave an herb garland.

QUILT LOVERS

· Fold or stack new or antique quilts in a hutch.
· Display old sewing notions in a basket.
· Fill an old sewing machine drawer with buttons, charms, and old jewelry.
· Put little quilts and antique dolls together in a doll bed or crib.
· Roll favorite fabric and stuff into an antique picnic basket.
· Frame up antique or leftover quilt blocks.

THE COUNTRY DECORATOR

MURPH'S TURF

GO!

Decoupage sports cards onto a used or unfinished bedside stand. For knobs and feet, drill baseballs into place.

COOL!

DINOSAURS
SPACE
SPORTS

TIME FOR TEA

To decorate a hutch, gather all your tea goodies together to create a pleasing arrangement.

FAMILY-ROOM RETREAT

YELLOWSTONE
OLD FAITHFUL
1

- Make a collage out of family memorabilia and souvenirs from trips.
- Build a cabin out of Lincoln Logs and display it with a miniature Log Cabin quilt.
- Collect leaves from the yard or park and spray them with metallic gold, copper, or silver paint. Add them to wreaths or show them off in a bowl or basket.
- Use old wagons to display vintage dolls and stuffed animals with companion quilts.
- Place soft-sculpture snowmen in a wreath for a wintertime accessory.
- Fill a basket with pinecones, nuts, and faux fruit.

- Group wooden toys together for a nostalgic yet functional display.

COZY NOOKS & CRANNIES

♥

Stack three vintage suitcases for an end table. Store games and puzzles inside.

THE BIRD BATH

- Stitch fun fabric borders to the edge of bathroom linens to create custom~ trimmed towels.
- Purchase and paint small wooden birdhouses for finials on your curtain rod.
- Stencil a sisal mat with birdhouses.

HOLIDAY FRONT DOOR

Fun finds from the flea market make for a welcoming front door:
- Vintage coal or snow shovel
- Pail of Christmas greenery
- Antique skis & snowshoes
- Old mittens
- Old sled
- Ice skates

FOR A SPECIAL GIRL

Create a stuffed Heart Garland to hang on her door or above her headboard. Put one letter from her name on each heart.

FRUITY KITCHEN

DEBBIE'S RECIPE

FOR A COUNTRY KITCHEN
- Bright red, golden, and green apples•
- Pears in tan and gold•
- Cheery red cherries•

Mix the fruits together with plenty of red and natural checkerboards. Add a hint of black for accent. Throw in a handful of green leaves and sprinkle liberally around your kitchen. Enjoy immediately!

COVERED BOXES

Use purchased papier~mâché boxes and decorate with fabrics and buttons.

Decoupage apple shapes to a purchased serving tray~

A perfect way to serve pie and coffee.

©Debbie Mumm

COZY COUNTRY DINING ROOM

Tea lovers, rejoice! The world's most popular beverage gets its just reward as the main feature in this coordinated dining room grouping. The delightful tea theme will set the mood for pleasant conversation no matter what you prefer in your cup! For a peek at the same room done up for Christmas, see page 31.

TEAPOT
TABLE QUILT

These teapots take their color cue from the rich reds and browns

of antique Staffordshire pottery. English potters in the late seventeenth century

capitalized on the rising popularity of tea with the creation of teapots, cups,

and saucers. Today's quilter can capitalize on easy patchwork and quick-fuse

appliqué to make this totally up-to-date Teapot Table Quilt. But don't reserve

this just for teatime—teapots around the table are also the perfect

accompaniment for breakfast, lunch, or dinner.

Finished Size: 34 inches square　　　**Finished Teapot Block: 9 × 7 inches**

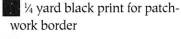

MATERIALS

(Obvious directional prints are not recommended.)

¼ yard red-and-black print for teapots

¼ yard light tan print for background

¼ yard tan-and-black print for block centers

⅝ yard green print for lattice and binding

¼ yard black print for patchwork border

¼ yard red print for patchwork border and corner squares

⅛ yard gold print for patchwork border

⅝ yard multicolor check for border

1⅛ yards fabric for backing

1⅛ yards cotton batting

Scraps, or ⅛-yard pieces, of several coordinated fabrics for appliqué pieces

Lightweight, sewable fusible web

Embroidery floss

4 assorted ⅝-inch buttons

CUTTING

Prewash and press all of your fabrics. Using a rotary cutter, see-through ruler, and cutting mat, prepare the pieces as described below. Measurements for all pieces include ¼-inch seam allowances.

FABRIC	FIRST CUT		SECOND CUT	
Color	**No. of Pieces**	**Dimensions**	**No. of Pieces**	**Dimensions**
Red-and-black print	**Teapots**			
	4	5½-inch squares	No second cut	
Light tan print	**Background**			
	3	2½ × 42-inch strips	4	2½ × 9½-inch pieces
			8	2½ × 5½-inch pieces
			16	1½-inch squares
Tan-and-black print	**Block centers**			
	1	6½-inch square	No second cut	
	4	5½-inch squares	No second cut	
Green print	**Lattice**			
	7	1 × 42-inch strips	2	1 × 25½-inch strips
			4	1 × 24½-inch strips
			2	1 × 9½-inch strips
			6	1 × 7½-inch strips
			2	1 × 6½-inch strips
	Binding			
	4	2¾ × 42-inch strips	No second cut	
Black print	**Patchwork border**			
	4	1½ × 42-inch strips	8	1½ × 14-inch strips
Red print	**Patchwork border**			
	2	1½ × 42-inch strips	4	1½ × 14-inch strips
	Corner squares			
	4	4½-inch squares	No second cut	
Gold print	**Patchwork border**			
	2	1½ × 42-inch strips	4	1½ × 14-inch strips
Multicolor check	**Border**			
	4	4½ × 25½-inch strips	No second cut	

Making the Teapot Blocks

You will be making four teapot blocks. Refer to "Making Quick Corner Triangles" on page 269 for instructions on making the corner triangle units. Refer to "Assembly Line Piecing" on page 268 for instructions on making the corner triangle units for all four blocks at the same time. Press the seams toward the triangle just added.

STEP 1. Sew four 1½-inch light tan print squares to each of the four 5½-inch red-and-black print squares. See **Diagram 1**. Press.

DIAGRAM 1

STEP 2. Using ¼-inch seams, sew the four units from Step 1 between the eight 2½ × 5½-inch light tan print pieces. Press, following the arrows in **Diagram 2**.

DIAGRAM 2

STEP 3. Sew the four 2½ × 9½-inch light tan print pieces to the four units from Step 2. See **Diagram 3**. Press. Each block will now measure 9½ × 7½ inches.

DIAGRAM 3

Appliqué

The appliqué pieces were added to the teapot blocks using the technique described in "Blanket Stitch Appliqué" on page 272. You can machine appliqué with either a satin stitch or blanket stitch if you prefer. Refer to "Machine Appliqué" on pages 271–272 for instructions on these techniques. Use a lightweight, sewable fusible web for all of these techniques.

STEP 1. Refer to "Quick-Fuse Appliqué" on pages 270–271. Trace four spouts, handles, lids, and daisies from the appliqué patterns on page 17.

STEP 2. Position and fuse the appliqué pieces to the teapots, referring to **Diagram 4** for placement.

DIAGRAM 4

STEP 3. Use two strands of embroidery floss to blanket stitch around the edges of the appliqué pieces.

Making the Center Block

STEP 1. Sew the 1 × 6½-inch lattice strips to the top and bottom of the 6½-inch tan-and-black print square. See **Diagram 5**. Press the seams toward the lattice.

DIAGRAM 5

STEP 2. Sew one 1 × 7½-inch lattice strip to each side, as shown in **Diagram 6**. Press.

DIAGRAM 6

STEP 3. Arrange four 1½ × 14-inch patchwork border strips (two black print, one red print, and one gold print) in the order shown in **Diagram 7**. Sew the strips together to make a 4½ × 14-inch strip set. Change sewing direction with each strip sewn, and press the seams toward the black print as you go. Cut this strip set into halves, approximately 7 inches each.

DIAGRAM 7

STEP 4. Resew the halves together to make an 8½ × 7-inch strip set. Using a rotary cutter and ruler, cut four 1½ × 8½-inch strips from this strip set. There should be eight squares in each strip. See **Diagram 8**.

8½"
7"
1½"

DIAGRAM 8

STEP 5. For the top and bottom borders, use a seam ripper to remove one black print square from each of two 1½ × 8½-inch patchwork border strips to make two strips with seven squares each. Set aside the black print squares for use in Step 6. Compare the strips to the top and bottom of the center block unit. You may need to take in or let out a few seams (⅟₁₆ inch or less) to make them fit. Referring to **Diagram 9** for placement, pin and sew the 1½ × 7½-inch patchwork border strips to the top and bottom. Press the seams toward the lattice.

7½"

DIAGRAM 9

STEP 6. Sew one 1½-inch black print square removed in Step 5 to the red print end of each remaining 1½ × 8½-inch patchwork border strip. See **Diagram 10**. Press.

Quick and Easy Window Treatment

Hang small wreaths at the upper corners of your window and drape a favorite fabric through. Gently entwine a garland of ivy with your fabric. Change the fabric or garland to reflect the season.

1½"   8½"
1½"   1½"

DIAGRAM 10

STEP 7. Referring to **Diagram 11** for placement, fit, pin, and sew the 1½ × 9½-inch patchwork border strips to the sides. Press. The center block will now measure 9½ inches square.

1½"   7½"   1½"
9½"   9½"

DIAGRAM 11

Making the Corner Blocks

STEP 1. Arrange five 1½ × 14-inch patchwork border strips (two black print, one red print, and two gold print) in the order shown in **Diagram 12**. Sew the strips together to make a 5½ × 14-inch strip set. Change sewing direction with each strip sewn, and press the seams toward the black print as

you go. Using a rotary cutter and ruler, cut eight 1½ × 5½-inch strips from this strip set. There should be five squares in each strip.

5½"
1½"
14"

DIAGRAM 12

STEP 2. Fit, pin, and sew the 1½ × 5½-inch patchwork border strips to the tops and bottoms of the four 5½-inch tan-and-black print squares. See **Diagram 13**. Press the seams toward the square.

5½"
1½"
5½"
1½"

DIAGRAM 13

STEP 3. Arrange the seven remaining 1½ × 14-inch patchwork border strips (four black print, two red print, and one gold print) in the order shown in **Diagram 14**. Sew the strips together to make a 7½ × 14-inch strip set. Change sewing direction with each strip sewn, and press the seams toward the black print as you go. Using a rotary cutter and ruler, cut eight 1½ × 7½-inch strips from this strip set. There should be seven squares in each strip.

DIAGRAM 14

STEP 4. Fit, pin, and sew the 1½ × 7½-inch patchwork border strips to the sides, as shown in **Diagram 15**. Press. Each corner block will now measure 7½ inches square.

DIAGRAM 15

Assembling the Top

STEP 1. Sew two 7½-inch corner blocks, two 1 × 7½-inch lattice strips, and one 9½ × 7½-inch teapot block together in the order shown in **Diagram 16**. Press. Repeat to make a second unit.

STEP 2. Sew the 1 × 24½-inch lattice strips to the tops and bottoms of the two units from Step 1. See **Diagram 17**. Press.

STEP 3. Sew the remaining two 9½ × 7½-inch teapot blocks, the two 1 × 9½-inch lattice strips, and the 9½-inch center block together in the order shown in **Diagram 18**. Press.

STEP 4. Sew the two units from Step 2 and the unit from Step 3 together in the order shown in **Diagram 19** on page 16. Press.

STEP 5. Sew the 1 × 25½-inch lattice strips to the sides. Press the seams toward the lattice.

STEP 6. Sew one 4½ × 25½-inch border strip each to the top and bottom. Press the seams toward the border.

STEP 7. Sew a 4½-inch red print square to each end of the remaining two 4½ × 25½-inch border strips. Press the seams toward the border. Pin and sew the border strips to the sides. Press.

Layering the Quilt

Arrange and baste the backing, batting, and top together, following the directions in "Layering the Quilt" on page 275. Trim the batting and backing to ¼ inch from the raw edges of the quilt top.

Make 2
DIAGRAM 16

DIAGRAM 17

DIAGRAM 18

Step 2
Unit

Step 3
Unit

Step 2
Unit

DIAGRAM 19

34"

34"

TABLE QUILT LAYOUT

Binding the Quilt

Using the four 2¾ × 42-inch binding strips, follow the directions for "Binding the Quilt" on pages 275–276.

Finishing Stitches

Machine or hand quilt in the seam lines of the teapots, lattice, corner squares, and patchwork border squares. Outline the appliqué designs by quilting ¹⁄₁₆ inch from the edges. Using a commercial quilting template, quilt a flower in the center block and each corner block. Quilt a 1¼-inch diagonal grid in each teapot block background and a 2-inch diagonal grid in the border. Sew a button to the lid of each teapot.

Fresh Flowers

Brighten up the table with a bouquet of fresh daisies in your favorite vase or teapot.

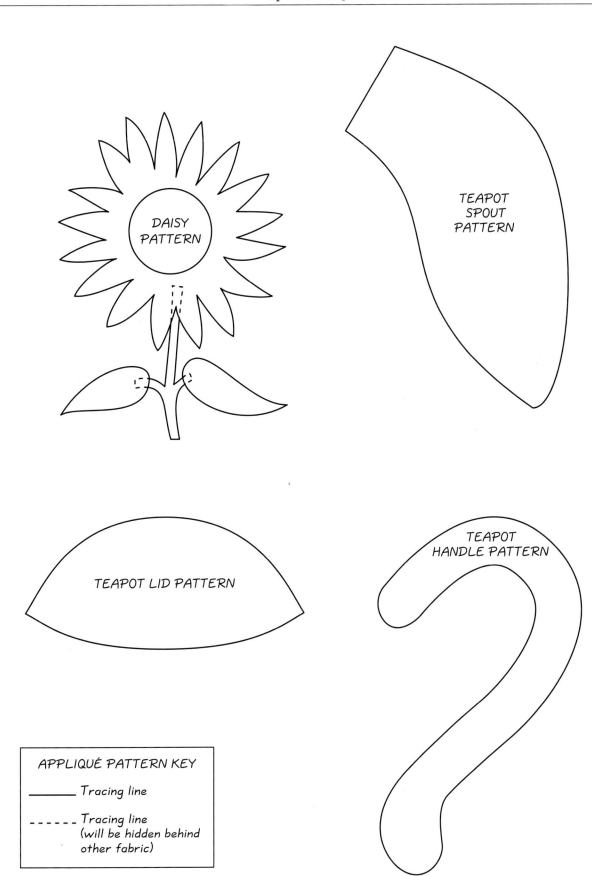

DAISY
PATTERN

TEAPOT
SPOUT
PATTERN

TEAPOT LID PATTERN

TEAPOT
HANDLE PATTERN

APPLIQUÉ PATTERN KEY

_____ Tracing line

- - - - - - Tracing line
(will be hidden behind
other fabric)

WEEKENDER

TEAPOT TRIO

Whether it's breakfast tea in the morning, low tea in the afternoon,

or high tea in the evening, any time is teatime when you have this captivating

trio of teapots hanging in your dining room. Craft your pots of folk art reds,

blacks, and golds, as shown in the photo, or choose lovely springtime florals

if that's more your cup of tea. (See the **Color Option** on page 21.)

Whatever your preference, the quick and easy techniques will have you

displaying your teapot colors in record time!

Finished Size: 18 × 32 inches   **Finished Teapot Block: 9 × 7 inches**

MATERIALS

(Obvious directional prints are not recommended.)

◼◻◼ ⅙ yard, or 4½-inch square, *each* of black, red, and multicolor prints for teapots

▦▦▦ ⅛ yard *each* of 3 tan prints for background

◼ ½ yard green print for lattice and binding

⅛ yard, or 1½ to 2½ × 32-inch strip, *each* of 7 fabrics for scrap border

⅔ yard fabric for backing

⅔ yard lightweight batting

Scraps, or ⅛-yard pieces, of several coordinated fabrics for appliqué pieces

Lightweight, sewable fusible web

Embroidery floss

3 assorted ⅝- to ¾-inch buttons

CUTTING

Prewash and press all of your fabrics. Using a rotary cutter, see-through ruler, and cutting mat, prepare the pieces as described below. Measurements for all pieces include ¼-inch seam allowances.

FABRIC	FIRST CUT		SECOND CUT	
Color	No. of Pieces	Dimensions	No. of Pieces	Dimensions
Black, red, and multicolor prints	**Teapots**—from *each* of the 3 fabrics, cut the following:			
	1	4½-inch square	No second cut	
Tan prints	**Background**—from *each* of the 3 fabrics, cut the following:			
	1	2½ × 42-inch strip	1	2½ × 9½-inch piece
			2	2½ × 5½-inch pieces
			4	1½-inch squares
Green print	**Lattice**			
	3	1½ × 42-inch strips	2	1½ × 25½-inch strips
			4	1½ × 9½-inch strips
	Binding		Cut *1* strip into the following:	
	3	2¾ × 42-inch strips	2	2¾ × 21-inch strips
Border fabrics	**Scrap border**			
	7	32-inch-long strips that vary in width from 1½ to 2½ inches	No second cut	

Making the Blocks

You will be making three teapot blocks, one each of three different fabric combinations. Before you start sewing, coordinate the fabrics for all combinations. Keep track of the combinations as you sew.

Refer to "Making the Teapot Blocks" and "Appliqué" on pages 12–13 to make three teapot blocks without daisies.

Assembling the Top

STEP 1. Using ¼-inch seams, sew one 1½ × 9½-inch lattice strip to the top of each block. See **Diagram 1**. Press the seams toward the lattice.

1½"   9½"

DIAGRAM 1

STEP 2. Sew the three blocks together and press. Sew the remaining 1½ × 9½-inch lattice strip to the bottom. See **Diagram 2**. Press.

STEP 3. Sew the 1½ × 25½-inch lattice strips to the sides. Press the seams toward the lattice.

1½"
9½"

DIAGRAM 2

Making the Scrap Border

STEP 1. Sew the seven 32-inch strips (one each of seven different fabrics) together to make an 11½ × 32-inch strip set. Change sewing direction with each strip sewn, and press the seams in one direction as you go. Using a rotary cutter and ruler, cut eight 3½ × 11½-inch strips from this strip set. See **Diagram 3**.

DIAGRAM 3

STEP 2. Pin and sew 3½ × 11½-inch scrap border strips to the top and bottom. Press the seams toward the lattice.

STEP 3. For the sides, sew two sets of three 3½ × 11½-inch scrap border strips together to make two 3½ × 33½-inch strips. Pin and sew the scrap border strips to the sides. Trim the excess length and press.

Layering the Quilt

Arrange and baste the backing, batting, and top together, following the directions in "Layering the Quilt" on page 275. Trim the batting and backing to ¼ inch from the raw edges of the quilt top.

Binding the Quilt

Using the two 2¾ × 21-inch binding strips for the top and bottom and the two 2¾ × 42-inch binding strips for the sides, follow the directions for "Binding the Quilt" on pages 275–276.

Finishing Stitches

Machine or hand quilt in the seam lines of the teapots, lattice, and scrap border pieces. Outline the appliqué designs by quilting ¹⁄₁₆ inch from the edges. Quilt a 1¼-inch diagonal grid in each block background. Sew a button to the lid of each teapot.

A Teacup Label

Use the teacups appliqué pattern from the Tea Sampler on page 26 to make a label for the back of your Teapot Trio quilt. Use a Pigma pen or Identipen to write your sentiment, name, and date on the cups. Fuse or appliqué the label to the back of the quilt.

QUILT LAYOUT

COLOR OPTION

Using florals and prints in shades of blue, pink, lavender, and peach can give your teapot quilt a springtime flavor.

TEA SAMPLER

The sipping of tea with guests as a sociable activity and token

of friendship has a long history—nearly 4,000 years. In celebration of the

enduring appeal of this beverage, make this sweet Tea Sampler and hang it

in a cozy nook to make your guests feel welcome in your home.

Finished Size: 15 × 14½ inches

MATERIALS AND CUTTING

Prewash and press all of your fabrics. Using a rotary cutter, see-through ruler, and cutting mat, prepare the pieces as described below. Measurements for all pieces include ¼-inch seam allowances.

FABRIC	YARDAGE	NO. OF PIECES	DIMENSIONS
Light to medium tan prints for background	⅛ to ¼ yard *each* of 5 fabrics	1	3 × 3½-inch piece (Block #1)
		1	3½-inch square (Block #2)
		1	3 × 3½-inch piece (Block #3)
		1	4 × 5½-inch piece (Block #4)
		1	5½-inch square (Block #5)
Green print for lattice	⅛ yard (cut into two 1 × 42-inch strips)	2	1 × 10-inch strips
		3	1 × 9½-inch strips
		1	1 × 5½-inch strip
		2	1 × 3½-inch strips
Red prints for border	⅛ yard *each* of 2 fabrics	1	2½ × 10½-inch strip *each*
Black prints for border	⅛ yard *each* of 2 fabrics	1	2½ × 14-inch strip *each*
Black solid for binding	⅛ yard (cut into two 1 × 42-inch strips)	2	1 × 15-inch strips
		2	1 × 14½-inch strips
Backing fabric	½ yard	—	—
Lightweight batting	½ yard	—	—
Several coordinated fabrics for appliqué pieces	Scraps, or ⅛-yard pieces	—	—
Lightweight, sewable fusible web; embroidery floss; ½-inch button			

Assembling the Background

Assemble the wallhanging top before adding the appliqué pieces. Refer to **Diagrams 1** through **3** for the measurements of the background blocks. Use ¼-inch seams and press the seams toward the lattice after each sewing step.

STEP 1. Sew background Block #2 between the two 1 × 3½-inch lattice strips. See **Diagram 1**. Press.

DIAGRAM 1

STEP 2. Sew the unit from Step 1 between background Blocks #1 and #3, as shown in **Diagram 2**. Press.

DIAGRAM 2

STEP 3. Sew the 1 × 5½-inch lattice strip between background Blocks #4 and #5. See **Diagram 3**. Press.

DIAGRAM 3

STEP 4. Sew one 1 × 9½-inch lattice strip between the units from Steps 2 and 3. See **Diagram 4**. Press.

DIAGRAM 4

STEP 5. Sew the remaining 1 × 9½-inch lattice strips to the top and bottom of the unit from Step 4. Press seams toward the lattice.

STEP 6. Sew the 1 × 10-inch lattice strips to the sides. Press.

STEP 7. Sew the 2½ × 10½-inch border strips to the top and bottom. Press the seams toward the border.

STEP 8. Sew the 2½ × 14-inch border strips to the sides. Press.

STEP 9. Sew the 1 × 14½-inch binding strips to the top and bottom. Press the seams toward the binding.

STEP 10. Sew the 1 × 15-inch binding strips to the sides. Press.

Appliqué

STEP 1. Refer to "Quick-Fuse Appliqué" on pages 270–271. Trace the teapot, teakettle, teacups, sugar bowl, and tea bag from the appliqué patterns on pages 25–26. Trace the lettering onto the tea bag tag before fusing.

STEP 2. Quick-fuse each appliqué design to the center of its corresponding background piece.

Position and fuse one design at a time, referring to the **Wallhanging Layout** on the opposite page for placement.

STEP 3. Use two strands of embroidery floss to stem stitch the lettering on the tea bag tag. Use one strand of embroidery floss to stem stitch the string and line on the tea bag and the steam lines on the teakettle. See "Decorative Stitches" on page 272 for instructions on stem stitching.

Flavored by Fabrics

For a totally different look, make this Tea Sampler with your favorite Japanese or batik fabrics.

Finishing Stitches

STEP 1. Position the top and backing with right sides together. Lay both pieces on top of the batting, with the backing next to the batting. Pin all three layers together. Using ¼-inch seams, sew around the edges, leaving a 3- to 4-inch opening for turning. Trim the backing and batting to the same size as the top. Trim the corners, turn the wallhanging right side out, hand stitch the opening closed, and press.

STEP 2. Machine or hand quilt in the seam lines of the lattice and binding. Outline the appliqué designs by quilting ¹⁄₁₆ inch from the edges. Quilt a 1¼-inch diagonal grid in the border. Sew the button to the lid of the teapot.

15"

14 1/2"

WALLHANGING LAYOUT

Stem stitch
embroider
this line

Tea

Lettering

TEA BAG PATTERN FOR BLOCK #3

SUGAR BOWL PATTERN
FOR BLOCK #1

Button

TEAPOT PATTERN
FOR BLOCK #5

APPLIQUÉ PATTERN KEY

———— Tracing line

- - - - Tracing line
(will be hidden behind
other fabric)

Stitching lines

TEA KETTLE PATTERN
FOR BLOCK #2

TEACUPS PATTERN
FOR BLOCK #4

TEATIME ACCESSORIES

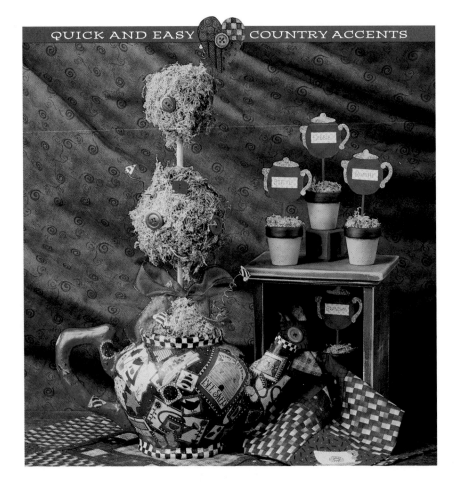

QUICK AND EASY   COUNTRY ACCENTS

Create your own tea ceremony, and from the moment they arrive, enchant your guests with this spirited Teapot Topiary, coordinating Teatime Napkins, Napkin Rings (directions on page 30), and Teapotted Place Cards (page 30). Make these accessories in folk art colors, as shown in the photo, or coordinate them with your favorite teapot or cups and saucers.

TEAPOT TOPIARY

Height: 18 inches

Materials

Papier-mâché teapot
Acrylic paint
Decoupage finish
Assorted fabric or paper motifs
Matte-finish spray varnish
Antiquing medium
Floral foam
3½-inch Styrofoam ball
2½-inch Styrofoam ball
¼-inch dowel, 16 inches long,
   stained
Tacky glue
Sheet moss
Assorted buttons
Medium-gauge wire
Glue gun and glue sticks
1 yard wire-edged ribbon

Assembly

STEP 1. Refer to "Decorative Painting" on page 53. Paint the papier-mâché teapot with acrylic paint and allow the paint to dry. (I painted the body of the teapot black and the handle red.) Add decorative painting touches, such as dots and checkerboards, as desired, and let dry.

STEP 2. Decoupage fabric or paper motifs to the teapot as directed on the container. Allow the decoupage to dry.

STEP 3. Spray the teapot with matte-finish varnish, and allow the varnish to dry thoroughly.

STEP 4. To antique the teapot, apply antiquing medium as directed on the container. Allow the medium to dry, and spray the teapot with a second coat of matte-finish varnish.

STEP 5. Fill the teapot with floral foam. Push the Styrofoam balls onto the dowel, leaving 1½ inches of space between them, and glue them in place with tacky glue. Insert the dowel into the teapot.

STEP 6. Coat the balls and the top of the floral foam base with tacky glue. Cover the glued areas with sheet moss.

STEP 7. Decorate the topiary with buttons and twisted wire pokes. Use the glue gun to add the buttons. To form twisted wire pokes, twist the medium-gauge wire around a dowel or pencil. Glue fabric or paper motifs to the ends of the wires.

STEP 8. Tie a bow of wire-edged ribbon around the stem of the topiary.

17"

17"

TEATIME NAPKINS

Finished Size: 17 inches square

(See the napkins in the photo on pages 8–9.)

Materials

To make 4 napkins:

¼ yard tan-and-black plaid
   for center square
⅓ yard green print for accent border
¼ yard black print for patchwork
   border
⅛ yard red print for patchwork
   border
⅛ yard gold print for patchwork
   border
¾ yard multicolor print for outer
   border
⅓ yard red-and-black print for
   corner squares
1⅛ yards fabric for backing
Scraps, or ⅛-yard pieces, of several
   coordinated fabrics for appliqué
   pieces
Lightweight, sewable fusible web
Embroidery floss

Assembling the Napkins

STEP 1. See "Cutting" on page 28. Using ¼-inch seams, sew the 1 × 6½-inch accent border strips to the tops and bottoms of the

CUTTING

Prewash and press all of your fabrics. Using a rotary cutter, see-through ruler, and cutting mat, prepare the pieces as described below. Measurements for all pieces include ¼-inch seam allowances.

FABRIC	FIRST CUT		SECOND CUT	
Color	No. of Pieces	Dimensions	No. of Pieces	Dimensions
Tan-and-black plaid	**Center square**			
	4	6½-inch squares	No second cut	
Green print	**Accent borders**			
	8	1 × 42-inch strips	8	1 × 10½-inch strips
			8	1 × 9½-inch strips
			8	1 × 7½-inch strips
			8	1 × 6½-inch strips
Black print	**Patchwork border**			
	4	1½ × 28-inch strips	No second cut	
Red print	**Patchwork border**			
	2	1½ × 28-inch strips	No second cut	
Gold print	**Patchwork border**			
	2	1½ × 28-inch strips	No second cut	
Multicolor print	**Outer border**			
	6	4 × 42-inch strips	16	4 × 10½-inch strips
Red-and-black print	**Corner squares**			
	2	4 × 42-inch strips	16	4-inch squares
Backing fabric	4	17½-inch squares	No second cut	

four 6½-inch tan-and-black plaid center squares. See **Diagram 1**. Press seams toward the accent border.

DIAGRAM 1

STEP 2. Sew the 1 × 7½-inch accent border strips to the sides, as shown in **Diagram 2**. Press.

DIAGRAM 2

STEP 3. Arrange the eight 1½ × 28-inch patchwork border strips (four black print, two red print, and two gold print) in the order shown in **Diagram 3** on the following page. Sew the strips together to make an 8½ × 28-inch strip set. Change sewing direction with each strip sewn, and press the seams toward the black print as you go. Using a rotary cutter and ruler, cut sixteen 1½ × 8½-

inch strips from this strip set. There should be eight squares in each strip.

8½"

1½"

28"

DIAGRAM 3

STEP 4. For the top and bottom borders, use a seam ripper to remove one black print square from each of eight 1½ × 8½-inch patchwork border strips to make eight strips with seven squares each. Set aside the black print squares for use in Step 5. Compare the strips to the tops and bottoms of the units from Step 2. You may need to take in or let out a few seams (¹⁄₁₆ inch or less) to make them fit. Referring to **Diagram 4** for placement, pin and sew the 1½ × 7½-inch patchwork border strips to the tops and bottoms of the units from Step 2. Press.

7½"

1½"

Step 2
Unit

DIAGRAM 4

STEP 5. Sew one 1½-inch black print square removed in Step 4 to the red print end of each of the remaining eight 1½ × 8½-inch

patchwork border strips. See **Diagram 5.** Press.

1½"   8½"

1½"   1½"

DIAGRAM 5

STEP 6. Referring to **Diagram 6** for placement, fit, pin, and sew the 1½ × 9½-inch patchwork border strips to the sides of the units from Step 4. Press.

1½"   *Step 4 Unit*   1½"

9½"   9½"

DIAGRAM 6

STEP 7. Sew the 1 × 9½-inch accent border strips to the tops and bottoms of the units from Step 6. Press the seams toward the accent border.

STEP 8. Sew the 1 × 10½-inch accent border strips to the sides. Press.

STEP 9. Sew 4 × 10½-inch outer border strips to the tops and bottoms of the units from Step 8. Press the seams toward the outer border.

STEP 10. Sew one 4-inch red-and-black print corner square to each end of the remaining eight 4 × 10½-inch outer border strips. Press the seams toward the outer border. Pin and sew the outer border strips to the sides. Press.

Appliqué

The appliqué pieces were added to the napkins using the technique described in "Blanket Stitch Appliqué" on page 272. You can machine appliqué with either a satin stitch or blanket stitch if you prefer. Refer to "Machine Appliqué" on pages 271–272. Use a lightweight, sewable fusible web for all of these techniques.

STEP 1. Refer to "Quick-Fuse Appliqué" on pages 270–271. Trace four teacups from the appliqué pattern on page 30.

STEP 2. Position and fuse a teacup to one corner square of each napkin, referring to the napkin layout on page 27 for placement. Be sure to allow for the ¼-inch seam allowances on the two raw edges of the corner squares when positioning the teacups.

STEP 3. Use two strands of embroidery floss to blanket stitch around the edges of the appliqué pieces.

Finishing

For each napkin, position the top and backing with right sides together. Using ¼-inch seams, sew around the edges, leaving a 3- to 4-inch opening for turning. Trim the corners, turn the napkin right side out, hand stitch the opening closed, and press.

NAPKIN RINGS

(See the napkin ring in the photo on pages 8–9.)

Materials

To make 4 napkin rings:

2½ × 30-inch strip red print
  for rings
2½ × 30-inch strip felt for backing
Lightweight, sewable fusible web
Embroidery floss
Four ⅞-inch buttons

Assembly

STEP 1. Refer to "Quick-Fuse Appliqué" on pages 270–271. Fuse the wrong side of the red print to the felt backing.

STEP 2. With a rotary cutter and ruler, cut four 1½ × 7-inch napkin ring strips.

STEP 3. Using two strands of embroidery floss, blanket stitch (page 272) around the edges of each napkin ring.

STEP 4. Sew a button to one end of each napkin ring. To make the buttonhole, cut a 1-inch slit in the opposite end of each napkin ring. Use two strands of embroidery floss to blanket stitch around each slit. Slip the button through the buttonhole to form a ring.

APPLIQUÉ PATTERN KEY

——— Tracing line

- - - - - Tracing line (will be hidden behind other fabric)

TEAPOTTED PLACE CARDS

Height: 5¼ inches

(See the place cards in the photo on page 26.)

Materials

To make 4 place cards:

Scraps, or ⅛-yard pieces, of
  several coordinated fabrics for
  appliqué pieces and backing
Fusible web
Permanent fine-point felt pen
Four 2-inch clay pots
Acrylic paint
Matte-finish spray varnish
Antiquing medium
Floral foam
Tacky glue
Sheet moss
⅛-inch dowel, at least 16
  inches long

Assembly

STEP 1. Refer to "Quick-Fuse Appliqué" on pages 270–271 and follow Steps 1 through 4. Use the teapot appliqué pattern below. Position and fuse the teapots to the wrong side of the backing fabric. Cut out along the edges of the fused teapots. Use the permanent felt pen to write a name on each.

STEP 2. Refer to "Decorative Painting" on page 53. Make sure the clay pots are clean and dry. Paint the outside of each pot and inside the rim with acrylic paint. Spatter-paint if desired.

STEP 3. Spray the pots with matte-finish varnish and let dry. Apply antiquing medium as directed on the container. Allow to dry, and spray the pots with a second coat of varnish.

STEP 4. Fill each pot with floral foam. Glue sheet moss to the top.

STEP 5. Cut four 4-inch lengths from the dowel. Paint the dowels with acrylic paint. Insert one dowel into each clay pot. Glue the teapots to the dowels with tacky glue.

TEACUP APPLIQUÉ PATTERN

TEAPOT PLACE CARD PATTERN

ANGELS ALL AROUND

Angels and stars are my very favorite Christmas theme. I love to fill my home with them and let them work their holiday magic. I've designed this set of projects to make it easy to transform your dining room into a heavenly scene for Christmas. But you can keep these angels on display year-round for a heaven-sent touch of charm.

WEEKENDER

CHRISTMAS ANGELS

These rag-doll–like angels are an irresistible duo that begs to be made.

The star-studded Angel Quilt hanging in the window is perfect for angel lovers

or anyone who likes to decorate for Christmas. (For a look that works year-

round, see the **Color Option** on page 37.) Checkerboards, stars, and angels

make the Angel Table Runner at the lower left (directions on page 38) extra

appealing. Your dining room will glimmer with warmth and good cheer.

Angel Quilt

Finished Size: 28 × 21½ inches   **Finished Angel Block: 8 × 12 inches**

MATERIALS

(Obvious directional prints are not recommended.)

▢ ⅛ yard tan solid for heads, arms, and legs

▨ ¼ yard tan-and-black print for background

▨ ▨ ⅛ yard *each* of 2 gold prints for wings

■ ■ ⅙ yard, or 4½ × 8½-inch piece, *each* of 2 red prints for dresses

■ ⅙ yard red print for lattice

■ ¾ yard black print for border and binding

¾ yard fabric for backing

¾ yard lightweight batting

Scraps, or ⅛-yard pieces, of several gold prints for appliqué stars

Fusible web

Yarn for hair (See "Quilting by Mail" on page 280 for ordering information.)

Embroidery floss

CUTTING

Prewash and press all of your fabrics. Using a rotary cutter, see-through ruler, and cutting mat, prepare the pieces as described below. Measurements for all pieces include ¼-inch seam allowances.

FABRIC	FIRST CUT		SECOND CUT	
Color	**No. of Pieces**	**Dimensions**	**No. of Pieces**	**Dimensions**
Tan solid	**Heads, arms, and legs**			
	1	2½ × 10-inch piece (heads)	No second cut	
	2	1½ × 15-inch pieces (arms)	No second cut	
	4	1 × 2½-inch pieces (legs)	No second cut	
Tan-and-black print	**Background**			
	2	2½ × 42-inch strips	2	2½ × 8½-inch pieces
			4	2½ × 3⅝-inch pieces
			4	2½ × 3½-inch pieces
			4	2½-inch squares
			2	2½ × 1¼-inch pieces
			4	1½-inch squares
	2	1 × 42-inch strips	4	1 × 13-inch strips
			2	1 × 8½-inch strips
Gold prints	**Wings**—from *each* of the 2 fabrics, cut the following:			
	1	2½ × 42-inch strip	2	2½ × 5½-inch pieces
			2	1½ -inch squares
Red prints	**Dresses**—from *each* of the 2 fabrics, cut the following:			
	1	4½ × 8½-inch piece	No second cut	
Red print	**Lattice**			
	3	1½ × 42-inch strips	2	1½ × 19½-inch strips
			2	1½ × 15-inch strips
			1	1½ × 13-inch strip
Black print	**Border**			
	4	3½ × 42-inch strips	2	3½ × 21½-inch strips
			2	3½ × 21-inch strips
	Binding			
	4	2¾ × 42-inch strips	No second cut	

Making the Heads and Arms

STEP 1. Make a template for the angel heads from the pattern on page 41.

STEP 2. Fold the 2½ × 10-inch tan solid piece in half crosswise with right sides together. Draw around the template to make two heads, leaving a generous ½-inch space between the heads. See **Diagram 1**.

Fold   2½"

5"

DIAGRAM 1

STEP 3. Sew on each drawn line, leaving the bottom edge open for turning. See **Diagram 2.** Cut out each head approximately ⅛ inch from the sewing line. Clip or pink the curves, turn the heads right side out, and press.

Fold

Leave open

DIAGRAM 2

STEP 4. To make the arms, fold each 1½ × 15-inch tan solid piece in half lengthwise with right sides together. Sew a ¼-inch seam on the edge opposite the fold, as shown in **Diagram 3.** Turn each tube right side out, press it, and cut it in half. You will now have four arms that measure ½ × 7½ inches each.

Fold

3/4" ⌐⌐⌐⌐⌐⌐⌐⌐⌐⌐⌐⌐⌐⌐⌐⌐⌐⌐⌐⌐⌐

15"

DIAGRAM 3

Turning Help

Use a bow whip or narrow loop turner to help turn the arms right side out. See "Quilting by Mail" on page 280 for ordering information.

Quick Corner Triangles

You will be making two angel blocks, one each of two different fabric combinations. Before sewing, coordinate the gold and red prints for the two combinations. The background is the same for both. Keep track of the combinations as you sew.

Refer to "Making Quick Corner Triangles" on page 269 for instructions on making the corner triangle units. Press the seams toward the triangle just added.

STEP 1. For the left wings, sew one 1½-inch and one 2½-inch tan-and-black print square to each of two 2½ × 5½-inch gold print pieces (one each of the two gold prints). See **Diagram 4.** Press.

LEFT WINGS
2½"

5½"

DIAGRAM 4

STEP 2. For the right wings, sew one 1½-inch and one 2½-inch tan-and-black print square to each of two 2½ × 5½-inch gold print pieces (one each of the two gold prints). Press. These corner triangles are sewn in the opposite direction from those in Step 1. See **Diagram 5** for proper placement.

RIGHT WINGS
2½"

5½"

DIAGRAM 5

STEP 3. With the arms centered and sandwiched between, sew two 1½-inch gold print squares to each of two 4½ × 8½-inch red print pieces (one each of the two different fabric combinations). See **Diagram 6.** Press.

4½"

8½"

DIAGRAM 6

Assembling the Blocks

Refer to "Assembly Line Piecing" on page 268 for instructions on completing the same steps for both angel blocks at the same time. Pay close attention that the corner triangle units are positioned as shown in the diagrams. Be sure to use ¼-inch seams and to press after each sewing step. Follow the arrows in the diagrams for pressing direction.

STEP 1. For the left wings, sew two 2½ × 5½-inch corner triangle units to two 2½ × 3½-inch tan-and-black print pieces. See **Diagram 7.** Press.

LEFT WINGS
2½"

5½"

3½"

DIAGRAM 7

STEP 2. For the right wings, sew two 2½ × 5½-inch corner triangle units to two 2½ × 3½-inch tan-and-black print pieces. See **Diagram 8**. Press.

RIGHT WINGS

DIAGRAM 8

STEP 3. Sew the 4½ × 8½-inch corner triangle units between the units from Step 1 and the units from Step 2. See **Diagram 9**. Press.

DIAGRAM 9

STEP 4. Sew two 3⅝ × 2½-inch tan-and-black print pieces, two 1 × 2½-inch tan solid pieces, and one 1¼ × 2½-inch tan-and-black print piece together in the order shown in **Diagram 10**. Press. Repeat to make two units.

DIAGRAM 10

STEP 5. Sew the two units from Step 3 to the two units from Step 4. See **Diagram 11**. Press.

DIAGRAM 11

STEP 6. Baste the angel heads to the centers of the two 8½ × 2½-inch tan-and-black print pieces. See **Diagram 12**.

DIAGRAM 12

STEP 7. Sew the two units from Step 6 to the two units from Step 5. See **Diagram 13**. Press. Each angel block will now measure 8½ × 12½ inches.

DIAGRAM 13

STEP 8. Sew a 1 × 8½-inch tan-and-black print strip to the top of each block, as shown in **Diagram 14**. Press.

DIAGRAM 14

STEP 9. Sew the 1 × 13-inch tan-and-black print strips to the sides of each block. See **Diagram 15**. Press. Each angel block will now measure 9½ × 13 inches.

DIAGRAM 15

Assembling the Top

STEP 1. Sew the 1½ × 13-inch lattice strip between the two blocks. Press the seams toward the lattice.

STEP 2. Sew the 1½ × 19½-inch lattice strips to the top and bottom. Press.

STEP 3. Sew the 1½ × 15-inch lattice strips to the sides. Press.

STEP 4. Sew the 3½ × 21½-inch border strips to the top and bottom. Press the seams toward the border.

STEP 5. Sew the 3½ × 21-inch border strips to the sides. Press.

Appliqué

STEP 1. Refer to "Quick-Fuse Appliqué" on pages 270–271. Trace five large stars and six small stars from the appliqué patterns on page 41.

STEP 2. Quick-fuse the stars to the border, referring to the **Quilt Layout** for placement.

Layering the Quilt

Arrange and baste the backing, batting, and top together, following the directions in "Layering the Quilt" on page 275. Trim the batting and backing to ¼ inch from the raw edges of the quilt top.

Binding the Quilt

Using the four 2¾ × 42-inch binding strips, follow the directions for "Binding the Quilt" on pages 275–276.

Star-Studded Details

For a celestial decorating theme, fuse stars to embellish your curtains or valances. Stencil or sponge stars on furniture, walls, ceilings, or floors.

Finishing Stitches

STEP 1. Machine or hand quilt in the seam lines of the wings, dresses, legs, lattice, and border. Quilt vertical lines ¾ inch apart in the dresses. Quilt a 1¼-inch diagonal grid in the background and random lines in the border. Outline the appliqué stars by quilting ¹⁄₁₆ inch from the edges.

STEP 2. Use yarn to add hair to the heads. Make French-knot eyes with embroidery floss, referring to "Decorative Stitches" on page 272 for instructions. Hand sew the heads in place. Tie a knot in the end of each arm and sew the arms in place.

QUILT LAYOUT

COLOR OPTION

Use pastels for a soft, ethereal look. This quilt could hang year-round.

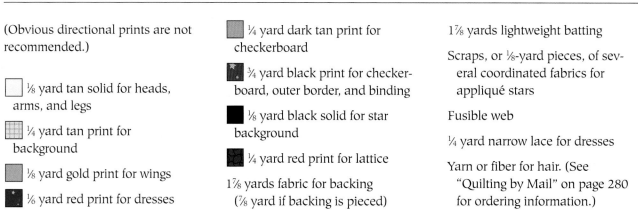

Angel Table Runner

Finished Size: 13 × 61 inches

Finished Angel Block: 8 × 12 inches

(See the table runner in the photo on page 32.)

MATERIALS

(Obvious directional prints are not recommended.)

⬜ ⅛ yard tan solid for heads, arms, and legs

▨ ¼ yard tan print for background

⬛ ⅛ yard gold print for wings

⬛ ⅙ yard red print for dresses

⬛ ¼ yard dark tan print for checkerboard

⬛ ¾ yard black print for checkerboard, outer border, and binding

⬛ ⅛ yard black solid for star background

⬛ ¼ yard red print for lattice

1⅞ yards fabric for backing (⅞ yard if backing is pieced)

1⅞ yards lightweight batting

Scraps, or ⅛-yard pieces, of several coordinated fabrics for appliqué stars

Fusible web

¼ yard narrow lace for dresses

Yarn or fiber for hair. (See "Quilting by Mail" on page 280 for ordering information.)

Embroidery floss

CUTTING

Prewash and press all of your fabrics. Using a rotary cutter, see-through ruler, and cutting mat, prepare the pieces as described below. Measurements for all pieces include ¼-inch seam allowances.

FABRIC	FIRST CUT		SECOND CUT	
Color	No. of Pieces	Dimensions	No. of Pieces	Dimensions
Tan solid ⬜	**Heads, arms, and legs**			
	1	2½ × 10-inch piece (heads)	No second cut	
	2	1½ × 15-inch pieces (arms)	No second cut	
	4	1 × 2½-inch pieces (legs)	No second cut	
Tan print ▨	**Background**			
	2	2½ × 42-inch strips	2	2½ × 8½-inch pieces
			4	2½ × 3⅝-inch pieces
			4	2½ × 3½-inch pieces
			4	2½-inch squares
			2	2½ × 1¼-inch pieces
			4	1½-inch squares

FABRIC	FIRST CUT		SECOND CUT	
Color	No. of Pieces	Dimensions	No. of Pieces	Dimensions
Gold print	**Wings**			
	1	2½ × 42-inch strip	4	2½ × 5½-inch pieces
			4	1½-inch squares
Red print	**Dresses**			
	2	4½ × 8½-inch pieces	No second cut	
Dark tan print	**Checkerboard**			
	4	1½ × 27-inch strips	No second cut	
Black print	**Checkerboard**			
	4	1½ × 27-inch strips	No second cut	
	Outer border		Cut 2 strips into the following:	
	4	2 × 42-inch strips	2	2 × 9½-inch strips
			2	2 × 21-inch strips
	Binding		Cut 2 strips into the following:	
	4	2¾ × 42-inch strips	2	2¾ × 14-inch strips
			2	2¾ × 26-inch strips
Black solid	**Star background**			
	1	3½ × 42-inch strip	4	3½ × 8½-inch pieces
Red print	**Lattice**		Cut 4 strips into the following:	
	7	1 × 42-inch strips	14	1 × 8½-inch strips

Making the Blocks

Refer to "Making the Heads and Arms" on pages 34–35 and "Quick Corner Triangles" on page 35 for instructions. You will be making two identical angel blocks.

Refer to "Assembling the Blocks" on pages 35–36 for instructions. Follow Steps 1 through 7. After assembly, each angel block will measure 8½ × 12½ inches.

Assembling the Top

STEP 1. To make the checkerboard, alternate the two colors and sew the eight 1½ × 27-inch checkerboard strips together to make an 8½ × 27-inch strip set. Change sewing direction with each strip sewn, and press the seams toward the darker fabric as you go. Using a rotary cutter and ruler, cut fourteen 1½ × 8½-inch checkerboard strips from this strip set. See **Diagram 16**.

DIAGRAM 16

STEP 2. Sew eight 1½ × 8½-inch checkerboard strips together in the order shown in **Diagram 17**. Press the seams, following the direction of the arrows in the diagram. The checkerboard unit will now measure 8½ inches square.

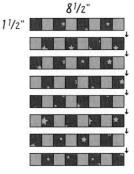

DIAGRAM 17

STEP 3. Sew the 8½-inch checkerboard unit, fourteen 1 × 8½-inch lattice strips, four 3½ × 8½-inch black solid star background pieces, six 1½ × 8½-inch checkerboard strips, and two angel blocks together as shown in **Diagram 18.** Press seams toward the lattice.

STEP 4. Cut one 1 × 42-inch lattice strip in half to make two 1 × 21-inch strips. Sew one 1 × 21-inch strip to each of the remaining two 1 × 42-inch lattice strips to make two strips approximately 1 × 63 inches each. Press. Sew the lattice strips to the sides. Trim the excess length and press.

STEP 5. Sew the 2 × 9½-inch outer border strips to the short ends of the table runner. Press the seams toward the outer border.

STEP 6. Sew one 2 × 21-inch outer border strip to each of the remaining two 2 × 42-inch outer border strips to make two strips approximately 2 × 63 inches each. Press. Sew the outer border strips to the sides. Trim the excess length and press.

Appliqué

STEP 1. Refer to "Quick-Fuse Appliqué" on pages 270–271. Trace 12 stars from the appliqué pattern on the opposite page.

STEP 2. Quick-fuse the stars to the star backgrounds, referring to the **Table Runner Layout** on the opposite page for placement.

DIAGRAM 18

Layering

Arrange and baste the backing, batting, and top together, following the directions in "Layering the Quilt" on page 275. Trim the batting and backing to ¼ inch from the raw edges of the table runner top.

Binding

Sew one 2¾ × 26-inch binding strip to each of the two 2¾ × 42-inch binding strips to make two strips approximately 2¾ × 68 inches each. Using the two 2¾ × 14-inch binding strips for the short ends and the two 2¾ × 68-inch binding strips for the sides, follow the directions for "Binding the Quilt" on pages 275–276.

Finishing Stitches

STEP 1. Machine or hand quilt in the seam lines of the wings, dresses, legs, checkerboards, lattice, and outer border. Quilt vertical lines ¾ inch apart in the dresses, or let your fabric suggest a quilting design. Quilt a 1¼-inch diagonal grid in the background of each angel block. In the outer border, quilt straight lines, approximately 2 inches apart, from the lattice to the binding. Outline the appliqué stars by quilting ¹⁄₁₆ inch from the edges.

STEP 2. Hand sew the lace to the bottoms of the dresses. Use yarn or fiber to add hair to the heads. Make French-knot eyes with embroidery floss, referring to "Decorative Stitches" on page 272. Hand sew the heads in place. Tie a knot in the end of each arm and sew the arms in place.

13"

61"

ANGEL HEAD
PATTERN

STAR PATTERNS FOR QUILT

STAR PATTERN FOR TABLE RUNNER

TABLE RUNNER LAYOUT

CELESTIAL NAPKINS, NAPKIN RINGS, AND TRAY

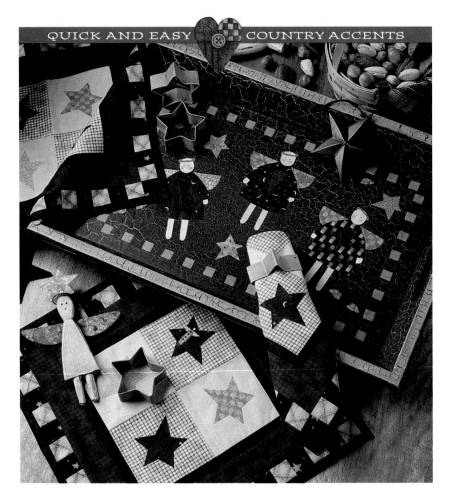

QUICK AND EASY COUNTRY ACCENTS

Stars and Angels Forever could be your entertaining motto with these Starry Napkins, Stellar Napkin Rings (directions on page 44), and Angelic Decoupage Tray (page 45). You'll have fun painting cookie cutters to transform them into napkin rings, and you can try both painting and decoupage on the wooden tray. The angels are made of fabric that is fused to the tray. (For a smaller version of the tray, see the photos on page 32 and the **Small Tray Layout** on page 45.)

STARRY NAPKINS

Finished Size: 15 inches square

Materials

To make 4 napkins:

⅙ yard *each* of 2 tan prints for background
⅓ yard black solid for accent border and binding
⅓ yard red plaid for wide border
⅓ yard dark tan print for checkerboard
⅓ yard black print for checkerboard
1 yard fabric for backing
Scraps, or ⅛-yard pieces, of several coordinated fabrics for appliqué stars
Lightweight, sewable fusible web
Embroidery floss

Assembling the Background

STEP 1. Using a ¼-inch seam, sew the two 4½ × 42-inch tan print background strips together to make an 8½ × 42-inch strip set. Press. Using a rotary cutter and ruler, cut eight 4½ × 8½-inch pieces from this strip set. See **Diagram 1** on the opposite page.

CUTTING

Prewash and press all of your fabrics. Using a rotary cutter, see-through ruler, and cutting mat, prepare the pieces as described below. Measurements for all pieces include ¼-inch seam allowances.

FABRIC	FIRST CUT		SECOND CUT	
Color	No. of Pieces	Dimensions	No. of Pieces	Dimensions
Tan prints	**Background**—from *each* of the 2 fabrics, cut the following:			
	1	4½ × 42-inch strip	No second cut	
Black solid	**Accent border and binding**			
	10	1 × 42-inch strips	8	1 × 15½-inch strips (binding)
			8	1 × 14½-inch strips (binding)
			8	1 × 9½-inch strips (accent border)
			8	1 × 8½-inch strips (accent border)
Red plaid	**Wide border**			
	5	2 × 42-inch strips	8	2 × 12½-inch strips
			8	2 × 9½-inch strips
Dark tan print	**Checkerboard**			
	6	1½ × 32-inch strips	No second cut	
Black print	**Checkerboard**			
	6	1½ × 32-inch strips	No second cut	
Backing fabric	4	15½-inch squares	No second cut	

DIAGRAM 1

STEP 2. Sew the 4½ × 8½-inch background pieces together in pairs to make four background units, as shown in **Diagram 2.** Press, following the direction of the arrow in the diagram.

DIAGRAM 2

STEP 3. Sew the 1 × 8½-inch accent border strips to the tops and bottoms of the four background units from Step 2. Press the seams toward the accent border.

STEP 4. Sew the 1 × 9½-inch accent border strips to the sides. Press.

STEP 5. Sew the 2 × 9½-inch wide border strips to the tops and bottoms. Press the seams toward the border.

STEP 6. Sew the 2 × 12½-inch wide border strips to the sides. Press.

Making the Checkerboard

STEP 1. Alternating the two colors, sew the twelve 1½ × 32-inch checkerboard strips together to make a 12½ × 32-inch strip set. Change sewing direction with each strip sewn, and press the seams toward the darker fabric as you go. Using a rotary cutter and ruler, cut eighteen 1½ × 12½-inch checkerboard strips from this strip set. There should be 12 squares in each strip. See **Diagram 3**.

12½"

1½"

32"

DIAGRAM 3

STEP 2. Compare eight 1½ × 12½-inch checkerboard strips to the tops and bottoms of the background units. You may need to take in or let out a few seams (¹⁄₁₆ inch or less) to make them fit. Pin and sew the checkerboard strips to the tops and bottoms of the background units. Press the seams toward the wide border.

STEP 3. Using a seam ripper, separate two 1½ × 12½-inch checkerboard strips into eight sets of 2 squares each. Sew one set of 2 squares to each of the remaining eight 1½ × 12½-inch checkerboard strips to make eight strips with 14 squares each. Press.

STEP 4. Fit, pin, and sew the 1½ × 14½-inch checkerboard strips to the sides. Press.

Appliqué

The stars were added to the napkins using the technique described in "Blanket Stitch Appliqué" on page 272. You can

machine appliqué with either a satin stitch or blanket stitch if you prefer. Refer to "Machine Appliqué" on pages 271–272 for instructions on either technique. Be sure to use a lightweight, sewable fusible web for all of these appliqué techniques.

STEP 1. Refer to "Quick-Fuse Appliqué" on pages 270–271. Trace 16 stars from the appliqué pattern on page 46.

STEP 2. Position and fuse the stars to the napkins, referring to the **Napkin Layout** below for placement.

STEP 3. Use two strands of embroidery floss to blanket stitch around the edges of the stars.

Finishing

STEP 1. Sew the 1 × 14½-inch binding strips to the tops and bottoms of the napkins. Press the seams toward the binding.

STEP 2. Sew the 1 × 15½-inch binding strips to the sides. Press.

STEP 3. For each napkin, position the top and backing with right

15"

15"

NAPKIN LAYOUT

sides together. Using ¼-inch seams, sew around the edges, leaving a 3- to 4-inch opening for turning. Trim the corners, turn the napkin right side out, hand stitch the opening closed, and press.

STELLAR NAPKIN RINGS

(See the napkin rings in the photo on page 42.)

Materials

To make 4 napkin rings:

4 star-shaped cookie cutters (approximately 2¾ inches each)
Spray primer
Acrylic paint
Matte-finish spray varnish
Antiquing medium

Assembly

STEP 1. Refer to "Decorative Painting" on page 53. Spray the cookie cutters with primer and allow the primer to dry thoroughly.

STEP 2. Paint with acrylic paint and allow the paint to dry. Apply a second coat if needed.

STEP 3. Spatter the cookie cutters with a contrasting paint, if desired, and allow the paint to dry.

STEP 4. Spray with matte-finish varnish and let dry.

STEP 5. Apply antiquing medium as directed on the container. Allow it to dry, and spray the cookie cutters with a second coat of matte-finish varnish.

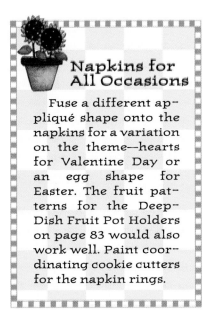

Napkins for All Occasions

Fuse a different appliqué shape onto the napkins for a variation on the theme—hearts for Valentine Day or an egg shape for Easter. The fruit patterns for the Deep-Dish Fruit Pot Holders on page 83 would also work well. Paint coordinating cookie cutters for the napkin rings.

ANGELIC DECOUPAGE TRAY

(See the tray in the photo on page 42.)

Materials

21 × 14-inch wooden tray
Acrylic paint
Crackle medium
Scraps, or ⅛-yard pieces, of
  several coordinated fabrics for
  appliqué pieces
Fusible web
Permanent fine-point felt pen
Red colored pencil
Bristle or foam brush
Decoupage finish
Matte-finish spray varnish
Press cloth

21"

14"

LARGE TRAY LAYOUT

Assembly

STEP 1. Refer to "Decorative Painting" on page 53. Paint the wooden tray with acrylic paint, and allow the paint to dry thoroughly.

STEP 2. Apply crackle medium and a second coat of paint as directed on the container. Allow the paint to dry thoroughly. Add decorative painting touches, such as checkerboards and contrasting borders, as desired, and let dry.

STEP 3. Refer to "Quick-Fuse Appliqué" on pages 270–271. Trace three angels, five small and/or large flying hearts, and three small and/or large stars from the appliqué patterns on page 46. Cover the appliqué pieces with a press cloth while quick-fusing them to the tray. Add eyes to the angels with the permanent felt pen and lightly blush the cheeks with the red colored pencil.

STEP 4. Use a bristle or foam brush to spread decoupage finish over the surface of the tray. Allow the finish to dry, and apply a second coat. When the second coat is dry, spray the tray with matte-finish varnish and let dry thoroughly.

13½"

10"

SMALL TRAY LAYOUT

Make a small angelic tray, like the one shown in the photo on page 32, to pair with the large tray.

APPLIQUÉ PATTERN KEY

—————— Tracing line

– – – – – Tracing line
(will be hidden behind
other fabric)

ANGEL PATTERN

SMALL STAR

LARGE STAR

STAR PATTERNS FOR TRAYS

FLYING HEART PATTERNS

Top

STAR PATTERN FOR NAPKINS

ANGEL TOPIARIES

QUICK AND EASY   COUNTRY ACCENTS

These fun and easy-to-make angel topiaries will be stellar additions to your collection of Christmas decorations. They coordinate with the Christmas Angels quilt and table runner on page 32 and can also function as decorations in their own right, adorning a mantel, table, or hutch with holiday or year-round cheer. I display the topiaries in my bedroom, where I can enjoy them all year long.

Materials

To make all 3 topiaries:

3 clay pots
Acrylic paint
Antiquing medium
Crackle medium
Matte-finish spray varnish
Floral foam
2 Styrofoam cones, each 9" tall
2 Styrofoam balls, measuring 1½"
  and 4" in diameter
Three ¼-inch dowels, stained (one
  14" long or two 5" long for Large
  Angel Topiary; 5" long for Small
  Angel Topiary; 6" long for
  Traditional Topiary Topiary)
Tacky glue

Sheet moss
Scraps of several coordinated
  fabrics and felt
Fusible web
Assorted buttons, raffia, and wire-
  edged ribbon
Medium-gauge wire
Glue gun and glue sticks
Permanent fine-point felt pen
Red colored pencil

Topiary Assembly

The assembly instructions for all three topiaries are the same. The specifics for decorating each topiary are listed after these steps.

STEP 1. Refer to "Decorative Painting" on page 53. Make sure the clay pot is clean and dry. Paint the pot with acrylic paint and allow to dry. Add decorative painting. Spray with matte-finish varnish and let dry.

STEP 2. Fill the pot with floral foam. Insert the dowel into the foam. Push the Styrofoam cone and/or ball onto the dowel, and glue in place with tacky glue.

STEP 3. Coat the topiary shape and the top of the floral foam base with tacky glue. Cover the glued areas with sheet moss.

STEP 4. Use a glue gun to decorate the topiary with fused shapes, buttons, bows, and twisted wire pokes.

LARGE ANGEL TOPIARY

Height: 21 inches

STEP 1. Refer to "Topiary Assembly" on page 47. Paint a checkerboard on the rim of the clay pot, spatter the pot with a contrasting color, and antique it.

STEP 2. Trace the angel wings, large flying heart, and small star from the appliqué patterns on the opposite page. Refer to Steps 1 through 4 in "Quick-Fuse Appliqué" on pages 270–271. To make two-sided shapes, position and fuse the designs to the wrong side of the backing fabric. Cut out along the edges of the fused shapes. Use the glue gun to glue the angel wings and flying heart to the topiary.

STEP 3. To form a wire poke, twist medium-gauge wire around a dowel or pencil. Use the glue gun to glue the star to one end of the wire, and insert the wire into the top of the topiary. Twist two pieces of wire together to form a halo, and insert the wire into the top of the topiary. Add a raffia bow to the neck, and glue buttons to the topiary.

SMALL ANGEL TOPIARY

Height: 18 inches

STEP 1. Refer to "Topiary Assembly" on page 47. Paint a checkerboard around the clay pot, spatter the pot with a contrasting color, apply crackle medium, and antique it.

STEP 2. Trace two of each of the stars from the appliqué patterns on the following page. Trace one large star from the appliqué patterns for the tray on page 46. Refer to Steps 1 through 4 in "Quick-Fuse Appliqué" on pages 270–271. To

make two-sided stars, position and fuse the stars to the wrong side of the backing fabric. Cut out along the edges of the fused stars.

STEP 3. To form five wire pokes, twist medium-gauge wire around a dowel or pencil. Use the glue gun to glue a star and button to one end of each wire. Insert one wire into the top of the topiary and the remaining wires into the pot.

STEP 4. Trace the angel from the appliqué pattern on page 46. Fuse to the back of the angel fabrics. Position and fuse the angel to the felt background. Cut around the angel approximately ⅛ inch from the edges. Add eyes to the angel with the permanent felt pen and lightly blush the cheeks with a red colored pencil. Glue the angel and assorted buttons to the topiary.

TRADITIONAL TOPIARY

Height: 12 inches

STEP 1. Refer to "Topiary Assembly" on page 47. Spatter the clay pot with a contrasting color and antique it. Use the glue gun to glue buttons to the rim.

STEP 2. Trace 12 to 15 hearts from the appliqué patterns below. Refer to Steps 1 through 4 in "Quick-Fuse Appliqué" on pages 270–271. To make two-sided hearts, position and fuse the hearts to the wrong side of the backing fabric. Cut out along the edges of the fused hearts. Add fused fabric wings to the hearts, or make dimensional wings by tearing small fabric strips, approximately 1 × 2½ inches each. Gather the center of each strip and glue one strip to the back of each fused heart.

STEP 3. Glue the hearts to the topiary. Tie a bow around the dowel with wire-edged ribbon.

STAR PATTERNS

ANGEL WINGS PATTERN

Use with or without wings

HEARTS PATTERNS

APPLIQUÉ PATTERN KEY

———— Tracing line

- - - - - Tracing line
(will be hidden behind
other fabric)

SHELF DOILIES

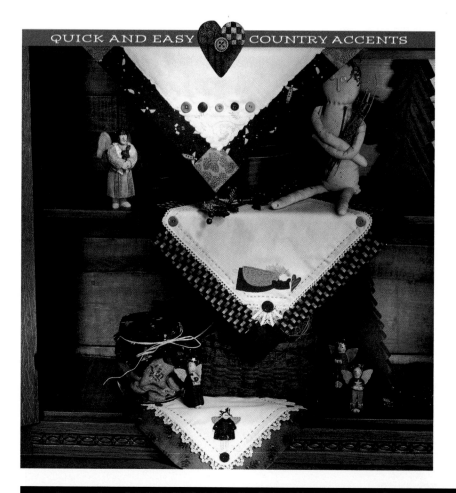

Adorn your shelves or furniture with doilies handmade quickly from purchased napkins or hankies. This is a perfect way to immortalize vintage linens. For the Angel Doily, *bottom*, Flying Angel Doily, *middle* (directions on page 51), and Button Doily, *top* (page 52), I used border fabrics in colors that coordinate with the Christmas Angels quilt and table runner shown on page 32.

MATERIALS AND CUTTING *(for Angel Doily)*

Prewash and press all of your fabrics. Using a rotary cutter, see-through ruler, and cutting mat, prepare the pieces as described below. Measurements for all pieces include ¼-inch seam allowances.

FABRIC	YARDAGE	NO. OF PIECES	DIMENSIONS
Light-color fabric for background square	⅓ yard, or 1 fat quarter	1	8½-inch square
Multicolor print for border	⅛ yard	4	3 × 8½-inch strips
Corner squares	⅛ yard	4	3-inch squares
Backing fabric	½ yard, or 1 fat quarter	1	13½-inch square
Several coordinated fabrics for appliqué pieces	Scraps, or ⅛-yard pieces	—	—

9½-inch napkin or hankie; lightweight, sewable fusible web; embroidery floss; 4 assorted ⁹⁄₁₆- to ¾-inch buttons

13"

13"

ANGEL DOILY

Finished Size: 13 inches square

Assembling the Doily

See "Materials and Cutting" on page 50.

STEP 1. Sew one 3 × 8½-inch border strip each to the top and bottom of the 8½-inch light-color background square. Press the seams toward the border.

STEP 2. Sew a 3-inch corner square to each end of the remaining two 3 × 8½-inch border strips. Press the seams toward the border. Pin and sew the border strips to the sides. Press.

STEP 3. Position the top and backing with right sides together. Using ¼-inch seams, sew around the edges, leaving a 3- to 4-inch opening for turning. Trim the corners, turn the doily right side out, hand stitch the opening closed, and press.

Appliqué

The appliqué pieces were added to the 9½-inch napkin using the technique described in "Blanket Stitch Appliqué" on page 272. Be sure to use a lightweight, sewable fusible web.

STEP 1. Refer to "Quick-Fuse Appliqué" on pages 270–271. Trace the angel from the appliqué pattern on page 46.

STEP 2. Position and fuse the appliqué pieces to the napkin, referring to the illustration at left for placement.

STEP 3. Use two strands of embroidery floss to blanket stitch around the edges of the angel. Using two strands of embroidery floss, add hair by tying five knots around the top of the head and clipping the ends to ⅜ inch in length. Make French-knot eyes with embroidery floss, referring to "Decorative Stitches" on page 272.

Finishing

Center the napkin over the background square and pin it securely. Use three strands of embroidery floss to make a running stitch around the edges of the napkin through all layers. Sew one button to each corner of the napkin.

Size Variations

The napkin used for the Angel Doily measures 13 inches square. However, you can adapt the instructions to fit any size napkin or hankie. Start by cutting the background square 1 inch smaller than the measurement of the napkin or hankie. Then adjust the border and backing to fit.

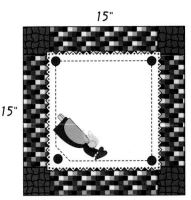

15"

15"

FLYING ANGEL DOILY

Finished Size: 15 inches square

(See the doily on the middle shelf in the photo on the opposite page.)

Assembling the Doily

See "Materials and Cutting" on page 52.

STEP 1. Sew one 3 × 10½-inch border strip each to the top and bottom of the 10½-inch light-color background square. Press the seams toward the border.

STEP 2. Sew a 3-inch corner square to each end of the remaining two 3 × 10½-inch border strips. Press the seams toward the border. Pin and sew the border strips to the sides. Press.

STEP 3. Position the top and backing with right sides together. Using ¼-inch seams, sew around the edges, leaving a 3- to 4-inch opening for turning. Trim the corners, turn the doily right side out, hand stitch the opening closed, and press.

Appliqué

The appliqué pieces were added to the 11½-inch napkin using the

MATERIALS AND CUTTING *(for Flying Angel Doily)*

Prewash and press all of your fabrics. Using a rotary cutter, see-through ruler, and cutting mat, prepare the pieces as described below. Measurements for all pieces include ¼-inch seam allowances.

FABRIC	YARDAGE	NO. OF PIECES	DIMENSIONS
Light-color fabric for background square	⅓ yard, or 1 fat quarter	1	10½-inch square
Multicolor print for border	¼ yard	4	3 × 10½-inch strips
Corner squares	⅛ yard	4	3-inch squares
Backing fabric	½ yard, or 1 fat quarter	1	15½-inch square
Several coordinated fabrics for appliqué pieces	Scraps, or ⅛-yard pieces	—	—

11½-inch napkin or hankie; lightweight, sewable fusible web; embroidery floss; 4 assorted ¾- to ⅞-inch buttons

technique described in "Blanket Stitch Appliqué" on page 272. Be sure to use a lightweight, sewable fusible web.

STEP 1. Refer to "Quick-Fuse Appliqué" on pages 270–271. Trace the flying angel from the appliqué pattern on page 53.

STEP 2. Position and fuse the appliqué pieces to the napkin, referring to the Flying Angel Doily illustration on page 51 for placement.

STEP 3. Use two strands of embroidery floss to blanket stitch around the edges of the flying angel. Backstitch the hair with two strands of embroidery floss, and make a French-knot eye with embroidery floss. See "Decorative Stitches" on page 272.

Finishing

Center the napkin over the background square and pin it securely. Use three strands of embroidery floss to make a running stitch around the edges of the napkin through all layers. Sew one button to each corner of the napkin.

BUTTON DOILY

Finished Size: 15 inches square

(See the doily on the top shelf in the photo on page 50.)

Making the Doily

The materials, cutting directions, and assembly instructions for the Button Doily are the same as those for the Flying Angel Doily on page 51, except that the

Button Doily does not require appliqué fabrics and uses five assorted buttons.

Finishing

Center the napkin over the background square and pin it securely. Hand stitch the edges of the napkin to the doily. Sew the buttons across one corner of the napkin, referring to the illustration at left for placement.

Use Sentimental Buttons

Snip the buttons off children's outgrown clothing, and sew them on a special keepsake doily. Select novelty print fabrics for the borders.

FLYING ANGEL
PATTERN

APPLIQUÉ PATTERN KEY

——— Tracing line

- - - - - Tracing line
(will be hidden behind
other fabric)

ANGEL PATTERN

Decorative Painting

Decorative painting can be done on almost any surface. Sand wood surfaces before painting and between coats with a fine-grit sandpaper. Always allow paint to dry thoroughly between steps.

STEP 1. Apply a base coat of acrylic paint. Many surfaces require two coats. Clay pots and papier-mâché are best painted with inexpensive foam brushes.

STEP 2. Add surface textures, such as sponging, spattering, or crackling. To sponge, apply contrasting color with a textured sponge. To spatter, apply contrasting color by running your thumb over a paint-filled toothbrush. To crackle, purchase a commercial crackle medium and follow the manufacturer's instructions.

STEP 3. Add detail painting, such as checkerboards, flowers, or hearts. To make checkerboards, use a commercial stencil or draw a graph for a checkerboard with a ruler. Paint every other square in contrasting colors.

STEP 4. Spray or brush on a coat of matte-finish varnish.

STEP 5. Add antiquing medium. Many products are available in both oil-base and latex formulas. Follow the manufacturer's instructions for best results.

STEP 6. Add a final coat of varnish in either matte, satin, or gloss finish.

HARVEST KITCHEN

There's nothing more comforting to me than a kitchen brimming with the harvest of fall's colorful bounty. The red apples, golden pears, and eye-catching checkerboard designs on these quilts and accessories will keep your kitchen filled with a warm country glow all through the year. Add country collectibles or accents from your garden for a look to call your own.

APPLE TABLE QUILT

Bright and bold red apples on the table make the perfect accompaniment to a home-cooked meal or an apple pie. The striking graphic accents in the blocks make this quilt irresistible whether you use it on your table or hang it on the wall. Keep an image of shiny Red Delicious apples in your head as you select the red print for the apple portion of the blocks.

Finished Size: 35 inches square   **Finished Apple Block: 4 × 6 inches**

MATERIALS

½ yard red print for apples

⅞ yard light tan print for background, four patches, and border

⅛ yard brown print for stems

¼ yard green print for triangles, corner squares, and center block

¼ yard tan print for triangles

¾ yard black solid for four patches, center block, lattice, and binding

⅛ yard red print for pieced blocks and center block

1⅛ yards fabric for backing

1⅛ yards cotton batting

Scraps of green print for appliqué leaves

Lightweight, sewable fusible web

Embroidery floss

CUTTING

Prewash and press all of your fabrics. Using a rotary cutter, see-through ruler, and cutting mat, prepare the pieces as described below. Measurements for all pieces include ¼-inch seam allowances.

FABRIC	FIRST CUT		SECOND CUT	
Color	No. of Pieces	Dimensions	No. of Pieces	Dimensions
Red print **Apples**				
	3	4½ × 42-inch strips	20	4½-inch squares
Light tan print **Background and four patches**				
	3	2¼ × 42-inch strips	40	2¼ × 2½-inch pieces (background)
	4	1½ × 42-inch strips	1	1½ × 30-inch strip (four patches)
			80	1½-inch squares (background)
	2	1½ × 42-inch strips (four patches)	No second cut	
Border				
	4	2½ × 30½-inch strips	No second cut	
Brown print **Stems**				
	2	1 × 42-inch strips	20	1 × 2½-inch pieces
Green print **Triangles, corner squares, and center block**				
	3	2½ × 42-inch strips	32	2½-inch squares (triangles)
			4	2½-inch squares (corner squares)
			4	2½ × 1½-inch pieces (center block)
Tan print **Triangles**				
	2	2½ × 42-inch strips	32	2½-inch squares
Black solid **Four patches and center block**			Cut *1* strip into the following:	
	3	1½ × 42-inch strips (use *2* for four patches)	1	1½ × 30-inch strip (four patches)
			4	1½-inch squares (center block)
Lattice				
	8	1 × 42-inch strips	2	1 × 30½-inch strips
			4	1 × 29½-inch strips
			2	1 × 16½-inch strips
			4	1 × 6½-inch strips
Binding				
	4	2¾ × 42-inch strips	No second cut	
Red print **Pieced blocks and center block**				
	1	2½ × 42-inch strip	9	2½-inch squares

Piecing the Blocks

You will be making 20 apple blocks, 8 pieced blocks, and 1 center block. Refer to "Making Quick Corner Triangles" on page 269 and "Assembly Line Piecing" on page 268. It is more efficient to do the same step for all blocks at the same time than to piece an entire block together at one time. Be sure to press after each sewing step, following the direction of the arrows in the diagrams unless instructed otherwise.

Making the Apple Blocks

STEP 1. Sew four 1½-inch light tan print squares to each of the twenty 4½-inch red print squares. See **Diagram 1**. In 12 of the units, press the seams toward the light tan print (Apple #1 Blocks). Press the seams in the remaining 8 units toward the red print (Apple #2 Blocks).

DIAGRAM 1

Be Creative with Extra Blocks

Stitch up some extra apple blocks to decorate kitchen towels, appliance covers, or an apron. You could also create chair cushions or place mats.

STEP 2. Using ¼-inch seams, sew the twenty 1 × 2½-inch brown print pieces between the forty 2¼ × 2½-inch light tan print pieces. See **Diagram 2**. Press.

DIAGRAM 2

STEP 3. Sew the 20 units from Step 2 to the 20 corner triangle units from Step 1, as shown in **Diagram 3**. Press the seams in the 12 Apple #1 Blocks toward the stems. Press the seams in the 8 Apple #2 Blocks toward the apples. Each apple block will now measure 4½ × 6½ inches.

Step 2 Unit

Step 1 Unit

DIAGRAM 3

Appliqué

The leaves were added to the apple blocks using the technique described in "Blanket Stitch Appliqué" on page 272. Be sure to use a lightweight, sewable fusible web.

STEP 1. Refer to "Quick-Fuse Appliqué" on pages 270–271. Trace 40 leaves from the appliqué pattern on page 62.

STEP 2. Allowing for ¼-inch seam allowances around the apple blocks, position and fuse the leaves in place.

Stitch the Leaves First

It is a good idea to complete the blanket stitch for each block before you assemble the Apple Table Quilt. The blocks will be easier to handle.

STEP 3. Use two strands of embroidery floss to blanket stitch around the edges of the leaves.

Making the Pieced Blocks

STEP 1. To make the green-and-tan corner triangle units, sew the thirty-two 2½-inch green print squares to the thirty-two 2½-inch tan print squares.

See **Diagram 4**. Press the seams toward the green print.

DIAGRAM 4

STEP 2. To make the four patches, use ¼-inch seams. Sew two 1½ × 42-inch light tan print strips and two 1½ × 42-inch black solid strips together in pairs to make two 2½ × 42-inch strip sets. Press the seams toward the black fabric. Using a rotary cutter and ruler, cut twenty-five 1½ × 2½-inch segments from each strip set. See **Diagram 5**.

DIAGRAM 5

STEP 3. Sew the 1½ × 30-inch light tan print strip to the 1½ × 30-inch black solid strip to make a 2½ × 30-inch strip set. Press the seam toward the black fabric. Using a rotary cutter and ruler, cut fourteen 1½ × 2½-inch segments from this strip set. See **Diagram 6.**

DIAGRAM 6

STEP 4. Sew the tan/black segments from Steps 2 and 3 together in pairs to make 32 four-patch units. See **Diagram 7.** Press.

DIAGRAM 7

STEP 5. Sew 16 of the four-patch units from Step 4 between the 32 corner triangle units from Step 1, as shown in **Diagram 8.** Press.

DIAGRAM 8

STEP 6. Sew eight 2½-inch red print squares between the remaining 16 four-patch units from Step 4. See **Diagram 9.** Press.

DIAGRAM 9

STEP 7. Sew the 8 units from Step 6 between the 16 units from Step 5, as shown in **Diagram 10.** Press. Each pieced block will now measure 6½ inches square.

DIAGRAM 10

Making the Center Block

STEP 1. Sew two 2½ × 1½-inch green print pieces between the four 1½-inch black solid squares. See **Diagram 11.** Press.

DIAGRAM 11

STEP 2. Sew the remaining 2½-inch red print square between the two remaining 1½ × 2½-inch green print pieces. See **Diagram 12.** Press.

DIAGRAM 12

STEP 3. Sew the unit from Step 2 between the two units from Step 1, as shown in **Diagram 13.** Press. The center block will now measure 4½ inches square.

DIAGRAM 13

Assembling the Top

STEP 1. Referring to **Diagram 14** for placement, sew two Apple #1 Blocks between four pieced blocks. Press.

DIAGRAM 14

STEP 2. Sew the center block between two Apple #1 Blocks. See **Diagram 15.** Press.

DIAGRAM 15

STEP 3. Sew the unit from Step 2 between the two units from Step 1. See **Diagram 16** on the opposite page. Press.

STEP 4. Alternating Apple #1 and Apple #2 Blocks, sew blocks together to make four rows with four blocks each. See **Diagram 17** on the opposite page. Press.

STEP 5. Sew the 1 × 6½-inch lattice strips to both ends of two rows of apples from Step 4. Press the seams toward the lattice.

STEP 6. Referring to **Diagram 18** on the opposite page for placement, sew the two units from Step 5 between the four remaining pieced blocks. Press.

STEP 7. Sew the 1 × 16½-inch lattice strips to the tops of the two remaining rows of apples from Step 4. Press.

STEP 8. Sew the unit from Step 3 between the two units from Step 7. See **Diagram 19**. Press.

STEP 9. Sew the 1 × 29½-inch lattice strips to the tops and bottoms of the two units from Step 6. Press.

STEP 10. Sew the unit from Step 8 between the two units from Step 9. See **Diagram 20** on page 62. Press.

STEP 11. Sew the 1 × 30½-inch lattice strips to the sides. Press.

STEP 12. Sew one 2½ × 30½-inch border strip each to the top and bottom. Press the seams toward the border.

STEP 13. Sew one 2½-inch green print corner square to each end of the remaining two 2½ × 30½-inch border strips. Press the seams toward the border. Pin and sew the border strips to the sides. Press.

Layering the Quilt

Arrange and baste the backing, batting, and top together, following the directions in "Layering the

Easing Extra Length

If one unit is slightly longer than the other, keep the longer unit on the bottom when stitching. The action of the feed dogs will help to ease in the longer piece to fit.

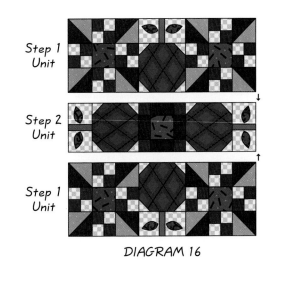

Step 1 Unit

Step 2 Unit

Step 1 Unit

DIAGRAM 16

APPLE #1   APPLE #2   APPLE #1   APPLE #2

DIAGRAM 17

Step 5 Unit

DIAGRAM 18

Step 7 Unit   Step 3 Unit   Step 7 Unit

DIAGRAM 19

Step 9
Unit

Step 8
Unit

Step 9
Unit

DIAGRAM 20

35"

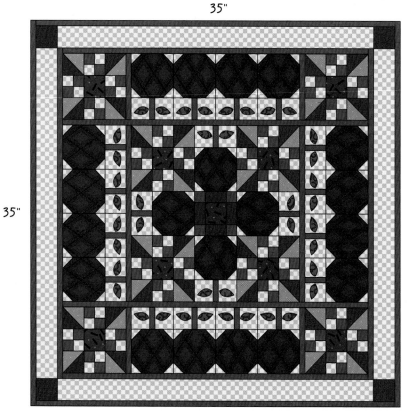

35"

TABLE QUILT LAYOUT

Quilt" on page 275. Trim the batting and backing to ¼ inch from the raw edges of the quilt top.

Binding the Quilt

Using the four 2¾ × 42-inch binding strips, follow the directions for "Binding the Quilt" on pages 275–276.

Finishing Stitches

Machine or hand quilt in the seam lines of the apples, stems, pieced blocks, center block, lattice, and corner squares. Outline the appliqué leaves by quilting ¹⁄₁₆ inch from the edges. Quilt an × in the center squares of the pieced blocks and in each corner square. Quilt a 1-inch diagonal grid in each apple. Quilt a 1¼-inch diagonal grid in the border.

LEAF
PATTERN

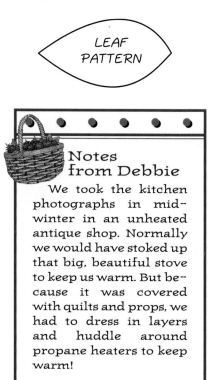

Notes from Debbie

We took the kitchen photographs in mid-winter in an unheated antique shop. Normally we would have stoked up that big, beautiful stove to keep us warm. But because it was covered with quilts and props, we had to dress in layers and huddle around propane heaters to keep warm!

FOUR-APPLE QUILT

Turn the page for a quilt that may bring back warm memories of

home or Grandma's kitchen. Maybe you remember helping to peel

apples for pie or snitching slices when no one was looking! One of my favorite

taste treats when helping my mom bake was to roll out the excess piecrust, top

it with cinnamon and sugar, and bake it for about ten minutes. Yummm!

This quilt would be sweet in any country kitchen. (If Granny Smith is your

favorite apple, see the **Color Option** on page 66.)

Finished Size: 22 inches square   **Finished Apple Block: 4 × 6 inches**

MATERIALS

⅙ yard red print for apples

¼ yard light tan print for background and four patches

⅛ yard, or 1 × 12-inch strip, brown print for stems

⅙ yard gold print for triangles and center block

⅛ yard green print for triangles

½ yard black solid for four patches, center block, and binding

⅙ yard red print for block centers and accent border

¼ yard green plaid for outer border

¾ yard fabric for backing

¾ yard lightweight batting

Scraps of green print for appliqué leaves

Lightweight, sewable fusible web

Embroidery floss

CUTTING

Prewash and press all of your fabrics. Using a rotary cutter, see-through ruler, and cutting mat, prepare the pieces as described below. Measurements for all pieces include ¼-inch seam allowances.

FABRIC	FIRST CUT		SECOND CUT	
Color	No. of Pieces	Dimensions	No. of Pieces	Dimensions
Red print	**Apples**			
	4	4½-inch squares	No second cut	
Light tan print	**Background and four patches**			
	1	2¼ × 42-inch strip	8	2¼ × 2½-inch pieces (background)
	2	1½ × 42-inch strips	2	1½ × 28-inch strips (four patches)
			16	1½-inch squares (background)
Brown print	**Stems**			
	4	1 × 2½-inch pieces	No second cut	
Gold print	**Triangles**			
	1	2½ × 42-inch strip	16	2½-inch squares
	Center block			
	1	1½ × 42-inch strip	4	1½ × 2½-inch pieces
Green print	**Triangles**			
	1	2½ × 42-inch strip	16	2½-inch squares
Black solid	**Four patches and center block**			
	2	1½ × 42-inch strips	2	1½ × 28-inch strips (four patches)
			4	1½-inch squares (center block)
	Binding			
	4	2¾ × 42-inch strips	No second cut	
Red print	**Block centers**			
	5	2½-inch squares	No second cut	
	Accent border			
	2	1 × 42-inch strips	2	1 × 17½-inch strips
			2	1 × 16½-inch strips
Green plaid	**Outer border**			
	2	2½ × 42-inch strips	2	2½ × 21½-inch strips
			2	2½ × 17½-inch strips

Making the Apple Blocks

You will be making four apple blocks. Refer to "Making Quick Corner Triangles" on page 269 for instructions on making the corner triangle units. Refer to "Assembly Line Piecing" on page 268 for instructions on making the same corner triangle units for all four blocks at the same time.

STEP 1. Follow Steps 1 through 3 under "Making the Apple Blocks" on page 59 to make four apple blocks. Press the seams in Step 1 toward the light tan print. Press the seams in Step 3 toward the apples.

STEP 2. Refer to "Appliqué" on page 59 to add the leaves to the apple blocks.

Making the Pieced Blocks

Refer to "Making the Pieced Blocks" on page 59 to make four pieced blocks. Use the sixteen 2½-inch gold print squares and the sixteen 2½-inch green print squares to make 16 gold-and-green corner triangle units. To make the four patches, use the two 1½ × 28-inch light tan print strips and the two 1½ × 28-inch black solid strips to make two strip sets. Cut these strip sets into thirty-two 1½ × 2½-inch segments. Follow the directions in Steps 5 through 7 to finish making four pieced blocks.

Making the Center Block

Refer to "Making the Center Block" on page 60 to make one center block. You will be using the gold print in place of the green print.

Assembling the Top

STEP 1. Follow Steps 1 through 3 under "Assembling the Top" on page 60.

STEP 2. Sew the 1 × 16½-inch accent border strips to the top and bottom. Press the seams toward the accent border.

STEP 3. Sew the 1 × 17½-inch accent border strips to the sides. Press.

STEP 4. Sew the 2½ × 17½-inch outer border strips to the top and bottom. Press the seams toward the outer border.

STEP 5. Sew the 2½ × 21½-inch outer border strips to the sides. Press.

Layering the Quilt

Arrange and baste the backing, batting, and top together, following the directions in "Layering the Quilt" on page 275. Trim the batting and backing to ¼ inch from the raw edges of the quilt top.

Binding the Quilt

Using the four 2¾ × 42-inch binding strips, follow the directions for "Binding the Quilt" on pages 275–276.

Finishing

Machine or hand quilt in the seam lines of the apples, stems, pieced blocks, center block, and accent border. Outline the appliqué leaves by quilting ¹⁄₁₆ inch from the edges. Quilt a 1-inch diagonal grid in each apple. In the outer border, quilt lines perpendicular to the binding, approximately 1 inch apart.

22"

22"

QUILT LAYOUT

COLOR OPTION

Here's a Granny Smith version of the quilt that will delight those who love the combination of blue, green, and gold.

FRESH FRUIT IN SEASON

The orchard-fresh Fruit Sampler and Apple Valance window dressing

on the next page look as if they've come straight from your favorite roadside

stand. The Fruit Sampler goes together easily with quick-fuse appliqué.

The Apple Valance (directions on page 71) is easy as apple pie

to make and can be adapted to fit any size window.

Fruit Sampler

Finished Size: 19 × 18 inches

MATERIALS AND CUTTING

Prewash and press all of your fabrics. Using a rotary cutter, see-through ruler, and cutting mat, prepare the pieces as described below. Measurements for all pieces include ¼-inch seam allowances.

FABRIC	YARDAGE	NO. OF PIECES	DIMENSIONS
Tan, green, and red prints for background (See Dimensions at right.)	⅛ to ¼ yard *each* of 7 fabrics	1	4 × 3½-inch piece *each* of 2 tan fabrics for cherries
		1	4 × 4½-inch piece *each* of 2 green fabrics for pears
		1	4 × 5½-inch piece *each* of 2 red fabrics for pineapples
		1	5½ × 7½-inch piece of tan print for apple basket
Tan print for checkerboard	⅛ yard	1	1½ × 24-inch strip
Black print for checkerboard	⅛ yard	1	1½ × 24-inch strip
Black solid for lattice	⅛ yard (cut into three 1 × 42-inch strips)	4	1 × 13½-inch strips
		2	1 × 12½-inch strips
		2	1 × 5½-inch strips
Gold prints for corner squares	⅛ yard, or 2½-inch square, *each* of 4 fabrics	1	2½-inch square *each*

(continued)

MATERIALS AND CUTTING – continued

FABRIC	YARDAGE	NO. OF PIECES	DIMENSIONS
Red prints for border	⅛ yard, or 2½ × 15-inch strip, *each* of 4 fabrics	1	2½ × 14½-inch strip *each* of 2 fabrics for sides
		1	2½ × 13½-inch strip *each* of 2 fabrics for top and bottom
Black solid for binding	⅛ yard (cut into two 1 × 42-inch strips)	4	1 × 18½-inch strips
Backing fabric	⅝ yard	—	—
Lightweight batting	⅝ yard	—	—
Several coordinated fabrics for appliqué pieces	Scraps, or ⅛-yard pieces	—	—
Fusible web			

Assembling the Background

Assemble the wallhanging top before adding the appliqué pieces. Referring to the **Wallhanging Layout** on page 71, lay out the background pieces in a pleasing arrangement. Keep track of your layout while sewing the background together. Be sure to use ¼-inch seams and to press after each sewing step.

STEP 1. For Row #1, sew one 4 × 4½-inch green pear background piece between one 4 × 3½-inch tan cherries background piece and one 4 × 5½-inch red pineapple background piece, as shown in **Diagram 1**. Press the seams, following the arrows in the diagrams.

ROW #1

DIAGRAM 1

STEP 2. For Row #2, sew the 1 × 5½-inch lattice strips to the top and bottom of the 5½ × 7½-inch tan apple basket background piece. See **Diagram 2**. Press.

ROW #2

DIAGRAM 2

STEP 3. Sew the two 1½ × 24-inch checkerboard strips together to make a 2½ × 24-inch strip set. Press the seam toward the darker fabric. Cut this strip set into thirds, approximately 8 inches each. See **Diagram 3**.

DIAGRAM 3

STEP 4. Resew the thirds together to make a 6½ × 8-inch strip set. Using a rotary cutter and ruler, cut four 1½ × 6½-inch strips from this strip set. There should be six squares in each strip. See **Diagram 4**. Use a seam ripper to remove one black square from two strips to make two 1½ × 5½-inch strips that begin and end with a tan square. Remove one tan square from the remaining two strips to make two 1½ × 5½-inch strips that begin and end with a black square.

DIAGRAM 4

STEP 5. Compare the 1½ × 5½-inch strips to the top and bottom of the unit from Step 2. You may need to take in or let out a few seams (¹⁄₁₆ inch or less) to make them fit. Make adjustments before you sew the checkerboard strips together into pairs. If you do make adjustments, make them in the same place on each strip so that the strips will still match up. Refer to "Fitting Pieced Borders" on page 274 for further instructions. Sew the checkerboard strips together in pairs, and press.

STEP 6. Referring to **Diagram 5** for placement of the light and dark squares, pin and sew the checkerboard to the unit from Step 2. Press.

STEP 7. For Row #3, sew the remaining 4 × 5½-inch red pineapple background piece between the 4 × 4½-inch green pear background piece and the 4 × 3½-inch tan cherries background piece, as shown in **Diagram 6**. Press.

STEP 8. Sew one 1 × 12½-inch lattice strip to each side of Row #2. Press the seams toward the lattice.

STEP 9. Sew Row #2 between Rows #1 and #3. Press the seams toward the lattice.

STEP 10. Sew one 1 × 13½-inch lattice strip each to the top and bottom. Press the seams toward the lattice.

STEP 11. Sew the two remaining 1 × 13½-inch lattice strips to the sides. Press.

ROW #2

Step 2 Unit

DIAGRAM 5

ROW #3

4"
4½"
5½"
3½"

DIAGRAM 6

Border and Binding

STEP 1. Lay out your border strips and corner squares in a pleasing arrangement. Keep track of your layout while sewing on the border. Sew the 2½ × 13½-inch border strips to the top and bottom. Press the seams toward the border.

STEP 2. Sew a 2½-inch corner square to each end of the 2½ × 12½-inch border strips. Press the seams toward the border. Pin and sew the border strips to the sides. Press.

Checkerboard Tips

The key to a successful checkerboard is selecting fabrics with good contrast. Making a scrap checkerboard is an option to give a different look to the Fruit Sampler wallhanging.

STEP 3. Sew one 1 × 18½-inch binding strip each to the top and bottom. Press the seams toward the binding.

STEP 4. Sew the two remaining 1 × 18½-inch binding strips to the sides. Press.

Appliqué

STEP 1. Refer to "Quick-Fuse Appliqué" on pages 270–271. Trace two clusters of cherries, two pears, two pineapples, and one apple basket from the appliqué patterns on pages 74–75.

STEP 2. Quick-fuse each appliqué design to the center of its corresponding background piece. Position and fuse one design at a time, referring to the photo on page 68 for placement.

Finishing Stitches

STEP 1. Position the top and backing with right sides together. Lay both pieces on top of the batting, with the backing next to the batting. Pin all three layers together. Using ¼-inch seams, sew around the edges, leaving a 3- to 4-inch opening for turning. Trim the backing and batting to the same size as the top. Trim the corners, turn the wallhanging right side out, hand stitch the opening closed, and press.

STEP 2. Machine or hand quilt in the seam lines of the lattice, checkerboard squares, corner squares, and binding. Outline the appliqué designs by quilting ¹⁄₁₆ inch from the edges. Quilt a 1¼-inch diagonal grid in the border.

19"

18"

WALLHANGING LAYOUT

Apple Valance

Finished Size: 6 × 10 inches

(See the valance in the photo on page 68.)

MATERIALS

You will need to measure your window(s) to determine how many 6-inch-wide valance panels you need to make. I used four panels in each of the two windows shown in the photo on pages 54–55. The following Materials list gives fabric requirements for both a single valance panel and a group of eight panels. Before buying fabric, use the Cutting directions on page 72 to customize the Materials list to fit your needs.

To make 1 valance panel:

☐ ¼ yard, or 6 × 8-inch piece, light tan print for background

☐ ⅛ yard, or 1½ × 42-inch strip, green print for border

☐ ⅛ yard, or 1½ × 18-inch piece, tan print for checkerboard

☐ ⅛ yard, or 1½ × 18-inch piece, red print for checkerboard

☐ ⅙ yard green plaid for tabs

¼ yard, or 8 × 12-inch piece, fabric for backing

Scraps, or ⅛-yard pieces, of several coordinated fabrics for appliqué pieces

Fusible web

To make 8 valance panels:

☐ ⅜ yard light tan print for background

☐ ⅓ yard green print for border

☐ ⅙ yard tan print for checkerboard

☐ ⅙ yard red print for checkerboard

☐ 1 yard green plaid for tabs

¾ yard fabric for backing

Scraps, or ⅛-yard pieces, of several coordinated fabrics for appliqué pieces

Fusible web

CUTTING

Prewash and press all of your fabrics. Using a rotary cutter, see-through ruler, and cutting mat, prepare the pieces as described below. Measurements for all pieces include ¼-inch seam allowances (to make 1 valance panel).

FABRIC	FIRST CUT		SECOND CUT	
Color	No. of Pieces	Dimensions	No. of Pieces	Dimensions
Light tan print	**Background**			
	1	Make a template for the background from the pattern on page 75	No second cut	
Green print	**Border**			
	1	1½ × 42-inch strip	2	1½ × 8-inch strips
			2	1½ × 6-inch strips
			1	1½ × 4½-inch strip
Tan print	**Checkerboard**			
	3	1½ × 5-inch strips	No second cut	
Red print	**Checkerboard**			
	3	1½ × 5-inch strips	No second cut	
Green plaid	**Tabs**			
	2	2 × 30-inch strips	No second cut	

Valance Assembly

STEP 1. Using a ¼-inch seam, sew the 1½ × 4½-inch border strip to the top of the light tan print background piece, as shown in **Diagram 7**. Press.

STEP 2. Sew one 1½ × 6-inch border strip to the lower left edge of the background piece. Press the seam toward the border. Trim the excess length from the border. See **Diagram 8**.

STEP 3. Sew the remaining 1½ × 6-inch border strip to the lower right edge of the background piece. Press. Trim, as shown in **Diagram 9**.

STEP 4. Sew the 1½ × 8-inch border strips to the sides. Press and trim. See **Diagram 10**.

STEP 5. Alternating the two colors, sew the six 1½ × 5-inch checkerboard strips together to make a 6½ × 5-inch strip set. Press the seams toward the darker

DIAGRAM 7   DIAGRAM 8   DIAGRAM 9   DIAGRAM 10

fabric as you go. Using a rotary cutter and ruler, cut two 1½ × 6½-inch strips from this strip set. See **Diagram 11**.

DIAGRAM 11

STEP 6. Compare the 1½ × 6½-inch strips to the top of the unit from Step 4. You may need to take in or let out a few seams (¹⁄₁₆ inch or less) to make them fit. Make adjustments before you sew the checkerboard strips together. If you do make adjustments, make them in the same place on each strip so that the strips will still match up. Refer to "Fitting Pieced Borders" on page 274 for further instructions. Sew the checkerboard strips together and press.

STEP 7. Referring to the **Valance Layout** for placement of the light and dark squares, pin and sew the checkerboard to the unit from Step 4. Press toward the green border.

Appliqué

STEP 1. Refer to "Quick-Fuse Appliqué" on pages 270–271. Trace one apple from the appliqué pattern on page 74.

STEP 2. Quick-fuse the apple to the center of the background piece, referring to the photo on page 68 for placement.

Finishing

STEP 1. To make the hanging tabs, fold each 2 × 30-inch green plaid tab strip in half lengthwise with right sides together. Sew a ¼-inch seam along the edge opposite the fold. Turn the tab right side out and press.

STEP 2. Fold the tabs in half and pin them in place, keeping the folds even with the top edge of the valance. The outside edge of each tab should line up with the seam of the first checkerboard square. Baste the tabs in place. They will be sewn into the seam when the valance is finished. See **Diagram 12**.

DIAGRAM 12

Try Other Fruits

If you like, substitute a pear or cherries on your valance, using the appliqué patterns for the Fruit Sampler on pages 74–75. You can also mix and match fruits within the window valance.

STEP 3. Position and pin the top and backing with right sides together. Make sure the tabs are tucked inside the valance so that they will not get caught in the seams. Using ¼-inch seams, sew around the edges, leaving a 3-inch opening for turning. Trim the backing to the same size as the top. Trim the corners, turn the valance right side out, hand stitch the opening closed, and press.

VALANCE LAYOUT

PEAR PATTERN

APPLE BASKET PATTERN

APPLE PATTERN

APPLIQUÉ PATTERN KEY

——— Tracing line

- - - - Tracing line
(will be hidden behind
other fabric)

BACKGROUND PATTERN

CHERRIES PATTERN

PINEAPPLE PATTERN

ORCHARD TRIO

Apples, pears, and plaids, oh my! This quilt and these two plaid towels

make a perfect trio. Make the Fruitful Towel Holder and Fruit Tea Towels

(directions on page 81) in a jiffy in your sewing room—you don't have to go to

the orchard to pick these fruits. Just pick your favorite plaids, whip up some

easy, quick-sew checkerboards, and quick-piece some fresh apples and pears.

Fruitful Towel Holder

Finished Size: 19 × 11 inches   **Finished Block: 4 × 6 inches**

(directions on page 81)

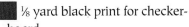
MATERIALS

(Obvious directional prints are not recommended.)

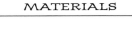 ⅙ yard, or 4½-inch square, *each* of 2 red prints for apples

¼ yard light tan print for background, tabs, and checkerboard

⅛ yard, or 1 × 2½-inch piece, *each* of 2 brown prints for apple stems

⅙ yard, or 4½ × 6½-inch piece, gold print for pear

⅛ yard, or 1 × 1½-inch piece, brown print for pear stem

⅛ yard green print for lattice

⅛ yard black print for checkerboard

⅛ yard black solid for binding

⅜ yard fabric for backing

⅜ yard lightweight batting

Scraps of green print for appliqué leaves

Lightweight, sewable fusible web

Green embroidery floss

½-inch wooden dowel, 19 inches long

CUTTING

Prewash and press all of your fabrics. Using a rotary cutter, see-through ruler, and cutting mat, prepare the pieces as described below. Measurements for all pieces include ¼-inch seam allowances.

FABRIC	FIRST CUT		SECOND CUT	
Color	**No. of Pieces**	**Dimensions**	**No. of Pieces**	**Dimensions**
Red print	**Apples**—from *each* of the 2 fabrics, cut the following:			
	1	4½-inch square	No second cut	
Light tan print	**Background, tabs, and checkerboard**			
	1	2½ × 42-inch strip	1	2½ × 12-inch strip (tabs)
			4	2½ × 2¼-inch pieces (apple background)
	2	1½ × 42-inch strips	1	1½ × 30-inch strip (checkerboard)
			2	1½ × 2½-inch pieces (pear background)
			2	1½ × 2¼-inch pieces (pear)
			8	1½-inch squares (apple)
			4	1½-inch squares (pear)
			2	1-inch squares (pear)
	1	1½ × 42-inch strip (checkerboard)	No second cut	
Brown print	**Apple stems**—from *each* of the 2 fabrics, cut the following:			
	1	1 × 2½-inch piece	No second cut	
Gold print	**Pear**			
	1	4½ × 3½-inch piece	No second cut	
	1	2½-inch square	No second cut	
Brown print	**Pear stem**			
	1	1 × 1½-inch piece	No second cut	
Green print	**Lattice**			
	2	1½ × 42-inch strips	2	1½ × 14½-inch strips
			2	1½ × 8½-inch strips
			2	1½ × 6½-inch strips
Black print	**Checkerboard**			
	1	1½ × 42-inch strip	No second cut	
	1	1½ × 30-inch strip	No second cut	
Black solid	**Binding**			
	2	1 × 42-inch strips	2	1 × 18½-inch strips
			2	1 × 11½-inch strips

Making the Blocks

You will be making two apple blocks, one each of two different apple and stem combinations. Before you start sewing, coordinate the fabrics for the two combinations. Keep track of the combinations as you sew. You will also be making one pear block.

Refer to "Making Quick Corner Triangles" on page 269. For each apple and pear block, the corner triangle units are made first and then the block is pieced. Pay close attention that the corner triangle units are positioned as shown in the diagrams. Press the seams toward the triangle just added.

STEP 1. Follow Steps 1 through 3 under "Making the Apple Blocks" on page 65 to make two apple blocks. Press the seams in Steps 1 and 3 toward the apples.

STEP 2. Refer to "Appliqué" on page 59 to add the leaves to the apple blocks.

STEP 3. To make the pear block, sew the four 1½-inch light tan print squares to the 4½ × 3½-inch gold print piece. See **Diagram 1.** Press.

DIAGRAM 1

STEP 4. Sew the two 1-inch light tan print squares to the 2½-inch gold print square, as shown in **Diagram 2.** Press.

DIAGRAM 2

STEP 5. Using ¼-inch seams, sew the corner triangle unit from Step 4 between the two 1½ × 2½-inch light tan print pieces. See **Diagram 3.** Press the seams, following the arrows in the diagram.

Step 4 Unit
1½" 2½" 1½"
2½"   2½"
DIAGRAM 3

STEP 6. Sew the 1 × 1½-inch brown print piece between the two 2¼ × 1½-inch light tan print pieces. See **Diagram 4.** Press.

2¼" 1" 2¼"
1½"   1½"
DIAGRAM 4

STEP 7. Sew the unit from Step 5 between the units from Steps 6 and 3, as shown in **Diagram 5.** Press. The pear block will now measure 4½ × 6½ inches.

Step 6 Unit
Step 5 Unit
Step 3 Unit
DIAGRAM 5

Adding the Lattice

STEP 1. Sew the pear block between two 1½ × 6½-inch lattice strips. Press toward the lattice.

STEP 2. Sew the unit from Step 1 between the two apple blocks. Press.

STEP 3. Sew the 1½ × 14½-inch lattice strips to the top and bottom. Press.

STEP 4. Sew the 1½ × 8½-inch lattice strips to the sides. Press.

Making the Checkerboard

STEP 1. For the top and bottom, sew the two 1½ × 42-inch checkerboard strips together to make a 2½ × 42-inch strip set. Press the seam toward the darker fabric. Cut this strip set into halves, approximately 21 inches each. See **Diagram 6.**

2½"
21"
42"
21"
DIAGRAM 6

STEP 2. Resew the halves together to make a 4½ × 21-inch strip set. Cut this strip set into fourths, approximately 5 inches each. See **Diagram 7.**

4½"
5"
5"
21"
5"
5"
DIAGRAM 7

STEP 3. Resew the quarters together to make a 16½ × 5-inch strip set. Using a rotary cutter and ruler, cut two 1½ × 16½-inch strips from this strip set. There should be 16 squares in each strip. See **Diagram 8.**

DIAGRAM 8

STEP 4. Compare the 1½ × 16½-inch strips to the top and bottom of the apple-pear unit. You may need to take in or let out a few seams (¹⁄₁₆ inch or less) to make them fit. Referring to the **Towel Holder Layout**, pin and sew the checkerboard strips to the top and bottom. Press the seams toward the lattice.

STEP 5. For the sides, sew the two 1½ × 30-inch checkerboard strips together to make a 2½ × 30-inch strip set. Press the seam toward the darker fabric. Cut this strip set into halves approximately 15 inches each. See **Diagram 9.**

DIAGRAM 9

STEP 6. Resew the halves together to make a 4½ × 15-inch strip set. Cut this strip set in thirds, approximately 5 inches each. See **Diagram 10.**

DIAGRAM 10

STEP 7. Resew the thirds together to make a 12½ × 5-inch strip set. Using a rotary cutter and ruler, cut two 1½ × 12½-inch strips from this strip set. See **Diagram 11.** Use a seam ripper to remove two squares from each strip to make two strips with 10 squares each.

DIAGRAM 11

STEP 8. Fit, pin, and sew the checkerboard strips to the sides. Press.

Binding
STEP 1. Sew the 1 × 18½-inch binding strips to the top and bottom. Press the seams toward the binding.

STEP 2. Sew the 1 × 11½-inch binding strips to the sides. Press.

Finishing Stitches
STEP 1. To make hanging tabs, fold the 2½ × 12-inch light tan print strip in half lengthwise with right sides together. Sew a ¼-inch seam along the raw edges. Turn the tab right side out, press, and cut into three 1 × 3½-inch pieces.

STEP 2. On the right side of the quilt top, space the tabs evenly across the bottom of the quilt. Position the tabs with the raw edges even with the raw edge of the quilt. Pin and then baste the tabs in place. They will be sewn into the seam when the quilt is finished.

STEP 3. Position the top and backing with right sides together. Lay both pieces on top of the batting, with the backing next to the batting. Pin all three layers together. Using ¼-inch seams, sew around the edges, leaving a 3- to 4-inch opening for turning. Trim the backing and batting to the same size as the top. Trim the corners, turn the towel holder right side out, hand stitch the opening closed, and press.

STEP 4. Machine or hand quilt in the seam lines of the apples, pear, lattice, checkerboard squares, and binding. Outline the appliqué leaves by quilting ¹⁄₁₆ inch from the edges. Paint the dowel and insert it through the hanging tabs.

TOWEL HOLDER LAYOUT

Fruit Tea Towels

(See the towels in the photo on page 76.)

MATERIALS

To make 1 tea towel:

These instructions are written for a tea towel that measures approximately 18 × 27 inches. You may have to adjust the length of your checkerboard and accent border to fit the size of your towel.

Purchased tea towel

⅛ yard gold or tan print for checkerboard

⅛ yard black print for checkerboard

⅛ yard, or 1 × 42-inch strip, red or green print for accent border

⅛ yard fabric for checkerboard backing

Scraps, or ⅛-yard pieces, of several coordinated fabrics for appliqué pieces

Lightweight, sewable fusible web

Embroidery floss

CUTTING

Prewash the tea towel and all of your fabrics. Press the fabrics. Using a rotary cutter, see-through ruler, and cutting mat, prepare the pieces as described below. Measurements for all pieces include ¼-inch seam allowances.

FABRIC	FIRST CUT		SECOND CUT	
Color	No. of Pieces	Dimensions	No. of Pieces	Dimensions
Gold or tan print	Checkerboard			
	2	1½ × 42-inch strips	3	1½ × 15-inch strips
Black print	Checkerboard			
	2	1½ × 42-inch strips	3	1½ × 15-inch strips
Red or green print	Accent border			
	2	1 × 18½-inch strips	No second cut	
Backing fabric	Checkerboard backing			
	1	3½ × 18½-inch piece	No second cut	

Assembling the Checkerboard

STEP 1. Alternating the two colors, sew the six 1½ × 15-inch checkerboard strips together to make a 6½ × 15-inch strip set. Press the seams toward the darker fabric as you go. Cut this strip set into thirds, approximately 5 inches each. See **Diagram 12.**

6½"

15"

5"

5"

5"

DIAGRAM 12

STEP 2. Resew the thirds together to make an 18½ × 5-inch strip set. Using a rotary cutter and ruler, cut two 1½ × 18½-inch strips from this strip set. There should be 18 squares in each strip. See **Diagram 13** on the following page.

18½"

5"   1½"

DIAGRAM 13

STEP 3. Compare the checkerboard to the tea towel. The sides of the checkerboard should extend ¼ inch beyond the sides of the tea towel. You may need to take in or let out a few seams (1⁄16 inch or less) to make them fit. Make adjustments before you sew the checkerboard strips together. See "Fitting Pieced Borders" on page 274 for further instructions. Sew the checkerboard strips together and press.

STEP 4. Sew the checkerboard from Step 3 between the two 1 × 18½-inch accent border strips. Press the seams toward the accent border.

STEP 5. Position the unit from Step 4 and the 3½ × 18½-inch backing strip with right sides together. Pin them together, keeping the raw edges even. (Remember to adjust the backing if you made a different-size checkerboard and accent border.) Using ¼-inch seams, sew around the edges, leaving a 3- to 4-inch opening for turning. Trim the corners, turn the checkerboard right side out, hand stitch the opening closed, and press.

STEP 6. Position the checkerboard approximately 3 inches up from the bottom edge of the towel. Pin it in place and topstitch around all the edges.

Appliqué

The appliqué pieces were added to the tea towels using the technique described in "Blanket Stitch Appliqué" on page 272. Be sure to use a lightweight, sewable fusible web.

Make Your Own Tea Towel

To make a tea towel, cut a fabric rectangle 1 inch larger than the desired finished size and narrow hem the edges.

STEP 1. Refer to "Quick-Fuse Appliqué" on pages 270–271. Trace three apples or two pears from the appliqué patterns below.

STEP 2. Position and fuse the apples or pears to the tea towel, referring to the photo on page 76 for placement.

STEP 3. Use two strands of embroidery floss to blanket stitch around the edges of the apples or pears.

18"

27"

TOWEL LAYOUT

PEAR PATTERN

APPLE PATTERN

APPLE LEAF PATTERN

APPLIQUÉ PATTERN KEY

——— Tracing line

- - - - - Tracing line (will be hidden behind other fabric)

DEEP-DISH FRUIT POT HOLDERS

QUICK AND EASY · COUNTRY ACCENTS

Mix and match your favorite fruits to hang as decorative accents or to use as practical but pretty pot holders. Stitch several to have on hand for hostess gifts after a backyard barbecue or picnic. And what could be better for a summer birthday gift than a cherry pie accompanied by a pair of cherry pot holders!

Finished Size: 7 inches square

Assembling the Background

See "Materials and Cutting" on the following page. Assemble the pot holder top before adding the appliqué pieces. Be sure to use ¼-inch seams and to press after each sewing step.

STEP 1. Sew the two 1½ × 24-inch checkerboard strips together to make a 2½ × 24-inch strip set. Press the seam toward the darker fabric. Cut this strip set into thirds, approximately 8 inches each. See **Diagram 1**.

STEP 2. Resew the thirds together to make a 6½ × 8-inch strip set. Using a rotary cutter and ruler, cut four 1½ × 6½-inch strips

from this strip set. There should be six squares in each strip. See **Diagram 2**.

2½"

8"

24"   8"

8"

DIAGRAM 1

6½"

1½"

8"

DIAGRAM 2

STEP 3. For the top and bottom, use a seam ripper to remove two squares each from two of the strips. Compare the strips to the top and bottom of the 4½-inch background square. You may need to take in or let out a few seams (1/16 inch or less) to make them fit.

MATERIALS AND CUTTING

Prewash and press all of your fabrics. Using a rotary cutter, see-through ruler, and cutting mat, prepare the pieces as described below. Measurements for all pieces include ¼-inch seam allowances (to make 1 pot holder).

FABRIC	YARDAGE	NO. OF PIECES	DIMENSIONS
Background square	⅛ yard	1	4½-inch square
Light tan print for checkerboard	⅛ yard	1	1½ × 24-inch strip
Red print for checkerboard	⅛ yard	1	1½ × 24-inch strip
Black solid for binding and tab	⅛ yard	2 2 1	1 × 7½-inch strips (binding) 1 × 6½-inch strips (binding) 1 × 4½-inch strip (tab)
Backing fabric	¼ yard	1	8-inch square
Cotton batting (See Note below.)	¼ yard	1	8-inch square
Several coordinated fabrics for appliqué pieces	Scraps, or ⅛-yard pieces	—	—

Fusible web

Note: If you plan to use your pot holder, use two layers of cotton batting. Use a lightweight, sewable fusible web and secure the edges of the appliqué pieces with machine or hand stitching.

STEP 4. Referring to **Diagram 3**, pin and sew the 1½ × 4½-inch checkerboard strips to the background square. Press the seams toward the background square.

DIAGRAM 3

STEP 5. Fit, pin, and sew the remaining 1½ × 6½-inch checker-board strips to the sides, as shown in **Diagram 4**. Press.

DIAGRAM 4

STEP 6. Sew the 1 × 6½-inch binding strips to the top and bottom. Press the seams toward the binding.

STEP 7. Sew the 1 × 7½-inch binding strips to the sides. Press.

Teakettle Revival

I picked up an old teakettle at a thrift shop, primed it with a spray primer, painted it with acrylic paint, antiqued it, and then sealed it with a spray sealer. It is **decorative** only!

Appliqué

STEP 1. Refer to "Quick-Fuse Appliqué" on pages 270–271. Trace an apple or a cluster of cherries from the appliqué patterns below or a pear from the Fruit Sampler patterns on page 74.

STEP 2. Quick-fuse the appliqué pieces to the center of the background square. If you plan to use your pot holder, remember to finish the edges of the appliqué pieces using machine appliqué (page 271) or hand blanket stitch (page 272).

7"
7"

POT HOLDER LAYOUT

Finishing Stitches

STEP 1. To make the hanging tab, fold the 1 × 4½-inch black tab strip in half lengthwise with wrong sides together. Press. Open the fabric and fold each long edge into the center fold. Press again. Topstitch along the open folded edges of the fabric strip. Fold the tab in half. Position and baste the tab to the top corner of the pot holder. See **Diagram 5**.

Basting stitches

DIAGRAM 5

STEP 2. Position the top and backing with right sides together. Lay both pieces on top of the batting, with the backing next to the batting. Pin all three layers together. Using ¼-inch seams, sew around the edges, leaving a 3-inch opening for turning. Trim the backing and batting to the same size as the top. Trim the corners, turn the pot holder right side out, hand stitch the opening closed, and press.

STEP 3. Machine or hand quilt in the seam lines of the center square, checkerboard, and binding. Outline the appliqué design by quilting ¹⁄₁₆ inch from the edges. If you plan to use your pot holder, do not machine quilt with a nylon monofilament thread, as it will melt.

CHERRIES PATTERN

APPLE PATTERN

APPLIQUÉ PATTERN KEY

_____ Tracing line

- - - - - - Tracing line (will be hidden behind other fabric)

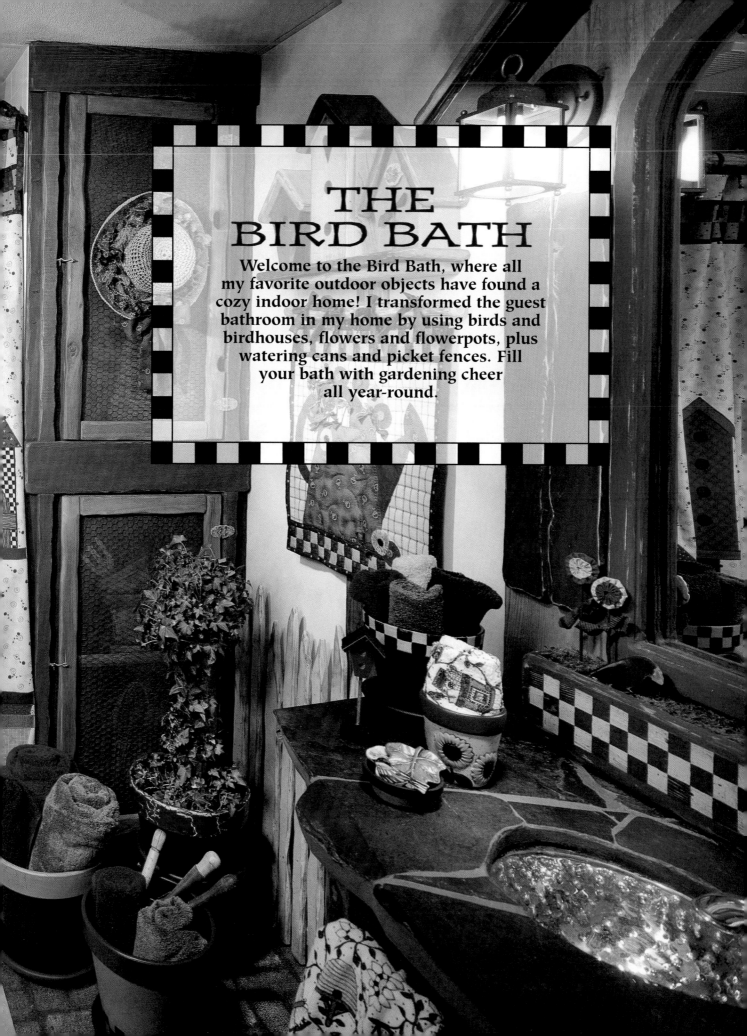

THE BIRD BATH

Welcome to the Bird Bath, where all my favorite outdoor objects have found a cozy indoor home! I transformed the guest bathroom in my home by using birds and birdhouses, flowers and flowerpots, plus watering cans and picket fences. Fill your bath with gardening cheer all year-round.

BIRD BATH SHOWER CURTAIN

You'll almost hear the birds singing when you shower behind this

colorful curtain decked out with birds and birdhouses, as shown in the

photo on pages 86–87. I love the big, bold birdhouse shapes, and they're

easy to cut and fuse. With the addition of country checkerboard borders,

you can create a wonderfully refreshing look for your bath.

Finished Size: 76 × 72 inches

MATERIALS FOR LARGE APPLIQUÉ PIECES

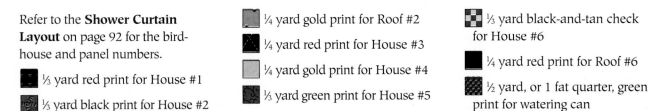

Refer to the **Shower Curtain Layout** on page 92 for the birdhouse and panel numbers.

⅓ yard red print for House #1

⅓ yard black print for House #2

¼ yard gold print for Roof #2

¼ yard red print for House #3

¼ yard gold print for House #4

⅓ yard green print for House #5

⅓ yard black-and-tan check for House #6

¼ yard red print for Roof #6

½ yard, or 1 fat quarter, green print for watering can

MATERIALS AND CUTTING

Prewash and press all of your fabrics. Using a rotary cutter, see-through ruler, and cutting mat, prepare the pieces as described below. Measurements for all pieces include ¼-inch seam allowances. (Obvious directional prints are not recommended.)

FABRIC	YARDAGE	NO. OF PIECES	DIMENSIONS
Light tan print for background and outer border	5 yards		Cut these first from the length of the fabric:
		2	3½ × 80-inch strips (outer border)
		1	26½ × 56½-inch piece (background Panel #2)
		2	25½ × 56½-inch pieces (background Panels #1 and #3)

FABRIC	YARDAGE	NO. OF PIECES	DIMENSIONS
■ Black print for accent border	⅓ yard	8	1 × 42-inch strips
▨ Gold print for checkerboard	⅝ yard	7	2½ × 42-inch strips
▨ Green print for checkerboard	⅝ yard	7	2½ × 42-inch strips
Green print for ties	¾ yard	12	2 × 36½-inch strips
Lining fabric	4½ yards	—	—
Several coordinated fabrics for yo-yos and small appliqué pieces	Scraps, or ⅛-yard pieces	—	—

6½ yards lightweight, sewable fusible web; thread to match appliqué pieces; 6½ yards Tear-Away fabric stabilizer; embroidery floss

Appliqué

STEP 1. Refer to "Quick-Fuse Appliqué" on pages 270–271. Be sure to use a lightweight, sewable fusible web. Trace the shapes from the appliqué patterns on pages 93–100 onto the paper side of the fusible web.

STEP 2. For the remaining appliqué shapes, draw the following rectangles on the paper side of the fusible web, leaving at least ½ inch between the rectangles. Label the rectangles as you go.

Birdhouse #1

House	9 × 11-inch rectangle
Roof	Two 1 × 8½-inch rectangles
Perch	½ × 3½-inch rectangle
Base	1 × 11-inch rectangle
Pole	1 × 13-inch rectangle

Birdhouse #2

House	11½ × 9-inch rectangle

Roof	13 × 6-inch rectangle
Windows	Two 1 × 3-inch rectangles
Door frame	Four ¾ × 5-inch rectangles
Door	3 × 5-inch rectangle
Base	1 × 13-inch rectangle
Pole	2 × 24-inch rectangle
	Two 1½ × 6-inch rectangles

Birdhouse #3

House	7 × 18-inch rectangle
Roof	Two 1 × 6½-inch rectangles
Base	1 × 9-inch rectangle
Pole	2 × 20-inch rectangle

Birdhouse #4

House	8 × 10-inch rectangle
Roof	Two 1½ × 8-inch rectangles
Pole	1 × 13-inch rectangle

Birdhouse #5

House	8 × 19-inch rectangle

Roof	Two 1½ × 8-inch rectangles
Base	1½ × 10-inch rectangle
Pole	2 × 26-inch rectangle
	Two 1½ × 5-inch rectangles

Birdhouse #6

House	15 × 11-inch rectangle
Roof	17 × 5-inch rectangle
Chimneys	Two 1 × 5-inch rectangles
Fence rail	1½ × 15-inch rectangle
Base	1 × 17-inch rectangle
Pole	3 × 23-inch rectangle

STEP 3. Fuse the traced shapes and drawn rectangles to the wrong side of your selected fabrics. Cut out each shape on the drawn line. As you cut, organize the appliqué pieces according to the birdhouse numbers. Remove the paper backing; a thin film will remain on the fabric.

STEP 4. Trim five of the rectangles, as shown in **Diagrams 1** through **5**, to create rooflines.

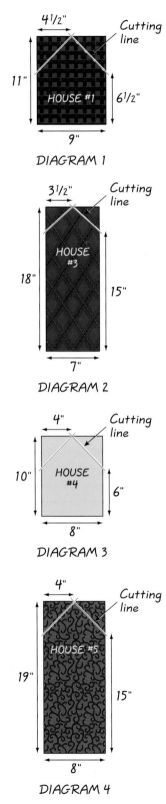

DIAGRAM 1

DIAGRAM 2

DIAGRAM 3

DIAGRAM 4

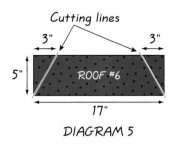

DIAGRAM 5

STEP 5. Position and fuse the appliqué pieces to the light tan print background panels, allowing for the ¼-inch seam allowances on the raw edges of the background panels. Refer to the **Shower Curtain Layout** on page 92 for placement. The roofs on Houses #1, #3, #4, and #5 are created by placing one end of the first rectangle over one end of the second rectangle, as shown in **Diagram 6**.

DIAGRAM 6

STEP 6. Referring to "Machine Appliqué" on pages 271–272, machine appliqué the pieces to the background panels. Use the Tear-Away fabric stabilizer on the wrong sides of the background panels for an even machine stitch. Remove the stabilizer after stitching.

Adding the Borders

STEP 1. Using ¼-inch seams, sew background Panels #1, #2, and #3 together. Refer to the **Shower Curtain Layout** on page 92 for placement. Press the seams open.

STEP 2. Sew the eight 1 × 42-inch accent border strips together in pairs to make four strips approximately 1 × 84 inches each. Press. Sew one 1 × 84-inch accent border strip each to the top and bottom of the shower curtain. Trim the excess length, and press the seams toward the accent border.

STEP 3. Alternating the two colors, sew the fourteen 2½ × 42-inch checkerboard strips together to make a 28½ × 42-inch strip set. Change sewing direction with each strip sewn, and press the seams toward the darker fabric as you go. Using a rotary cutter and ruler, cut twelve 2½ × 28½-inch strips from this strip set. There should be 14 squares in each strip. See **Diagram 7**.

DIAGRAM 7

Add a Touch of Rustic Authenticity

I added a long branch above my traditional curtain rod. I tied the Bird Bath Shower Curtain to this branch and used the regular rod for the plastic shower curtain liner.

STEP 4. Sew eight 2½ × 28½-inch checkerboard strips together in pairs to make four 2½ × 56½-inch checkerboard strips.

STEP 5. Sew the four remaining 2½ × 28½-inch checkerboard strips to the four checkerboard strips made in Step 4. You will now have four 2½ × 84½-inch checkerboard strips.

STEP 6. Using a seam ripper, remove 4 squares from each checkerboard strip to make four 2½ × 76½-inch strips with 38 squares each.

STEP 7. Compare the strips to the top and bottom of the shower curtain. You may need to take in or let out a few seams (¹⁄₁₆ inch or less) to make them fit. Make adjustments before you sew the checkerboard strips together in pairs. If you do make adjustments, make them in the same place on each strip so that the strips will still match up. Refer to "Fitting Pieced Borders" on page 274 for further instructions. Sew the strips together in pairs and press.

STEP 8. Pin and sew the checkerboards to the top and bottom of the shower curtain. Press the seams toward the accent border.

STEP 9. Sew the two remaining 1 × 84-inch accent border strips to the top and bottom of the shower curtain. Trim the excess length, and press the seams toward the accent border.

STEP 10. Sew the 3½ × 80-inch outer border strips to the top and

bottom of the shower curtain. Trim the excess length, and press the seams toward the accent border.

Assembly

STEP 1. Refer to "Making Yo-yos" on pages 272–273. Make two yo-yos flowers from the pattern on page 93. Sew the yo-yos above the bird standing on the pot in Panel #1, referring to the **Shower Curtain Layout** on page 92 for placement. Use six strands of embroidery floss to stem stitch bird legs and flower stems. Make French-knot eyes on the birds with embroidery floss. See "Decorative Stitches" on page 272.

STEP 2. Cut the 4½-yard piece of lining fabric into two 2¼-yard

lengths. Trim the selvage edges off both lining pieces. With right sides together, sew the halves together to make one piece approximately 80 × 81 inches. Press the seams open.

STEP 3. With right sides together, position and pin the shower curtain top and lining together. Using ¼-inch seams, sew around the edges, leaving an 8- to 10-inch opening for turning. Trim the lining to the same size as the top. Trim the corners, turn the shower curtain right side out, hand stitch the opening closed, and press.

STEP 4. Mark placement and make twelve 1-inch buttonholes ½ inch down from the top edge. The first and last buttonholes are spaced 1 inch from the sides, and

Debbie's Decorating Diary

The Bird Bath, shown in the photo on pages 86–87, was created from a very ordinary guest bathroom, right off my home art studio. Because the room is small, the custom vanity was pared down in size with a bar-size brass sink. Slate countertops add an outdoorsy feel. The mirror is surrounded by shutters, a window box, a peaked roof, and outdoor lighting fixtures.

We laid green carpet down and stenciled it with brown and terra-cotta brick shapes to look like a patio with moss growing around stone pavers. The floor cloth was painted on pretreated canvas and was antiqued before varnishing. The walls and ceiling are faux painted with blue sky and billowy clouds. A picket fence lines the walls of the room throughout.

The storage cupboards to the right of the shower represent gardeners' cupboards, with hook-and-eye latches mimicking old-fashioned screen doors. Chicken wire that was spray painted green adds an interesting texture to these cupboard doors.

What you can't see in the corner is our updated outhouse, complete with roof, shelves on the wall, and a carved moon.

the remaining ten buttonholes are spaced approximately 6½ inches apart.

STEP 5. To make the ties, fold the twelve 2 × 36½-inch strips in half lengthwise with right sides together. Sew a ¼-inch seam on the edge opposite the fold and on one short side on each tie. Trim the

corners, turn the ties right side out, and press. Fold in the remaining end and stitch the opening closed. Topstitch the edges.

STEP 6. Insert the ties through the buttonholes and tie them in bows, attaching the curtain to the shower curtain rod.

Time-Saver

A bow whip or narrow loop turner will make turning the long, narrow tubes of fabric for the shower curtain ties much easier. See "Quilting by Mail" on page 280 for ordering information.

SHOWER CURTAIN LAYOUT

STAR PATTERN
FOR HOUSE #4

YO-YO PATTERN

APPLIQUÉ PATTERN KEY

———— Tracing line

– – – – Tracing line
(will be hidden behind
other fabric)

CHIMNEY PATTERN
FOR HOUSE #1

NEST PATTERN
FOR HOUSE #1

MOON
PATTERN
FOR
HOUSE #5

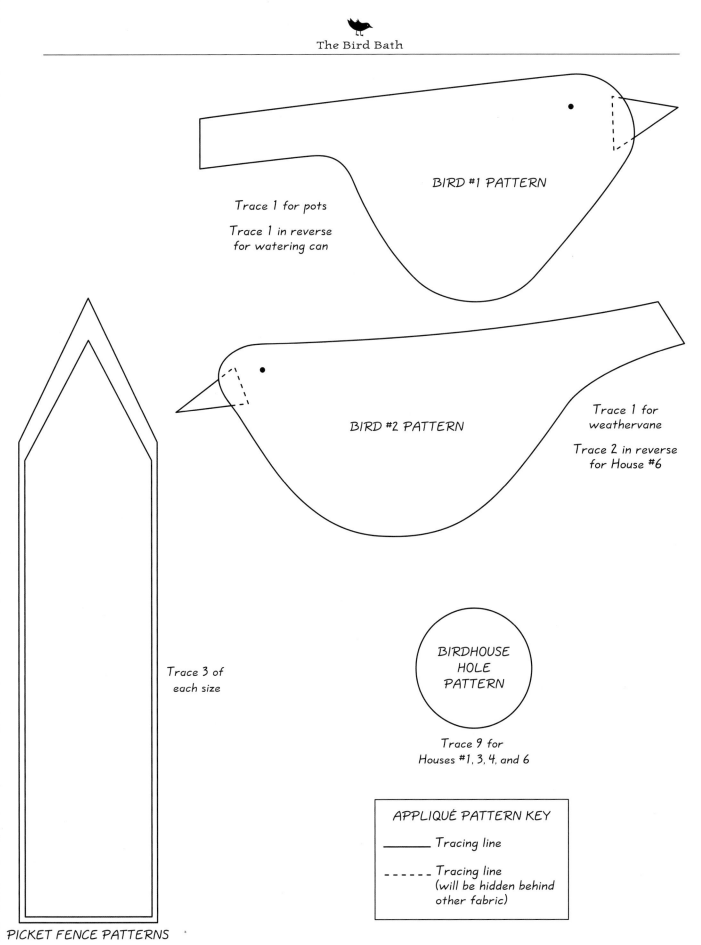

BIRD #1 PATTERN

Trace 1 for pots

Trace 1 in reverse
for watering can

BIRD #2 PATTERN

Trace 1 for
weathervane

Trace 2 in reverse
for House #6

Trace 3 of
each size

BIRDHOUSE
HOLE
PATTERN

Trace 9 for
Houses #1, 3, 4, and 6

APPLIQUÉ PATTERN KEY

————— Tracing line

- - - - - Tracing line
(will be hidden behind
other fabric)

PICKET FENCE PATTERNS
FOR HOUSE #6

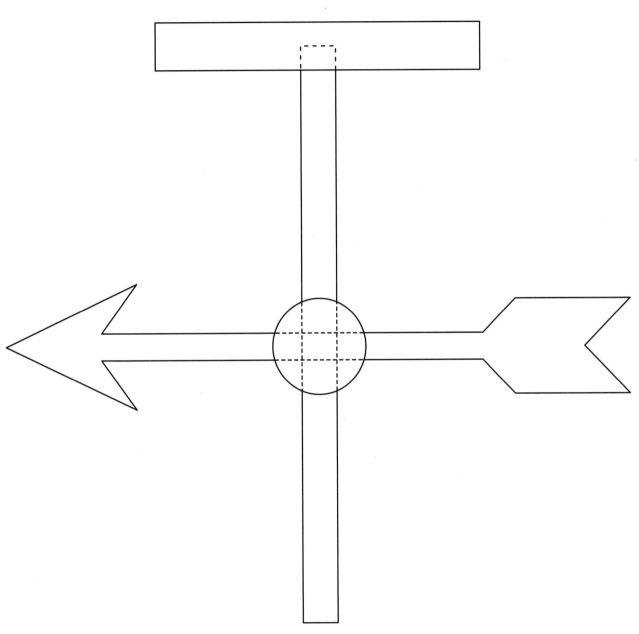

WEATHERVANE PATTERN FOR HOUSE #2

FLOWERPOT PATTERNS

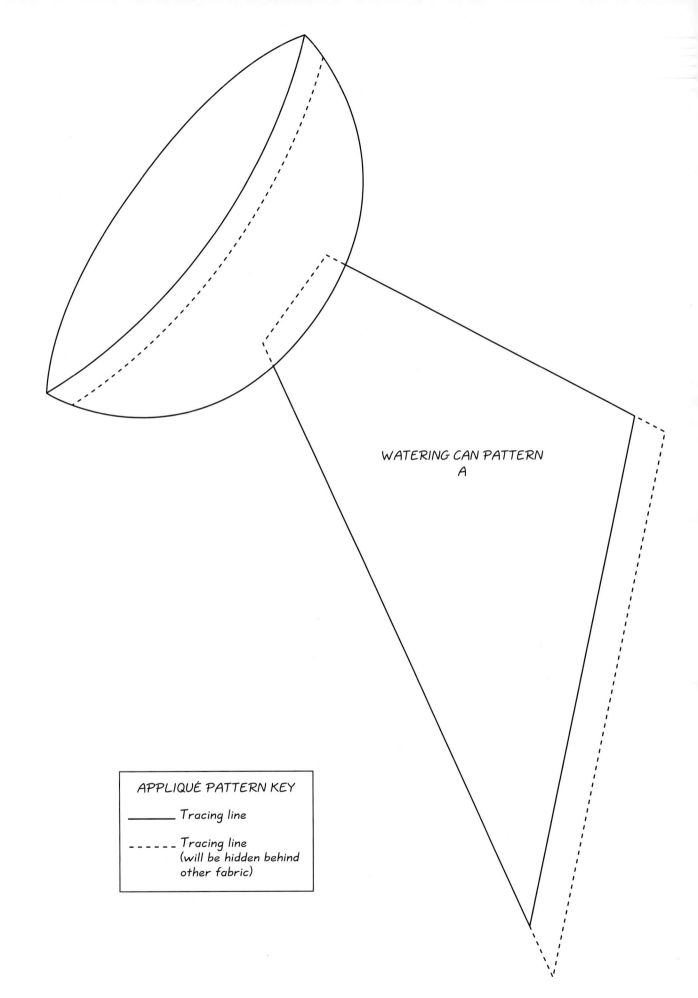

WATERING CAN PATTERN
A

APPLIQUÉ PATTERN KEY

———— Tracing line

------- Tracing line
(will be hidden behind
other fabric)

Watering Can Pattern D goes here

Watering Can Pattern A goes here

WATERING CAN PATTERN
B

Align with red line of Watering Can Pattern C

WATERING CAN PATTERN
C

Align with red line of Watering Can Pattern B

BIRDHOUSE #5
DOOR PATTERN

Watering Can
Pattern E
goes here

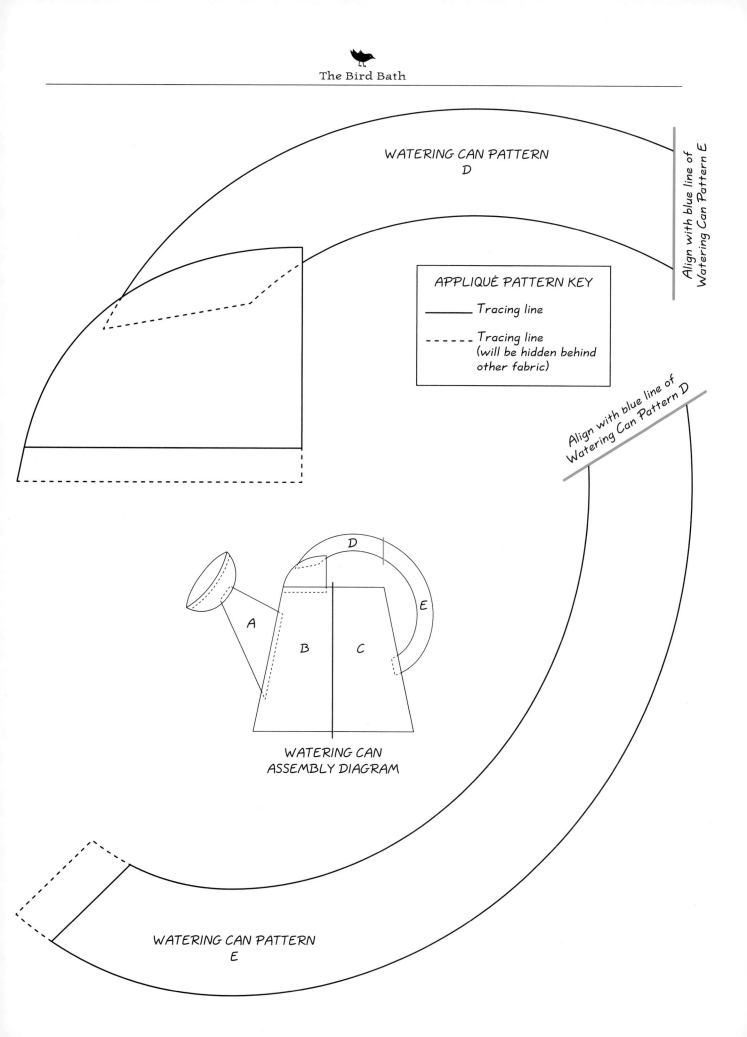

WATERING CAN PATTERN
D

Align with blue line of Watering Can Pattern E

APPLIQUÉ PATTERN KEY

—————— Tracing line

- - - - - - Tracing line
(will be hidden behind
other fabric)

Align with blue line of
Watering Can Pattern D

A

B   C

D

E

WATERING CAN
ASSEMBLY DIAGRAM

WATERING CAN PATTERN
E

WATERING CAN WALLHANGING

Watering cans are so quaint and picturesque. I love their shape

and like to collect all sizes of antique and reproduction versions. The

wallhanging you see on the next page is perfect for a gardening friend and

would be right at home in any room, nook, or hallway. (For a more

summery look, see the **Color Option** on page 104.)

Finished Size: 19 × 21 inches

(For a more summery look, see the **Color Option** on page 104.)

MATERIALS AND CUTTING

Prewash and press all of your fabrics. Using a rotary cutter, see-through ruler, and cutting mat, prepare the pieces as described below. Measurements for all pieces include ¼-inch seam allowances.

FABRIC	YARDAGE	NO. OF PIECES	DIMENSIONS
Tan plaid for background	½ yard	1	15½ × 18½-inch piece
Black print for accent border and binding	⅙ yard (cut into three 1 × 42-inch strips)	2	1 × 18½-inch strips (accent border)
		2	1 × 21½-inch strips (binding)
		2	1 × 18½-inch strips (binding)
Gold print for checkerboard	¼ yard	3	1½ × 24-inch strips
Green print for checkerboard	¼ yard	3	1½ × 24-inch strips
Backing fabric	⅔ yard	—	—
Lightweight batting	⅔ yard	—	—

(continued)

WEEKENDER

MATERIALS AND CUTTING — CONTINUED

FABRIC	YARDAGE	NO. OF PIECES	DIMENSIONS
Green print for appliqué watering can	12 × 16-inch piece	—	—
Several coordinated fabrics for remaining appliqué pieces and dimensional leaves	Scraps, or ⅛- to ¼-yard pieces	—	—
Lightweight, sewable fusible web; embroidery floss; 11 assorted buttons			

Assembling the Background

Assemble the wallhanging top before adding the appliqué pieces. Be sure to use ¼-inch seams and to press after each sewing step.

STEP 1. Sew the 1 × 18½-inch accent border strips to the top and bottom of the 18½ × 15½-inch tan plaid background piece. Press the seams toward the accent border.

STEP 2. Alternating the two colors, sew the six 1½ × 24-inch checkerboard strips together to make a 6½ × 24-inch strip set. Change sewing direction with each strip sewn, and press the seams toward the darker fabric as you go. Cut this strip set into thirds, approximately 8 inches each. See **Diagram 1.**

DIAGRAM 1

STEP 3. Resew the thirds together to make an 18½ × 8-inch strip set. Using a rotary cutter and ruler, cut four 1½ × 18½-inch strips from this strip set. There should be 18 squares in each strip. See **Diagram 2.**

DIAGRAM 2

STEP 4. Compare the strips to the top and bottom of the wallhanging. You may need to take in or let out a few seams (1/16 inch or less) to make them fit. Make adjustments before you sew the checkerboard strips together into pairs. If you do make adjustments, make them in the same place on each strip so that the strips will still match up. Refer to "Fitting Pieced Borders" on page 274 for further instructions. Sew the checkerboard strips together in pairs and press.

STEP 5. Pin and sew the checkerboards to the top and bottom of the wallhanging. Press the seams toward the accent border.

STEP 6. Sew the 1 × 18½-inch binding strips to the top and bottom. Press the seams toward the binding.

STEP 7. Sew the 1 × 21½-inch binding strips to the sides. Press.

Appliqué

The appliqué pieces were added to the background using the technique described in "Blanket Stitch Appliqué" on page 272. You can machine appliqué with either a satin stitch or blanket stitch if you prefer. Refer to "Machine Appliqué" on pages 271–272 for instructions on either technique. Be sure to use a lightweight, sewable fusible web for all of these appliqué techniques.

STEP 1. Refer to "Quick-Fuse Appliqué" on pages 270–271. Trace the watering can from the appliqué pattern on pages 97–100 and trace 11 flowers from the appliqué pattern on page 104.

STEP 2. Position and fuse the appliqué pieces to the background, referring to the **Wallhanging Layout** on the following page for placement.

STEP 3. Use two strands of embroidery floss to blanket stitch around the edges of the appliqué pieces. Use six strands of embroidery floss to chain stitch the flower stems, referring to "Decorative Stitches" on page 272 for instructions on chain stitching.

Finishing Stitches

STEP 1. Position the top and backing with right sides together. Lay both pieces on top of the batting, with the backing next to the batting. Pin all three layers together. Using ¼-inch seam allowances, sew around the edges, leaving a 3- to 4-inch opening for turning. Trim the backing and batting to the same size as the top. Trim the corners, turn the wallhanging right side out, hand stitch the opening closed, and press.

STEP 2. Machine or hand quilt in the seam lines of the accent border, checkerboard squares, and binding. Outline the appliqué design by quilting 1/16 inch from the edges. Quilt a 1½-inch grid in the background.

For Yo-yo Lovers

If you want to make the flowers for the wallhanging out of yo-yos, cut circles of fabric at least twice the diameter of the flower appliqué pattern at right. Refer to "Making Yo-yos" on pages 272–273, and use a blanket stitch to attach the yo-yos to the background.

STEP 3. Cut several 1 × 3-inch strips of fabric for the leaves. Tie a knot in the center of each strip. Sew the leaves to the flower stems, and sew a button to the center of each flower.

FLOWER PATTERN

19"

21"

WALLHANGING LAYOUT

COLOR OPTION

Country blues with accents of red, pink, and yellow add a summery touch to the wallhanging.

STACKED CROWS WALLHANGING

Caw, caw, caw! The whimsical and endearing crows on the next page will win over even the most ardent gardener, despite the raucous reputation of the real birds. Hearts, a checkerboard border, a star, and a picket fence all capture the country spirit perfectly, making this wallhanging suitable for any spot in the house.

Finished Size: 13 × 19 inches

MATERIALS AND CUTTING

Prewash and press all of your fabrics. Using a rotary cutter, see-through ruler, and cutting mat, prepare the pieces as described below. Measurements for all pieces include ¼-inch seam allowances.

FABRIC	YARDAGE	NO. OF PIECES	DIMENSIONS
Tan check for background	⅓ yard	1	9½ × 15½-inch piece
Dark green print for accent border	⅛ yard (cut into two 1 × 42-inch strips)	2	1 × 16½-inch strips
		2	1 × 9½-inch strips
Dark red print for checkerboard	¼ yard	3	1½ × 24-inch strips
Tan print for checkerboard	¼ yard	3	1½ × 24-inch strips
Dark green print for binding	⅛ yard (cut into two 1 × 42-inch strips)	2	1 × 19½-inch strips
		2	1 × 12½-inch strips
Backing fabric	½ yard	—	—
Lightweight batting	½ yard	—	—
Several coordinated fabrics for appliqué pieces	Scraps, or ⅛- to ¼-yard pieces	—	—
Lightweight, sewable fusible web; embroidery floss			

Assembling the Background

Assemble the wallhanging top before adding the appliqué pieces. Be sure to use ¼-inch seams and to press after each sewing step.

STEP 1. Sew the 1 × 9½-inch accent border strips to the top and bottom of the 9½ × 15½-inch tan check background piece. Press the seams toward the accent border.

STEP 2. Sew the 1 × 16½-inch accent border strips to the sides. Press.

STEP 3. Alternating the two colors, sew the six 1½ × 24-inch checkerboard strips together to make a 6½ × 24-inch strip set. Change sewing direction with each strip sewn, and press the seams toward the darker fabric as you go. Cut this strip set into thirds, approximately 8 inches each. See **Diagram 1**.

6½"

8"

24"

8"

8"

DIAGRAM 1

STEP 4. Resew the thirds together to make an 18½ × 8-inch strip set. Using a rotary cutter and ruler, cut four 1½ × 18½-inch strips from this strip set. There should be 18 squares in each strip. See **Diagram 2**.

STEP 5. For the top and bottom, use a seam ripper to remove 8 squares from two checkerboard strips to make two strips with 10 squares each. Compare the 1½ × 10½-inch strips to the top and bottom of the wallhanging. You may need to take in or let out a few seams (¹⁄₁₆ inch or less) to make them fit. Referring to the **Wallhanging Layout** on page 108 for placement of the light and dark squares, pin and sew the 1½ × 10½-inch checkerboard strips to the top and bottom. Press the seams toward the accent border.

STEP 6. Fit, pin, and sew the 1½ × 18½-inch checkerboard strips to the sides. Press.

STEP 7. Sew the 1 × 12½-inch binding strips to the top and bottom. Press the seams toward the binding.

STEP 8. Sew the 1 × 19½-inch binding strips to the sides. Press.

Appliqué

The appliqué pieces were added to the background using the technique described in "Blanket Stitch Appliqué" on page 272. Be sure to use a lightweight, sewable fusible web.

STEP 1. Refer to "Quick-Fuse Appliqué" on pages 270–271. Trace the birdhouse, star, fence, birds, and hearts from the appliqué patterns on pages 108–109.

STEP 2. Position and fuse the appliqué pieces to the background, referring to the **Wallhanging Layout** on page 108 for placement.

STEP 3. Use two strands of embroidery floss to blanket stitch around the edges of the appliqué pieces. Using three strands of embroidery floss, stem stitch the legs and make French-knot eyes on the birds. Refer to "Decorative Stitches" on page 272.

Finishing Stitches

STEP 1. Position the top and backing with right sides together. Lay both pieces on top of the batting, with the backing next to the batting. Pin all three layers together. Using ¼-inch seam allowances, sew around the edges, leaving a 3- to 4-inch opening for turning. Trim the backing and batting to the same size as the top. Trim the corners, turn the wallhanging right side out, hand stitch the opening closed, and press.

STEP 2. Machine or hand quilt in the seam lines of the accent border, checkerboard squares, and binding. Outline the appliqué design by quilting ¹⁄₁₆ inch from the edges. Quilt a 1-inch diagonal grid in the background.

18½"

1½"

8"

DIAGRAM 2

13"

19"

WALLHANGING LAYOUT

BIRD #1 PATTERN

Stem stitch

Align bird #1 legs here

BIRD #2 PATTERN

Stem stitch

Align bird #2 legs here

BIRD #3 PATTERN

Stem stitch

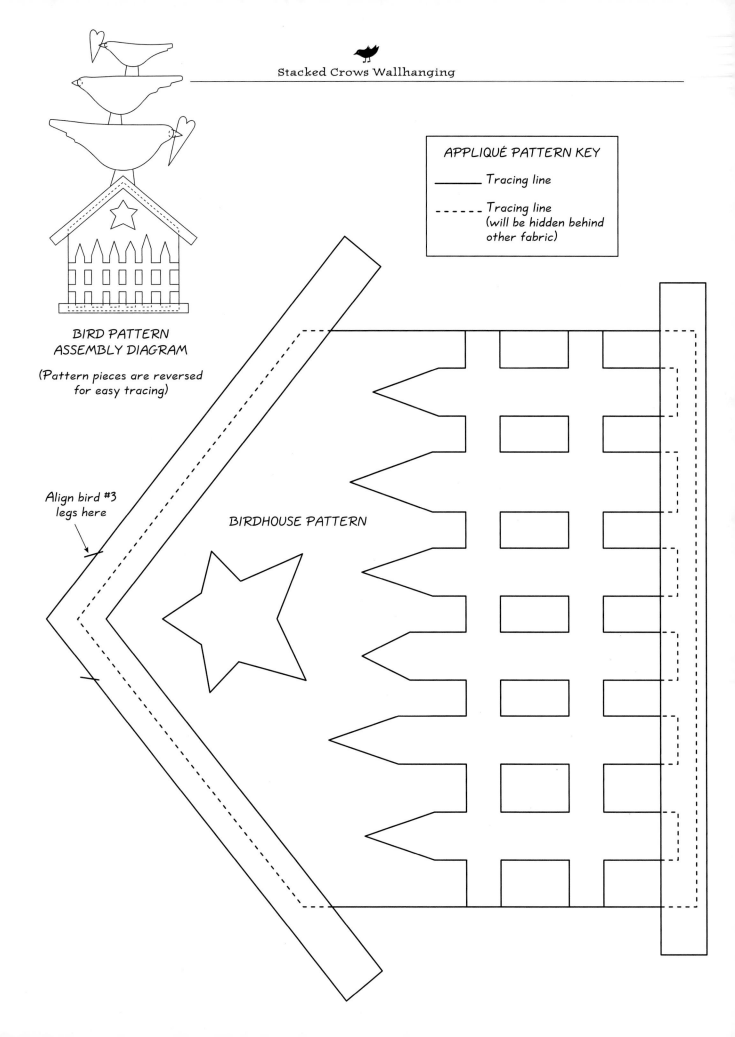

APPLIQUÉ PATTERN KEY

———— Tracing line

– – – – Tracing line
(will be hidden behind
other fabric)

BIRD PATTERN
ASSEMBLY DIAGRAM

(Pattern pieces are reversed
for easy tracing)

Align bird #3
legs here

BIRDHOUSE PATTERN

GARDEN GUEST TOWELS

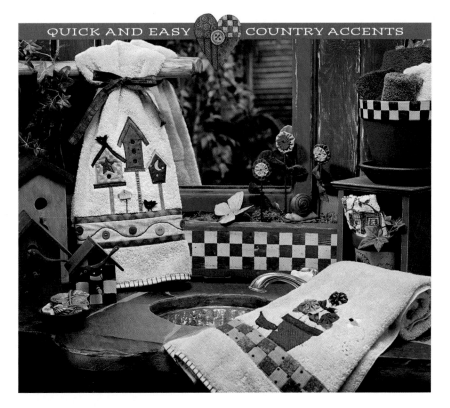

Complete your birds-in-the-garden theme with these sweet hand towels. The Gardener's Delight Towel, *right*, and the Birdhouse Towel, *left* (directions on page 112), are perfect accessories for any bath, so while you're making a set of your own, make an extra set for a gift, too.

Towel size (unfolded) is 20" × 34"

GARDENER'S DELIGHT TOWEL

These instructions are written for a hand towel that measures approximately 20 × 34 inches. You may have to adjust the length of your checkerboard to fit the size of your towel.

Assembling the Checkerboard

See "Materials and Cutting" on the opposite page.

STEP 1. Sew the two 1½ × 42-inch checkerboard strips together to make a 2½ × 42-inch strip set. Press the seams toward the darker fabric. Using a rotary cutter and ruler, cut twenty 1½ × 2½-inch segments from this strip set. See **Diagram 1**.

2½"

1½"

42"

DIAGRAM 1

MATERIALS AND CUTTING *(for Gardener's Delight Towel)*

Prewash the hand towel and all of your fabrics. Press the fabrics. Using a rotary cutter, see-through ruler, and cutting mat, prepare the pieces as described below. Measurements for all pieces include ¼-inch seam allowances.

FABRIC	YARDAGE	NO. OF PIECES	DIMENSIONS
Gold print for checkerboard	⅛ yard	1	1½ × 42-inch strip
Green print for checkerboard	⅛ yard	1	1½ × 42-inch strip
Backing for checkerboard	⅛ yard	1	2½ × 20½-inch strip
Several coordinated fabrics for appliqué pieces, yo-yos, and dimensional leaves	Scraps, or ⅛-yard pieces	—	—

Purchased hand towel; lightweight, sewable fusible web; thread to match appliqué pieces; Tear-Away fabric stabilizer; embroidery floss

Adjust for Size

It's easy to make adjustments for a smaller hand towel. I cut 20 segments to fit a 20-inch towel. A 17-inch towel would take 17 segments.

STEP 2. Alternating placement of the light and dark squares, sew the 20 checkerboard segments together, as shown in **Diagram 2**. Press the seams in one direction, following the arrows in the diagram.

STEP 3. Compare the checkerboard to the hand towel. The sides of the checkerboard should extend ¼ inch beyond the sides of the towel. You may need to take in or let out a few seams (⅟₁₆ inch or less) to make the checkerboard fit.

STEP 4. Position the checkerboard and the 2½ × 20½-inch backing strip with right sides together. Pin them together, keeping the raw edges even. (Remember to adjust the backing if you made a different-size checkerboard.) Using ¼-inch seams, sew around the edges, leaving a 3- to 4-inch opening for turning. Trim the corners, turn the

checkerboard right side out, hand stitch the opening closed, and press.

STEP 5. Position the checkerboard approximately 3 inches up from the bottom edge of the towel. Pin it in place and topstitch around all the edges.

Appliqué

The appliqué pieces were added to the hand towel using the technique described in "Machine Appliqué" on pages 271–272. Be sure to use a lightweight, sewable fusible web.

STEP 1. Refer to "Quick-Fuse Appliqué" on page 270. Trace the flowerpot, bird, and bee from the appliqué patterns on page 115.

STEP 2. Position and fuse the appliqué pieces to the center of the towel, above the checkerboard,

1½"

2½"

DIAGRAM 2

referring to the Gardener's Delight Towel layout on page 110 for placement.

STEP 3. Machine appliqué around the edges of the pieces. Use the Tear-Away fabric stabilizer on the wrong side of the hand towel for an even machine stitch. Remove the stabilizer after stitching.

Finishing

STEP 1. Refer to "Making Yo-yos" on pages 272–273. Make three yo-yo flowers from the pattern on the opposite page. Sew the yo-yos to the towel, above the pot.

STEP 2. Use six strands of embroidery floss to blanket stitch the lower edge of the towel. Use six strands of embroidery floss to stem stitch the bird legs and flower stems and two strands to make a French-knot eye on the bird. See "Decorative Stitches" on page 272. Stitch a meandering bee path, using six strands of embroidery floss.

STEP 3. Cut three 1 × 3-inch strips for leaves. Tie a knot in the center of each strip, and sew one strip to each flower stem.

BIRDHOUSE TOWEL

(See the towel on the left in the photo on page 110.)

See "Materials and Cutting" on the opposite page. These instructions are written for a hand towel that measures approximately 20 × 34 inches. You may have to adjust the length of your border to fit your towel size.

Assembling the Border

STEP 1. Sew the 2 × 20½-inch wide border strip between the two 1 × 20½-inch narrow border strips. Press the seams toward the narrow borders.

STEP 2. Position the border and the 3 × 20½-inch backing strip with right sides together. Pin them together, keeping the raw edges even.

Using ¼-inch seams, sew around the edges, leaving a 3- to 4-inch opening for turning. Trim the corners, turn the border right side out, hand stitch the opening closed, and press.

STEP 3. Position the border approximately 3 inches up from the bottom edge of the towel. Pin it in place and topstitch around all the edges.

Appliqué

The appliqué pieces were added to the hand towel using the technique described in "Machine Appliqué" on pages 271–272. Be sure to use a lightweight, sewable fusible web.

STEP 1. Refer to "Quick-Fuse Appliqué" on pages 270–271. Trace the birdhouses, poles, and birds from the appliqué patterns on page 114.

STEP 2. Position and fuse the appliqué pieces to the center of the towel, above the border, referring to the Birdhouse Towel layout for placement.

STEP 3. Machine appliqué around the edges of the pieces. Use the Tear-Away fabric stabilizer on the wrong side of the hand towel for an even machine stitch. Remove the stabilizer after stitching.

MATERIALS AND CUTTING *(for Birdhouse Towel)*

Prewash the hand towel and all of your fabrics. Press the fabrics. Using a rotary cutter, see-through ruler, and cutting mat, prepare the pieces as described below. Measurements for all pieces include ¼-inch seam allowances.

FABRIC	YARDAGE	NO. OF PIECES	DIMENSIONS
Gold print for wide border	⅛ yard	1	2 × 20½-inch strip
Green print for narrow border	⅛ yard	2	1 × 20½-inch strips
Backing for border	⅛ yard	1	3 × 20½-inch strip
Several coordinated fabrics for appliqué pieces	Scraps, or ⅛-yard pieces	—	—

Purchased hand towel; lightweight, sewable fusible web; thread to match appliqué pieces; Tear-Away fabric stabilizer; embroidery floss; assorted buttons; ceramic buttons (optional). (See "Quilting by Mail" on page 280 for information on ordering ceramic buttons.)

Finishing

Use six strands of embroidery floss to blanket stitch the lower edge of the towel. Use six strands of embroidery floss to stem stitch the bird legs and a vine in the wide border strip (the vine can also be stitched by machine, using a satin stitch). Use two strands to make a French-knot eye on each bird. See "Decorative Stitches" on page 272. Sew assorted buttons to the wide border strip and to the appliqué design.

YO-YO PATTERN

APPLIQUÉ PATTERN KEY

———— Tracing line

- - - - Tracing line
(will be hidden behind
other fabric)

BIRDHOUSE
TOWEL PATTERNS

Button

Button

Stem stitch or satin stitch

Yo-yos

Running stitch

Flower stems and bird legs
are embroidered using stem stitch

Torn fabric strips

GARDENER'S DELIGHT
TOWEL PATTERNS

French knot

Checkerboard border

PINE LODGE FAMILY ROOM

Create a private retreat in your family room
with this relaxing lodge look, whether you live in
the heart of the city or on the edge of the woods.
Use deep, rich, and colorful fabrics to create a
warm, friendly, and inviting hideaway that
you'll escape to every chance you get.
Build a fire, get out the checkers,
relax, and enjoy!

HEARTHSIDE PINEY WOODS

Bring a touch of the pine woods into your home with this quilt for

your mantel. You can just imagine the sunlight filtering down through

the pine boughs in the quiet of the afternoon. (For a more contemporary

look, see the **Color Option** on page 127.) Pair the quilt with the Mantel

Doilies (directions on page 128), or scatter the doilies about the

room on tables, chests, or the backs of chairs.

Piney Woods Quilt

Finished Size: 46½ × 26¾ inches　　　　**Finished Block: 7 inches square**

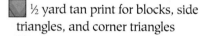

MATERIALS

(Obvious directional prints are not recommended.)

 ⅛ yard black print for center squares

⅛ yard brown print for blocks

⅛ yard red print for corner squares

½ yard dark brown print for blocks, side units, and corner triangle

⅛ yard multicolor print for corner squares

⅛ yard green print for corner squares

½ yard tan print for blocks, side triangles, and corner triangles

⅓ yard light brown print for blocks

⅝ yard black solid for accent border and binding

⅛ yard, or 2 to 3 × 40-inch strip, *each* of 7 assorted fabrics for scrap border

1⅜ yards fabric for backing

1⅜ yards lightweight batting

Scraps, or ⅛-yard pieces, of assorted green prints for appliqué trees

Lightweight, sewable fusible web

Embroidery floss

CUTTING

Prewash and press all of your fabrics. Using a rotary cutter, see-through ruler, and cutting mat, prepare the pieces as described below. Measurements for all pieces include ¼-inch seam allowances.

FABRIC	FIRST CUT		SECOND CUT	
Color	No. of Pieces	Dimensions	No. of Pieces	Dimensions
Black print	**Center squares**			
	1	3½ × 42-inch strip	11	3½-inch squares
Brown print	**Blocks**			
	1	3½ × 42-inch strip	1	3½ × 12-inch strip
			6	3½ × 1½-inch strips
Red print	**Corner squares**			
	2	1½ × 42-inch strips	2	1½ × 28-inch strips
			2	1½ × 12-inch strips
Dark brown print	**Blocks**			
	1	5½ × 42-inch strip	1	5½ × 12-inch strip
			6	5½ × 1½-inch strips
	Side triangle units			
	1	6⅞ × 42-inch strip	1	6⅞ × 11-inch strip
			10	6⅞ × 1½-inch strips
	Corner triangle units			
	1	1½ × 42-inch strip	4	1½ × 7⅞-inch strips
Multicolor print	**Corner squares**			
	2	1½ × 42-inch strips	1	1½ × 28-inch strip
			1	1½ × 12-inch strip
			1	1½ × 11-inch strip
Green print	**Corner squares**			
	2	1½ × 42-inch strips	1	1½ × 28-inch strip
			1	1½ × 12-inch strip
			2	1½-inch squares
Tan print	**Blocks**			
	1	3½ × 42-inch strip	1	3½ × 28-inch strip
			6	3½ × 1½-inch strips
	1	1½ × 42-inch strip	10	1½ × 3½-inch strips
	Side triangles and corner triangles			
	1	9¾ × 42-inch strip	2	9¾-inch squares (side triangles)
			2	5½-inch squares (corner triangles)

FABRIC	FIRST CUT		SECOND CUT	
Color	No. of Pieces	Dimensions	No. of Pieces	Dimensions
Light brown print	**Blocks**			
	1	5½ × 42-inch strip	1	5½ × 28-inch strip
			7	5½ × 1½-inch strips
	2	1½ × 42-inch strips	9	1½ × 5½-inch strips
Black solid	**Accent border**			
	4	1 × 42-inch strips	No second cut	
	Binding		Cut *1* strip into the following:	
	5	2¾ × 42-inch strips	2	2¾ × 21-inch strips
Assorted fabrics	**Scrap border**			
	7	40-inch-long strips that vary in width from 2 to 3 inches	No second cut	

Piecing the Blocks

You will be making 11 blocks, 3 of Block #1 and 8 of Block #2. For Block #1, use the brown and dark brown print strips. For Block #2, use the tan and light brown print strips. Refer to "Assembly Line Piecing" on page 268. Use ¼-inch seams and press after each sewing step. Follow the arrows in the diagrams for pressing directions.

Making Block #1

STEP 1. Sew three 3½-inch black print center squares between the six 1½ × 3½-inch brown print strips, as shown in **Diagram 1**. Press.

DIAGRAM 1

STEP 2. Sew the 3½ × 12-inch brown print strip between the two 1½ × 12-inch red print strips to make a 5½ × 12-inch strip set. See **Diagram 2**. Press.

DIAGRAM 2

STEP 3. Using a rotary cutter and ruler, cut six 1½ × 5½-inch strips from the strip set made in Step 2. See **Diagram 3**.

STEP 4. Sew the three units from Step 1 between the six units from Step 3, as shown in **Diagram 4**. Press.

DIAGRAM 3

DIAGRAM 4

STEP 5. Sew the three units from Step 4 between the six 1½ × 5½-inch dark brown print strips. See **Diagram 5** on page 122. Press.

5½"

1½"

Step 4
Unit

5½"

1½"

DIAGRAM 5

STEP 6. Sew the 5½ × 12-inch dark brown print strip between the 1½ × 12-inch multicolor print strip and the 1½ × 12-inch green print strip to make a 7½ × 12-inch strip set. See **Diagram 6**. Press.

1½" 5½" 1½"

12" 12"

DIAGRAM 6

STEP 7. Using a rotary cutter and ruler, cut six 1½ × 7½-inch strips from the strip set made in Step 6. See **Diagram 7**.

7½"

1½"

12"

DIAGRAM 7

STEP 8. Sew the three units from Step 5 between the six units from Step 7, referring to **Diagram 8** for placement of the corner

squares. Each Block #1 will now measure 7½ inches square.

BLOCK #1
Step 5 Unit

Step 7 Units

DIAGRAM 8

Making Block #2

STEP 1. Sew the remaining eight 3½-inch black print center squares between the sixteen 1½ × 3½-inch tan print strips. See **Diagram 9**. Press.

3½"

1½"

3½"

1½"

DIAGRAM 9

STEP 2. Sew the 3½ × 28-inch tan print strip between the two 1½ × 28-inch red print strips to make a 5½ × 28-inch strip set. See **Diagram 10**. Press.

1½" 3½" 1½"

28" 28"

DIAGRAM 10

STEP 3. Using a rotary cutter and ruler, cut sixteen 1½ × 5½-inch strips from the strip set made in Step 2. See **Diagram 11**.

5½"

1½"

28"

DIAGRAM 11

STEP 4. Sew the 8 units from Step 1 between the 16 units from Step 3, as shown in **Diagram 12**. Press.

Step 1 Unit

Step 3 Units

DIAGRAM 12

STEP 5. Sew the 8 units from Step 4 between the sixteen 1½ × 5½-inch light brown print strips. See **Diagram 13**. Press.

5½"

1½"

Step 4
Unit

5½"

1½"

DIAGRAM 13

STEP 6. Sew the 5½ × 28-inch light brown print strip between the 1½ × 28-inch multicolor print strip and the 1½ × 28-inch green print strip to make a 7½ × 28-inch strip set. See **Diagram 14**. Press.

1½" 5½" 1½"

28" 28"

DIAGRAM 14

STEP 7. Using a rotary cutter and ruler, cut sixteen 1½ × 7½-inch strips from the strip set made in Step 6. See **Diagram 15**.

7½"

1½"

28"

DIAGRAM 15

STEP 8. Sew the 8 units from Step 5 between the 16 units from Step 7, referring to **Diagram 16** for placement of the corner squares. Each Block #2 will now measure 7½ inches square.

BLOCK #2
Step 5 Unit

Step 7 Units

DIAGRAM 16

Making the Side Triangles

STEP 1. Cut the two 9¾-inch tan print squares in half diagonally in each direction to make eight triangles, as shown in **Diagram 17**.

Cut 9¾" Cut

9¾"

Arrows indicate straight of grain

DIAGRAM 17

STEP 2. Sew one 1½ × 6⅞-inch dark brown print strip to each of

Twiggy Accessories

To bring a bit of the outdoors into your family room, gather interesting branches and twigs to tuck into baskets or crockery. Or bundle the branches together, tie them with raffia, twine, or strips of fabric, and stack them next to your fireplace.

the eight tan print triangles from Step 1. See **Diagram 18**. Press. After pressing, the top of the dark brown strip will be longer than the triangle. It will be trimmed later.

6⅞" 9¾"

1½" 6⅞"

DIAGRAM 18

STEP 3. Sew the 1½ × 11-inch multicolor print strip to the 6⅞ × 11-inch dark brown strip to make a 7⅞ × 11-inch strip set. See **Diagram 19**. Press.

1½" 6⅞"

11" 11"

DIAGRAM 19

STEP 4. Using a rotary cutter and ruler, cut six 1½ × 7⅞-inch strips from the strip set made in Step 3. See **Diagram 20**.

7⅞"

1½"

11"

DIAGRAM 20

STEP 5. Sew six units from Step 2 to the six units from Step 4, as shown in **Diagram 21**. Press. These side triangles with the multicolor corner squares will be used for the top and bottom of the quilt.

Step 2 Unit

Step 4 Unit

DIAGRAM 21

STEP 6. Sew the two 1½-inch green print squares to the two remaining 1½ × 6⅞-inch dark brown print strips. See **Diagram 22**. Press.

1½" 6⅞"
1½" 1½"

DIAGRAM 22

STEP 7. Sew the two units from Step 6 to the two remaining units from Step 2, as shown in **Diagram 23**. Press. These side triangles with the green corner squares will be used for the sides of the quilt.

Step 2 Unit

Step 6 Unit

DIAGRAM 23

Making the Corner Triangles

STEP 1. Cut the two 5½-inch tan print squares in half diagonally to make four triangles, as shown in **Diagram 24**.

Don't Stretch the Bias

To avoid stretching the bias edge of the triangle, sew with the triangle on the bottom.

Cut

5½"

5½"

Arrow indicates straight of grain
DIAGRAM 24

STEP 2. Sew the four 1½ × 7⅞-inch dark brown print strips to the four triangles from Step 1, as shown in **Diagram 25**. Press.

5½"   5½"

1½"
7⅞"

DIAGRAM 25

Assembling the Top

The quilt top is sewn together in rows, and then the rows are joined. Pay close attention that the green and multicolor corner squares are positioned as shown in the diagrams. When sewing the side triangles to the blocks, be sure to match the seams of the corner squares. The side triangles will be longer than the blocks; these will be trimmed after the quilt top is assembled. Be sure to use ¼-inch seams throughout.

STEP 1. For Rows #1 and #5, sew one corner triangle to one Block #2. The blocks are slightly smaller than the corner triangles and should be centered on the corner triangles. See **Diagram 26**. Press.

BLOCK #2

DIAGRAM 26

STEP 2. Sew each of the two units from Step 1 between one side triangle with a green corner square and one side triangle with a multicolor corner square, as shown in **Diagram 27**. Press.

ROWS #1 AND #5

Step 1 Unit

Make 2
DIAGRAM 27

STEP 3. For Rows #2 and #4, sew one corner triangle, two Block #2s, one Block #1, and one side triangle with a multicolor corner square together as shown in **Diagram 28** on the opposite page. Press.

STEP 4. For Row #3, sew two side triangles with multicolor corner squares, two Block #2s, and one Block #1 together in the order shown in **Diagram 29.** Press.

STEP 5. Sew the rows together, as shown in **Diagram 30.** Press all the seams in one direction.

STEP 6. The raw edges of the quilt top will be uneven. Use a rotary cutter and ruler to carefully trim the edges ¼ inch from the corner points of the quilt blocks. See **Diagram 31** on the following page.

ROWS #2 AND #4

Block #2

Block #1

Block #2

Make 2
DIAGRAM 28

ROW #3

Block #2

Block #1

Block #2

DIAGRAM 29

Pressed for Time?

Make one tree block, add corner triangles, and frame it for a quick, but heartfelt, gift.

Appliqué

The trees were added to the block centers using the technique described in "Blanket Stitch Appliqué" on page 272. You can machine appliqué with either a satin stitch or blanket stitch if you prefer. Refer to "Machine Appliqué" on pages 271–272. Be sure to use a lightweight, sewable fusible web.

STEP 1. Refer to "Quick-Fuse Appliqué" on pages 270–271. Trace 11 trees from the appliqué pattern on page 127.

ROW #1

ROW #2

ROW #3

ROW #4

ROW #5

DIAGRAM 30

DIAGRAM 31

DIAGRAM 33

STEP 5. For the top and bottom, sew two sets of two 3 × 29½-inch strips together to make two 3 × 58½-inch strips. Pin and sew the scrap border strips to the top and bottom. Trim the excess length, and press the seams toward the accent border.

STEP 6. Pin and sew the remaining two 3 × 29½-inch scrap border strips to the sides. Trim the excess length and press.

Layering the Quilt

Arrange and baste the backing, batting, and top together, following the directions in "Layering the Quilt" on page 275. Trim the batting and backing to ¼ inch from the raw edges of the quilt top.

Binding the Quilt

Sew one 2¾ × 21-inch binding strip to each of two 2¾ × 42-inch binding strips to make two 2¾ × 62½-inch binding strips. Using the two 2¾ × 62½-inch binding strips for the top and bottom and the remaining two 2¾ × 42-inch binding strips for the sides, follow the directions for "Binding the Quilt" on pages 275–276.

STEP 2. Position and fuse the trees to the centers of the black print background squares.

STEP 3. Use two strands of embroidery floss to blanket stitch around the edges of the trees.

Adding the Borders

STEP 1. Sew one 1 × 42-inch accent border strip each to the top and bottom. Trim the excess length, and press the seams toward the accent border.

STEP 2. Sew the two remaining 1 × 42-inch accent border strips to the sides. Trim the excess length and press.

STEP 3. For the scrap border, sew the seven 40-inch strips (one each of seven different fabrics) together to make a 15 × 40-inch strip set. Change sewing direction with each

strip sewn, and press the seams in one direction as you go. Cut this strip set in halves, approximately 20 inches each. See **Diagram 32**.

DIAGRAM 32

STEP 4. Resew the halves together to make a 29½ × 20-inch strip set. Using a rotary cutter and ruler, cut six 3 × 29½-inch strips from this strip set. See **Diagram 33**.

46¹/₂"

26³/₄"

QUILT LAYOUT

Try colors of blue, green, purple, and gold with the green trees.

COLOR OPTION

Finishing Stitches

Machine or hand quilt in the seam lines of the blocks, side and corner triangle units, accent border, and scrap border. Outline the appliqué trees by quilting ¹/₁₆ inch from the edges. Quilt a 1¹/₄-inch diagonal grid in the side and corner triangles.

TREE PATTERN

Mantel Doilies

Finished Size: 8 inches square

(See the doilies on the mantel in the photo on page 118.)

MATERIALS

Doilies are made in sets of three. Two sets, each using a different fabric combination, were made for the mantel shown in the photo. Measure your mantle or shelf to determine how many sets you need to make. The doilies measure 11¼ inches from point to point.

To make 3 doilies:

⅛ yard black print for center squares

⅛ yard brown print for border

⅛ yard, or 1½ × 25-inch strip, red print for corner squares

¼ yard dark brown print for outer border

⅛ yard, or 1½ × 12-inch strip, multicolor print for corner squares

⅛ yard, or 1½ × 12-inch strip, green print for corner squares

⅙ yard black print for binding

⅓ yard fabric for backing

CUTTING

Prewash and press all of your fabrics. Using a rotary cutter, see-through ruler, and cutting mat, prepare the pieces as described below. Measurements for all pieces include ¼-inch seam allowances.

FABRIC		FIRST CUT		SECOND CUT	
Color		No. of Pieces	Dimensions	No. of Pieces	Dimensions
Black print		**Center squares**			
		3	3½-inch squares	No second cut	
Brown print		**Border**			
		1	3½ × 42-inch strip	1	3½ × 12-inch strip
				6	3½ × 1½-inch strips
Red print		**Corner squares**			
		1	1½ × 25-inch strip	2	1½ × 12-inch strips
Dark brown print		**Outer border**			
		1	5½ × 42-inch strip	1	5½ × 12-inch strip
				6	5½ × 1½-inch strips
Multicolor print		**Corner squares**			
		1	1½ × 12-inch strip	No second cut	

FABRIC	FIRST CUT		SECOND CUT	
Color	No. of Pieces	Dimensions	No. of Pieces	Dimensions
Green print	**Corner squares**			
	1	1½ × 12-inch strip	No second cut	
Black print	**Binding**			
	3	1 × 42-inch strips	6	1 × 8½-inch strips
			6	1 × 7½-inch strips
Backing fabric	3	8½-inch squares	No second cut	

Making the Doilies

STEP 1. Refer to "Making Block #1" on page 121 for instructions. Follow the directions in Steps 1 through 8 to make three blocks.

STEP 2. Sew the 1 × 7½-inch binding strips to the tops and bottoms of the blocks. Press the seams toward the border.

STEP 3. Sew the 1 × 8½-inch binding strips to the sides. Press.

Finishing

For each doily, position the top and backing with right sides together. Using ¼-inch seams, sew around the edges, leaving a 3- to 4-inch opening for turning. Trim the corners, turn the doily right side out, hand stitch the opening closed, and press. Decorate as desired.

DOILY LAYOUT

Notes from Debbie

We were so thrilled to find such a gorgeous location to photograph the family room projects. The home is a log cabin situated on the beach of beautiful Hayden Lake in Idaho. Many of the photo shoots that I am on are in dark photo studios. This time we lucked out! Not only was the setting spectacular, but we could see the lake through picture windows on one whole side of the home. As we began to shoot, unfortunately we found that there was too much light coming in. We had to cover the windows with huge black blankets—so we were back in the dark again!

CABIN-IN-THE-PINES QUILT

Soften the walls of your family room with this traditional Log Cabin quilt. Or use it on an overstuffed chair or sofa to cuddle up with on cold autumn and winter evenings. Of course, it would be equally at home on a bed. The enduring appeal of this well-loved pattern will guarantee that this quilt will have a place in your decorating scheme for a long time to come.

Finished Size: 82 inches square   **Finished Block: 13½ inches square**

MATERIALS

⅛ yard gold print for center squares

¼ yard *each* of 18 to 22 red prints for logs

⅛ yard *each* of 30 to 40 assorted prints (no reds or golds) for logs

¾ yard black print for binding

6¼ yards fabric for backing

Lightweight queen-size batting (90 × 108 inches)

CUTTING

Prewash and press all of your fabrics. Using a rotary cutter, see-through ruler, and cutting mat, prepare the pieces as described below. Measurements for all pieces include ¼-inch seam allowances.

FABRIC	FIRST CUT		SECOND CUT	
Color	No. of Pieces	Dimensions	No. of Pieces	Dimensions
Gold print	**Center squares**			
	2	2 × 42-inch strips	36	2-inch squares
Red prints	**Logs**			
	36	2 × 12½-inch strips	No second cut	
	36	2 × 11-inch strips	No second cut	
	36	2 × 9½-inch strips	No second cut	

(continued)

CUTTING—CONTINUED				
FABRIC	**FIRST CUT**		**SECOND CUT**	
Color	**No. of Pieces**	**Dimensions**	**No. of Pieces**	**Dimensions**
Red prints— continued	36	2 × 8-inch strips	No second cut	
	36	2 × 6½-inch strips	No second cut	
	36	2 × 5-inch strips	No second cut	
	36	2 × 3½-inch strips	No second cut	
	36	2 × 2-inch squares	No second cut	
Assorted prints	**Logs**			
	36	2 × 14-inch strips	No second cut	
	36	2 × 12½-inch strips	No second cut	
	36	2 × 11-inch strips	No second cut	
	36	2 × 9½-inch strips	No second cut	
	36	2 × 8-inch strips	No second cut	
	36	2 × 6½-inch strips	No second cut	
	36	2 × 5-inch strips	No second cut	
	36	2 × 3½-inch strips	No second cut	
Black print	**Binding**			
	9	2¾ × 42-inch strips	No second cut	

Making the Blocks

You will be making 36 blocks, each with a gold print center square, eight strips of assorted red prints, and eight strips of assorted prints. Pay close attention to the color placement in the diagrams when piecing your blocks. For a scrappy look, try to avoid using the same fabric twice in the same block. Refer to "Assembly Line Piecing" on page 268. Use ¼-inch seams and press after each sewing step, following the direction of the arrows in the diagrams.

STEP 1. Sew one 2-inch red print square to each 2-inch gold print center square. See **Diagram 1**. Press.

DIAGRAM 1

STEP 2. Sew the 2 × 3½-inch red print strips to the units from Step 1, as shown in **Diagram 2**. Press.

DIAGRAM 2

STEP 3. Sew the units from Step 2 to the 3½ × 2-inch assorted print strips. See **Diagram 3**. Press.

DIAGRAM 3

STEP 4. Sew the units from Step 3 to the 2 × 5-inch assorted print strips. See **Diagram 4**. Press.

DIAGRAM 4

STEP 5. Sew the 5 × 2-inch red print strips to the units from Step 4, as shown in **Diagram 5**. Press.

DIAGRAM 5

STEP 6. Sew the 2 × 6½-inch red print strips to the units from Step 5. See **Diagram 6**. Press.

DIAGRAM 6

STEP 7. Sew the units from Step 6 to the 6½ × 2-inch assorted print strips. See **Diagram 7.** Press.

DIAGRAM 7

STEP 8. Sew the units from Step 7 to the 2 × 8-inch assorted print strips, as shown in **Diagram 8.** Press.

DIAGRAM 8

STEP 9. Sew the 8 × 2-inch red print strips to the units from Step 8. See **Diagram 9.** Press.

DIAGRAM 9

STEP 10. Sew the 2 × 9½-inch red print strips to the units from Step 9. See **Diagram 10.** Press.

DIAGRAM 10

STEP 11. Sew the units from Step 10 to the 9½ × 2-inch assorted print strips, as shown in **Diagram 11.** Press.

DIAGRAM 11

STEP 12. Sew the units from Step 11 to the 2 × 11-inch assorted print strips. See **Diagram 12.** Press.

DIAGRAM 12

STEP 13. Sew the 11 × 2-inch red print strips to the units from Step 12. See **Diagram 13.** Press.

DIAGRAM 13

STEP 14. Sew the 2 × 12½-inch red print strips to the units from Step 13, as shown in **Diagram 14.** Press.

DIAGRAM 14

STEP 15. Sew the units from Step 14 to the 12½ × 2-inch assorted print strips. See **Diagram 15.** Press.

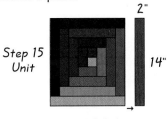

DIAGRAM 15

STEP 16. Sew the units from Step 15 to the 2 × 14-inch assorted print strips, as shown in **Diagram 16.** Press. Each Log Cabin block will now measure 14 inches square.

DIAGRAM 16

Assembling the Top

STEP 1. Referring to **Diagram 17** for placement, sew the blocks together in pairs to make 18 two-block units. Press the seams in one way in 9 units; press the seams in the opposite direction in the other 9 units.

DIAGRAM 17

STEP 2. Sew the two-block units from Step 1 together in pairs to make 9 four-block units. See **Diagram 18** on page 134. Press.

DIAGRAM 18

Make 3 rows
DIAGRAM 19

STEP 3. Sew the four-block units from Step 2 together to make three rows, as shown in **Diagram 19**. Press the seams in the middle row in the opposite direction of the seams in the top and bottom rows.

STEP 4. Sew the three rows from Step 3 together and press. The quilt top will now measure 81½ inches square.

Making the Backing

Cut the backing fabric into two 88-inch lengths and one 44-inch length. Remove the selvage edges from all pieces. Cut a 35-inch-wide segment from the entire length of each 88-inch piece. Cut two 20 × 44-inch segments from the 44-inch piece. Sew the two 20 × 44-inch pieces together to make one approximately 20 × 88-inch piece. Sew the pieces together, as shown in **Diagram 20**.

Layering the Quilt

Arrange and baste the backing, batting, and top together, following the directions in "Layering the Quilt" on page 275.

Finishing Stitches

Machine or hand quilt as desired. The quilt shown in the photo on page 130 was machine quilted in a large overall stipple pattern. Trim the batting and

backing to ¼ inch from the raw edges of the quilt top.

Binding the Quilt

Cut one 2¾ × 42-inch binding strip into four 2¾ × 10-inch strips. Sew one 2¾ × 10-inch binding strip and two 2¾ × 42-inch binding strips together in sets to make four binding strips approximately 2¾ × 94 inches each. Follow the directions for "Binding the Quilt" on pages 275–276.

DIAGRAM 20

QUILT LAYOUT

HEARTHSIDE GAMES

Nothing beats a fireside game of checkers and a mug of hot cider on a chilly night. This gameboard (shown on the next page) is a great way to use up scraps and makes a super gift. See the Checkers Storage Bag (page 138) to dye your own buttons for checkers and to make a storage bag. Stitch up quick and easy coordinating Coasters (directions on page 139).

Fireside Checkers Gameboard

Finished Size: 19 × 26 inches

MATERIALS

¼ yard tan print for checkerboard squares

Scrap, or 2½-inch square, *each* of 32 dark fabrics for checkerboard squares

⅜ yard black solid for accent border and binding

Scrap, or 3½ × 4-inch piece, *each* of 12 assorted fabrics for patchwork border

¾ yard fabric for backing

¾ yard lightweight batting

Scraps, or ⅛-yard pieces, of several coordinated fabrics for appliqué pieces

Lightweight, sewable fusible web

Embroidery floss

CUTTING

Prewash and press all of your fabrics. Using a rotary cutter, see-through ruler, and cutting mat, prepare the pieces as described below. Measurements for all pieces include ¼-inch seam allowances.

FABRIC	FIRST CUT		SECOND CUT	
Color	**No. of Pieces**	**Dimensions**	**No. of Pieces**	**Dimensions**
Tan print	**Checkerboard squares**			
	3	2½ × 42-inch strips	32	2½-inch squares
Dark fabrics	**Checkerboard squares**—from *each* of the 32 fabrics, cut the following:			
	1	2½-inch square	No second cut	

(continued)

WEEKENDER

CUTTING — CONTINUED				
FABRIC	**FIRST CUT**		**SECOND CUT**	
Color	**No. of Pieces**	**Dimensions**	**No. of Pieces**	**Dimensions**
Black solid	**Accent border**			
	2	1½ × 42-inch strips	2	1½ × 18½-inch strips
			2	1½ × 16½-inch strips
Binding fabric	**Binding**		Cut 1 strip into the following:	
	3	2¾ × 42-inch strips	2	2¾ × 21-inch strips
Assorted fabrics	**Patchwork border**—from *each* of the 12 fabrics, cut the following:			
	1	3½ × 4-inch piece	No second cut	

Assembly

STEP 1. Alternating the tan print and the dark fabrics, lay out the 2½-inch checkerboard squares in a pleasing arrangement of eight rows with eight squares each. Keep track of your layout while sewing the checkerboard together. Using ¼-inch seams, sew together each of the eight rows of eight squares. See **Diagram 1.** Press the seams toward the dark squares.

STEP 2. Sew the eight rows together to form a 16½-inch-square checkerboard, as shown in **Diagram 2.** Press the seams in one direction.

STEP 3. Sew the 1½ × 16½-inch accent border strips to the top and bottom of the checkerboard. Press the seams toward the accent border.

STEP 4. Sew the 1½ × 18½-inch accent border strips to the sides. Press.

STEP 5. Referring to the photo on the opposite page for placement, lay out the 3½ × 4-inch patchwork border pieces in a pleasing arrangement of two rows of six pieces each. Sew the pieces together to make two 18½ × 4-inch patchwork border strips. See **Diagram 3.** Press the seams in one direction.

STEP 6. Sew the 18½ × 4-inch patchwork border strips to the top and bottom. Press the seams toward the accent border.

Appliqué

The appliqué pieces were added to the patchwork border using the technique described in "Blanket Stitch Appliqué" on page 272. Use a lightweight, sewable fusible web.

STEP 1. Refer to "Quick-Fuse Appliqué"on pages 270–271. Trace six trees from the pattern on page 127 and six stars from the pattern on page 140.

STEP 2. Alternating trees and stars, position and fuse them in place. Be sure to allow for ¼-inch seams on the raw edges of the patchwork border.

DIAGRAM 1

DIAGRAM 2

DIAGRAM 3

STEP 3. Use two strands of embroidery floss to blanket stitch around the edges of the trees and stars.

Layering the Quilt

Arrange and baste the backing, batting, and top together, following the directions in "Layering the Quilt" on page 275. Trim the batting and backing to ¼ inch from the raw edges of the quilt top.

Binding the Quilt

Using the two 2¾ × 21-inch binding strips for the top and bottom and the two 2¾ × 42-inch binding strips for the sides, follow the directions for "Binding the Quilt" on pages 275–276.

Finishing Stitches

Machine or hand quilt in the seam lines of the borders. Outline the trees and stars by quilting ¹⁄₁₆ inch from the edges. Quilt diagonal lines through the checkerboard squares.

19"

26"

GAMEBOARD LAYOUT

Checkers Storage Bag

Finished Size of Bag: approximately 5 × 7 inches

(See the Checkers Storage Bag in the photo on page 136.)

Materials

12 *each* of 2 colors, or 24 light-color, 1⅜-inch plastic buttons
Rit dye (optional)
■ 7¾ × 10½-inch piece of red print for storage bag
▨ 3½-inch square of gold print for appliqué star
Lightweight, sewable fusible web
Embroidery floss
15-inch-long piece of crochet thread
1⅜-inch buttons—12 *each* of 2 colors, or 24 light-color plastic buttons

Making the Bag

STEP 1. For checkers, use 12 each of two colors of buttons. Or create custom colors by dyeing light-color buttons with Rit dye. See "How to Dye Buttons" on the opposite page.

STEP 2. For the storage bag, make a narrow hem on one 10½-inch edge of the red print piece. Fold ¼ inch to the wrong side, fold another ¼ inch to the wrong side, and stitch along the folded edge.

STEP 3. Fold the bag in half with wrong sides together. Refer to

"Quick-Fuse Appliqué" on pages 270–271. Trace one star from the appliqué pattern on page 140. Position and fuse the star to the bottom center of the bag. See **Diagram 4.** Use two strands of embroidery floss to blanket stitch around the edges of the star.

Hemmed edges

Fold

DIAGRAM 4

STORAGE BAG

STEP 4. Fold the bag in half with right sides together. Sew a ¼-inch seam on the bottom and on the edge opposite the fold. Trim the corners, turn the bag right side out, and press.

STEP 5. Use the crochet thread to make a drawstring. Starting above the star, sew a long running stitch 1 inch from the top of the bag.

How to Dye Buttons

Be sure to use an old saucepan, spoon, and strainer. Wear an old shirt or apron and rubber gloves.

STEP 1. Bring approximately 2 cups of water to a boil. Lower the heat and add small amounts of Rit dye to the water until the desired color is reached. Stir well.

STEP 2. Add light-color plastic buttons to the dye. Some buttons will dye very quickly while others may take up to 20 minutes. Stirring frequently, let the

buttons simmer until the desired color is reached. If you need to add more dye, do so while stirring.

STEP 3. Remove the buttons and place them in a strainer. Rinse them thoroughly with cold water. Set them on a paper towel to dry.

Note: Be cautious when using dyed buttons on clothing or quilts because the dye may bleed when the buttons get wet.

Coasters

Finished Size: 4 inches square

(See the coasters in the photo on page 136.)

MATERIALS AND CUTTING

Prewash and press all of your fabrics. Using a rotary cutter, see-through ruler, and cutting mat, prepare the pieces as described below. Measurements for all pieces include ¼-inch seam allowances (to make 4 coasters).

FABRIC	YARDAGE	NO. OF PIECES	DIMENSIONS
■ Black print for center squares	⅛ yard	4	3½-inch squares
■■■□ Assorted fabrics for patchwork border	⅛ yard *each* of 4 fabrics	1	1 × 40-inch strip *each*
Backing fabric	⅙ yard	4	4½-inch squares
Flannel for batting	⅙ yard	4	4½-inch squares
Several coordinated fabrics for appliqué stars	Scraps, or ⅛-yard pieces	—	—
Lightweight, sewable fusible web; embroidery floss			

Assembly

STEP 1. For the patchwork border, arrange the four 1 × 40-inch patchwork border strips in a pleasing order. Sew the strips together to make a 2½ × 40-inch strip set. Change sewing direction with each strip sewn, and press the seams in one direction. Cut this strip set in halves, approximately 20 inches each. See **Diagram 5.**

DIAGRAM 5

STEP 2. Resew the halves together to make a 4½ × 20-inch strip set. Using a rotary cutter and ruler, cut sixteen 1 × 4½-inch strips from this strip set. There should be eight squares in each strip. See **Diagram 6.**

DIAGRAM 6

STEP 3. For the top and bottom, use a seam ripper to remove two squares each from eight 1 × 4½-inch patchwork border strips to make eight strips with six squares each. Pin and sew the 1 × 3½-inch patchwork border strips to the tops and bottoms of the four

3½-inch black print center squares. See **Diagram 7.** Press the seams toward the center square.

DIAGRAM 7

STEP 4. Pin and sew the remaining eight 1 × 4½-inch patchwork border strips to the sides, as shown in **Diagram 8.** Press.

DIAGRAM 8

Appliqué

The stars were added to the center squares using the technique

described in "Blanket Stitch Appliqué" on page 272. You can machine appliqué with either a satin stitch or blanket stitch if you prefer. Refer to "Machine Appliqué" on pages 271–272. Be sure to use a lightweight, sewable fusible web for all of these techniques.

STEP 1. Refer to "Quick-Fuse Appliqué" on pages 270–271. Trace four stars from the appliqué pattern below.

STEP 2. Position and fuse the stars to the center squares.

STEP 3. Use two strands of embroidery floss to blanket stitch around the edges of the stars.

Finishing

For each coaster, position the top and backing with right sides together. Lay both pieces on top of the flannel and pin all three layers together. Using ¼-inch seams, sew around the edges, leaving a 3-inch opening for turning. Trim the corners, turn the coaster right side out, hand stitch the opening closed, and press.

STAR PATTERN

COASTER LAYOUT

SNOWMAN BRIGADE

When it snows, make snowmen! Better yet, make the fun projects shown on the next page before it snows, and you'll be ahead of the game and ready for instant decorating. Hang the Snowfall Friends Banner next to the fireplace, and don't worry about meltdown. The irresistible three-dimensional Snow Buddies (directions on page 145) are made from batting and other scraps that you probably have on hand.

Snowfall Friends Banner

Finished Size: 14 × 30 inches

MATERIALS AND CUTTING

Prewash and press all of your fabrics. Using a rotary cutter, see-through ruler, and cutting mat, prepare the pieces as described below. Measurements for all pieces include ¼-inch seam allowances.

FABRIC	YARDAGE	NO. OF PIECES	DIMENSIONS
Black prints for background	¼ yard *each* of 3 fabrics	1	7½-inch square *each*
Assorted fabrics for patchwork lattice	⅛ yard *each* of 8 fabrics	1	1½ × 18-inch strip *each*
Black star print for border	¼ yard	2 2	2½ × 29½-inch strips 2½ × 9½-inch strips

(continued)

MATERIALS AND CUTTING — CONTINUED

FABRIC	YARDAGE	NO. OF PIECES	DIMENSIONS
▨ Gold print for binding	¼ yard	2 2	2¾ × 42-inch strips 2¾ × 21-inch strips
Backing fabric	½ yard	—	—
Lightweight batting	½ yard	—	—
Several coordinated fabrics for appliqué pieces	Scraps, or ⅛-yard pieces	—	—

Fusible web; embroidery floss; permanent fine-point felt pen; assorted buttons; ceramic buttons (optional). (See "Quilting by Mail" on page 280 for information on ordering ceramic buttons.)

Assembling the Background

Assemble the banner top before adding the appliqué pieces. Be sure to use ¼-inch seams and to press after each sewing step.

STEP 1. For the patchwork lattice, arrange the eight 1½ × 18-inch patchwork lattice strips in a pleasing order. Sew the strips together to make an 8½ × 18-inch strip set. Change sewing direction with each strip sewn, and press the seams in one direction. Using a rotary cutter and ruler, cut ten 1½ × 8½-inch strips from this strip set. There should be 8 squares in each strip. See **Diagram 1**.

DIAGRAM 1

STEP 2. For the horizontal lattice strips, use a seam ripper to remove 1 square each from four 1½ × 8½-inch lattice strips to make four 1½ × 7½-inch lattice strips. There should be 7 squares in each strip. Set aside 2 squares for use in Step 3.

STEP 3. For the vertical lattice strips, sew two sets of three 1½ × 8½-inch lattice strips and one 1½-inch square removed in Step 2 to make two 1½ × 25½-inch lattice strips. There should be 25 squares in each strip. See **Diagram 2**.

Scrappy Lattice

If the patchwork lattice looks too orderly or planned and you want to maintain a random appearance, use a seam ripper to separate and rearrange the squares in the horizontal lattice strips. Then resew them together. It is easier to rearrange the horizontal strips than the vertical strips.

DIAGRAM 2

STEP 4. Lay out your lattice strips and black print background squares in a pleasing arrangement.

Keep track of your layout while sewing on the lattice strips.

STEP 5. Pin and sew one 1½ × 7½-inch horizontal lattice strip to the top of each 7½-inch black print background square and to the bottom of the bottom square. Press the seams toward the background squares. Join the blocks and press.

STEP 6. Compare the 1½ × 25½-inch vertical lattice strips to the sides. You may need to take in or let out a few seams (⅟₁₆ inch or less) to make them fit. Pin and sew the lattice strips to the sides. Press the seams toward the background squares.

STEP 7. Sew the 2½ × 9½-inch border strips to the top and bottom. Press the seams toward the border.

STEP 8. Sew the 2½ × 29½-inch border strips to the sides. Press.

Appliqué

STEP 1. Refer to "Quick-Fuse Appliqué" on pages 270–271. Trace the snowmen and other shapes from the appliqué patterns on pages 146–148.

STEP 2. Position and fuse one design at a time to the center of its corresponding background square. Refer to the photo on page 142 for placement. Note that you have the option of using ceramic buttons for some of the fusible shapes. Buttons should be sewn on after the banner has been quilted.

STEP 3. To embroider the tree trunk, use six strands of embroidery floss to stem stitch three rows of stitching very close together. Use two strands of embroidery floss to stem stitch the branches on the tree and the holly vine on the birdhouse. See "Decorative Stitches" on page 272.

STEP 4. Use a permanent felt pen to draw design details such as eyes and mouths.

Layering the Banner

Arrange and baste the backing, batting, and top together, following the directions in "Layering the Quilt" on page 275. Trim the batting and backing to ¼ inch from the raw edges of the banner top.

Binding the Banner

Using the two 2¾ × 21-inch binding strips for the top and bottom and the two 2¾ × 42-inch binding strips for the sides, follow the directions for "Binding the Quilt" on pages 275–277.

Finishing Stitches

Machine or hand quilt in the seam lines of the backgrounds, patchwork lattice, and border. Outline the appliqué designs by quilting ⅟₁₆ inch from the edges. Quilt a 1¼-inch diagonal grid in the border. Sew assorted buttons to the banner, referring to the appliqué patterns on pages 146–148 for placement.

14"

30"

BANNER LAYOUT

Snow Buddies

Height of Large Snowman: 12 inches
Height of Small Snowman: 10 inches

(See the three-dimensional snowmen in the photo on page 142.)

Materials

To make 1 snowman:

⅓ yard cotton batting
Polyester fiberfill stuffing
1½ cups plastic pellet bean-bag fill
8½-inch square of ribbing
   for hat
Glue gun and glue sticks
5 × 29-inch strip of wool or
   brushed cotton for scarf (for
   small snowman)
Tacky glue
Assorted buttons
⅛ yard wool or flannel for vest (for
   large snowman)
Twigs for arms

Assembly

STEP 1. To make the snowman, use the body pattern on pages 149–150 and the base pattern on page 147. Cut out two bodies and one base from the cotton batting.

STEP 2. With right sides together, pin and sew around the body, using ¼-inch seam allowances. Leave the armholes open as marked and the bottom edge open between the dots. Clip the curves and turn the body right side out.

STEP 3. Stuff the body with the polyester fiberfill to desired firmness, leaving 1 inch unstuffed for the plastic pellets.

STEP 4. Pin and sew the base to the body with wrong sides together, leaving a 2-inch opening. Add the plastic pellets, and sew the opening closed.

STEP 5. To make the hat, fold the square of ribbing in half, and sew a ¼-inch seam on the edge opposite the fold. Turn the ribbing right side out. Gather one raw edge tightly ¼ inch from the edge, and tie a knot. Turn the remaining raw edge up twice. Use the glue gun to glue the hat to the snowman.

STEP 6. To make the scarf for the small snowman, tie the strip of wool or brushed cotton around the neck, trim the ends to the desired length, and fray them.

STEP 7. Glue face details in place with tacky glue. Glue buttons to the front of the snowman.

STEP 8. To make the vest for the large snowman, use the vest patterns on page 151. Cut out two vest front pieces and one vest back piece from the wool or flannel. Sew the front pieces to the back at the sides, leaving an opening for each twig arm as marked.

STEP 9. To add twig arms, put tacky glue on one end of each twig, and insert the twigs through the holes in the seams on both sides of the body.

Just for Fun

Try using an old sock or sweater cuff instead of ribbing for the hat. Decorate the hat with fused patches, buttons, or small sprigs of greenery. Create a bow tie or neck tie out of fabric, and add it to the snowman, too.

For the face details, make a carrot nose and little chunks of coal, using a colorful modeling compound such as FIMO or Sculpey. Bake the shapes according to the manufacturer's directions, and glue them in place with tacky glue.

Make a Wreath

Arrange and attach a few pinecones and Snow Buddies to a wreath.

APPLIQUÉ PATTERN KEY

———— Tracing line

----- Tracing line
(will be hidden behind
other fabric)

Button

Button

Button

Button

Button

Button

Stitching line

SNOWMAN #1 PATTERN

BASE PATTERNS FOR 3-D SNOWMEN

Small snowman

Large snowman

Button

Button

SNOWMAN #2 PATTERN

SNOWMAN #3 PATTERN

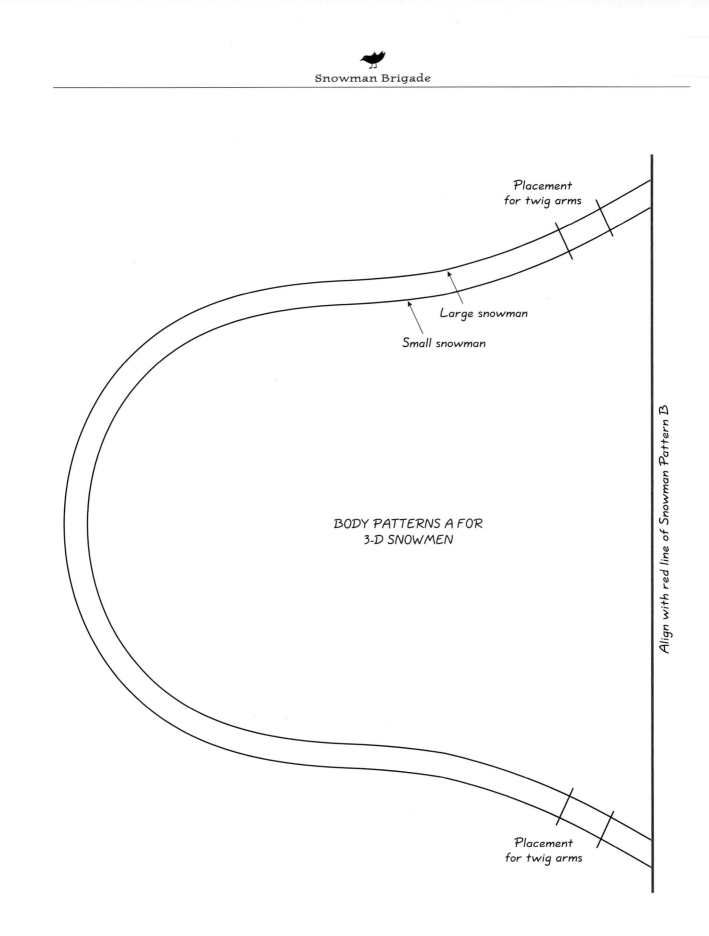

Placement
for twig arms

Large snowman

Small snowman

Align with red line of Snowman Pattern B

BODY PATTERNS A FOR
3-D SNOWMEN

Placement
for twig arms

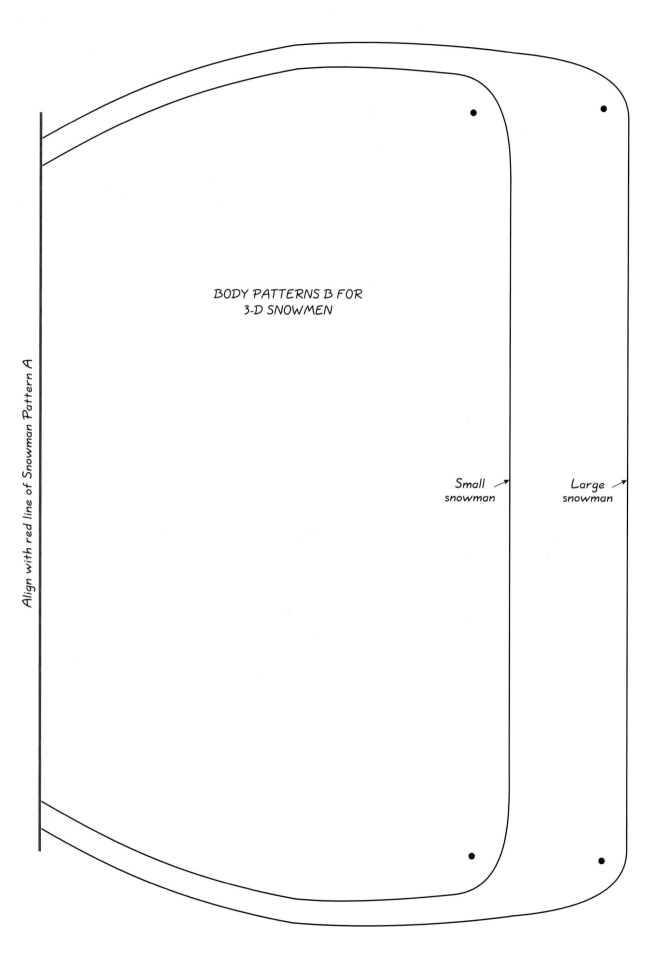

Align with red line of Snowman Pattern A

BODY PATTERNS B FOR
3-D SNOWMEN

Small
snowman

Large
snowman

Leave open
for twig arms

VEST FRONT PATTERN FOR
LARGE SNOWMAN

Cut 2

Arrow indicates straight of grain

Leave open
for twig arms

VEST BACK PATTERN FOR
LARGE SNOWMAN

Cut 1

Place on fold

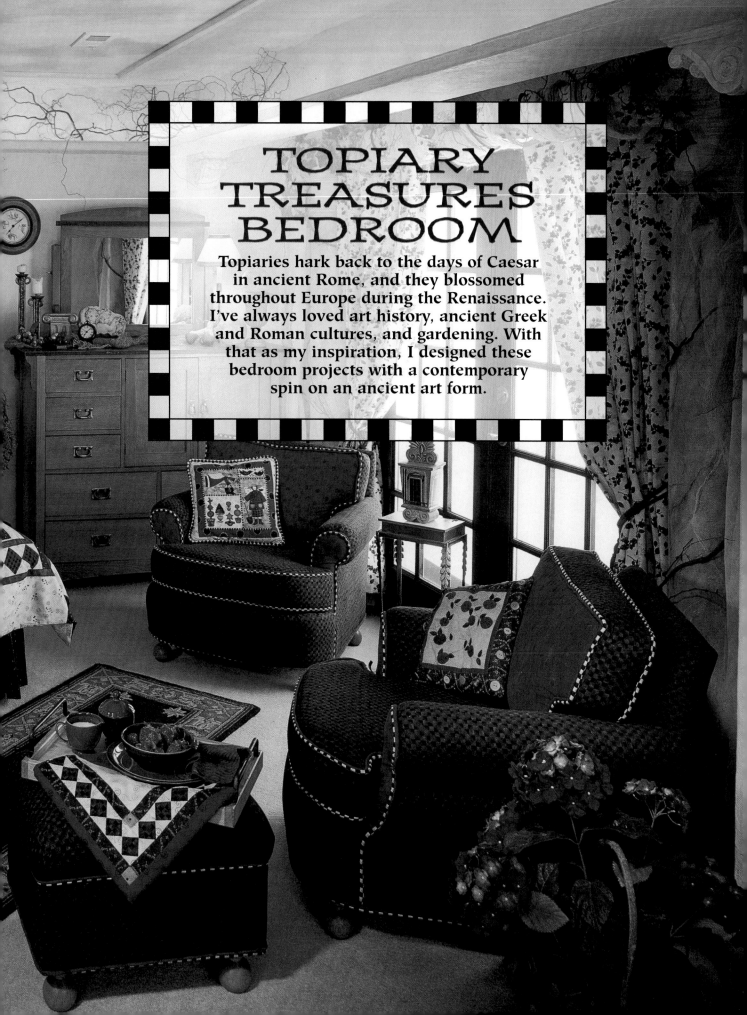

TOPIARY TREASURES BEDROOM

Topiaries hark back to the days of Caesar in ancient Rome, and they blossomed throughout Europe during the Renaissance. I've always loved art history, ancient Greek and Roman cultures, and gardening. With that as my inspiration, I designed these bedroom projects with a contemporary spin on an ancient art form.

TOPIARY TREASURES

With this inviting duvet cover, you'll imagine yourself strolling

through the gardens of a country estate in ancient Rome or an elegant English

manor house of the seventeenth century. Cypress, boxwood, and rosemary were

clipped into various shapes, from smooth balls and cones to spirals, pyramids,

and animals. I've put my topiaries in pots with coordinating vines and bows.

Ruffled pillow shams (directions on page 165) and assorted throw pillows (page

187) will beckon you to kick back and dream your own garden fantasy.

King-Size Duvet Cover

Finished Size: 100 inches square   **Finished Block: 10 × 14 inches**

MATERIALS

The king-size duvet cover is shown in the photo. To make the queen-size version, see page 160. Since there are often size variations in king-size duvets, you may have to adjust the borders of your cover to fit the size of your duvet.

(Obvious directional prints are not recommended.)

6⅛ yards tan print for block and lattice backgrounds

2 yards green print for 1-inch block and outer borders

3 yards red-and-black check for lattice squares

⅝ yard black print for lattice corner squares

2⅛ yards tan floral print for border

¼ yard black print for border corner squares

⅜ yard *each* of 2 green prints for appliqué topiary circles

¼ yard *each* of 2 black prints for appliqué pots

Scraps, or ⅛-yard pieces, of several coordinated fabrics for small appliqué pieces

9½ yards fabric for backing

4½ yards lightweight, sewable fusible web

Thread to match appliqué pieces

3½ yards Tear-Away fabric stabilizer

Ten 1-inch buttons

CUTTING

Prewash and press all of your fabrics. Using a rotary cutter, see-through ruler, and cutting mat, prepare the pieces as described below. Measurements for all pieces include ¼-inch seam allowances.

FABRIC	FIRST CUT		SECOND CUT	
Color	No. of Pieces	Dimensions	No. of Pieces	Dimensions
Tan print	**Block background**			
	7	14½ × 42-inch strips	20	10½ × 14½-inch pieces
	Lattice background			
	43	2½ × 42-inch strips	684	2½-inch squares
Green print	**1-inch block border**			
	34	1½ × 42-inch strips	40	1½ × 10½-inch strips
			40	1½ × 16½-inch strips
	1-inch outer border		Cut *1* strip into the following:	
	9	1½ × 42-inch strips	4	1½ × 10-inch (approximate) strips
Red-and-black check	**Lattice squares**			
	22	4½ × 42-inch strips	171	4½-inch squares
Black print	**Lattice corner squares**			
	4	4½ × 42-inch strips	30	4½-inch squares
Tan floral print	**Border**		Cut *1* strip into the following:	
	9	7½ × 42-inch strips	4	7½ × 10-inch (approximate) strips
Black print	**Border corner squares**			
	1	7½ × 42-inch strip	4	7½-inch squares

Block Borders

STEP 1. Sew the 1½ × 10½-inch green print block border strips to the tops and bottoms of the twenty 10½ × 14½-inch tan print block background pieces. Press the seams toward the border.

STEP 2. Sew the 1½ × 16½-inch green print block border strips to the sides. Press.

Appliqué

The topiaries were added to the background pieces using the technique described in "Machine Appliqué" on pages 271–272. I used a machine blanket stitch, but you can use a machine satin stitch if you prefer. Be sure to use a lightweight, sewable fusible web.

STEP 1. Refer to "Quick-Fuse Appliqué" on pages 270–271. Trace ten topiaries with bows and ten topiaries with vines from the appliqué patterns on pages 162–164.

STEP 2. Position and fuse the topiaries to the background pieces, referring to the **King-Size Duvet Cover Layout** on page 159 for placement.

STEP 3. Stitch around the edges of the topiaries with a machine blanket stitch. Use the Tear-Away fabric stabilizer on the wrong side of the background pieces for an even machine stitch. Remove the stabilizer after stitching.

Piecing the Lattice

You will be making 171 lattice blocks. Refer to "Making Quick Corner Triangles" on page 269 for instructions on making the corner triangle units, and review "Assembly Line Piecing" on page 268. Press the seams toward the triangle just added.

STEP 1. Sew two 2½-inch tan print lattice background squares to each of the 4½-inch red-and-black check lattice squares. See **Diagram 1**. Press.

DIAGRAM 1

STEP 2. Sew two additional 2½-inch tan print lattice background squares to the units from Step 1. See **Diagram 2**. Press.

DIAGRAM 2

STEP 3. Using ¼-inch seams, sew 75 units from Step 2 together, as shown in **Diagram 3**, to make 25 units with three squares each. Press the seams, following the arrows in the diagram. Each of these units will now measure 4½ × 12½ inches. Compare the lattice units to the tops and bottoms of the topiary blocks. You may need to take in or let out a few seams (¹⁄₁₆ inch or less) to make them fit.

Make 25 units for king-size
Make 20 units for queen-size
DIAGRAM 3

Make It Reversible!

Purchase a fabulous fabric that you love for the backing of your Topiary Treasures Duvet Cover, and the cover will be reversible.

STEP 4. Sew the remaining 96 units from Step 2 together, as shown in **Diagram 4**, to make 24 units with four squares each. Press. Each of these units will now measure 4½ × 16½ inches. Compare the lattice units to the sides of the topiary blocks, and adjust as necessary.

Make 24 units for king-size
Make 20 units for queen-size
DIAGRAM 4

Assembling the Top

STEP 1. Referring to the **King-Size Duvet Cover Layout** on page 159 for placement, arrange the topiary blocks and lattice units in their proper positions. Keep track of your layout while sewing the blocks and lattice together.

STEP 2. For Rows #1 and #3, sew 4½ × 16½-inch lattice units and

topiary blocks together in the order shown in **Diagram 5** on the following page. These rows will begin and end with bow blocks. Press the seams toward the blocks.

STEP 3. For Rows #2 and #4, sew 4½ × 16½-inch lattice units and topiary blocks together as in Step 2, but these rows will begin and end with vine blocks. Press the seams toward the blocks.

STEP 4. Sew the 4½-inch black print lattice corner squares and the 4½ × 12½-inch lattice units together, as shown in **Diagram 6** on the following page, to make five rows. Press the seams toward the lattice corner squares.

STEP 5. Sew the lattice rows from Step 4 and the rows of blocks from Steps 2 and 3 together. Press the seams toward the blocks.

Adding Borders

STEP 1. Sew the eight 1½ × 42-inch green print outer border strips together in pairs to make four strips approximately 1½ × 84 inches each. Press the seams to one side. Sew one 1½ × 10-inch green print outer border strip to one end of each 1½ × 84-inch outer border strip, and press.

STEP 2. Pin and sew one outer border strip on to the top and bottom of the duvet cover. Trim the excess length, and press the seams toward the outer border.

STEP 3. Pin and sew the remaining outer border strips to the sides. Trim the excess length and press.

ROWS 1 AND 3

Four-square lattice unit

4½"

Note: for queen-size omit this block and lattice strip

16½"

16½"

DIAGRAM 5

Note: for queen-size omit this lattice strip and lattice corner block

Three-square lattice unit

4½"

12½"   4½"

4½"

DIAGRAM 6

STEP 4. Sew the eight 7½ × 42-inch tan floral print border strips together in pairs to make four strips approximately 7½ × 84 inches each. Press. Sew one 7½ × 10-inch tan floral print border strip to one end of each 7½ × 84-inch border strip. Press the seams to one side. Measure the outer edges of the duvet cover. Trim the border strips to these measurements.

STEP 5. Pin and sew one border strip to the top and one to the bottom of the duvet cover. Press the seams toward the border.

STEP 6. Sew one 7½-inch black print border corner square to each end of the two remaining border strips. Press the seams toward the border. Pin and sew the border strips to the sides. Press.

Adding the Backing

STEP 1. Cut the backing fabric into three equal lengths, about 110

inches each. Trim the selvage edges off all three pieces.

STEP 2. With right sides together, sew two backing pieces together lengthwise to make one piece approximately 80 × 110 inches. Press. Fold and press ¼ inch to the wrong side along one long edge. Fold again 1 inch to the wrong side. Press. Topstitch along the folded edge to make a hem.

STEP 3. Fold and press ¼ inch to the wrong side along one long edge of the remaining backing piece. Fold again 3 inches to the wrong side. Press. Topstitch along the folded edge to make a hem. Mark placement and make ten vertical buttonholes on the hemmed edge. The first and last buttonholes are spaced 13 inches from the sides, and the remaining eight buttonholes are spaced approximately 9 inches apart.

STEP 4. Position the top and backing piece from Step 3 with right sides together. Center the top

on the backing so that an equal amount of backing extends on each side. The backing will extend beyond the top edge of the duvet cover top by approximately 5 inches. See **Diagram 7.** Pin the two layers together. Using ¼-inch seams, sew around the sides and top edge of the duvet cover where the top is pinned to the backing. Trim the backing to the same size as the top.

Backing piece from Step 3

110"

5"

Duvet cover top wrong side up

DIAGRAM 7

STEP 5. Position the top and backing piece from Step 2 with right sides together, and pin them in place. The hemmed edge of this

Queen-size does not include this vertical row of blocks and lattice units

100"

100"

KING-SIZE DUVET COVER LAYOUT

backing piece will overlap by 3 inches the hemmed edge of the backing piece already sewn to the top. Center the top on the backing so that an equal amount extends on each side. See **Diagram 8.** Pin the two layers together. Using ¼-inch seams, sew around the sides and bottom of the duvet

cover. Trim the backing to the same size as the top. Trim the corners, turn the duvet cover right side out, and press.

STEP 6. Mark placement of the buttons on the bottom backing piece, and sew the buttons in place. Insert your duvet inside the cover.

3"   3"

Duvet cover top wrong side up

Backing piece from Step 2
DIAGRAM 8

Queen-Size Duvet Cover

Finished Size: 84 × 100 inches
Finished Block: 10 × 14 inches

(Obvious directional prints are not recommended.)

5¼ yards tan print for block and lattice backgrounds

1¾ yards green print for 1-inch block and outer borders

2½ yards red-and-black check for lattice squares

⅝ yard black print for lattice corner squares

2⅛ yards tan floral print for border

¼ yard black print for border corner squares

⅜ yard *each* of 2 green prints for appliqué topiary circles

¼ yard *each* of 2 black prints for appliqué pots

Scraps, or ⅛-yard pieces, of several coordinated fabrics for small appliqué pieces

8 yards fabric for backing

4 yards lightweight, sewable fusible web

Thread to match appliqué pieces

2½ yards Tear-Away fabric stabilizer

Ten 1-inch buttons

CUTTING

Prewash and press all of your fabrics. Using a rotary cutter, see-through ruler, and cutting mat, prepare the pieces as described below. Measurements for all pieces include ¼-inch seam allowances.

FABRIC	FIRST CUT		SECOND CUT	
Color	**No. of Pieces**	**Dimensions**	**No. of Pieces**	**Dimensions**
Tan print	**Block background**			
	6	14½ × 42-inch strips	16	10½ × 14½-inch pieces
	Lattice background			
	35	2½ × 42-inch strips	560	2½-inch squares
Green print	**1-inch block border**			
	27	1½ × 42-inch strips	32	1½ × 10½-inch strips
			32	1½ × 16½-inch strips
	1-inch outer border		Cut *1* strip into the following:	
	9	1½ × 42-inch strips	2	1½ × 11-inch strips
Red-and-black check	**Lattice squares**			
	18	4½ × 42-inch strips	140	4½-inch squares

FABRIC	FIRST CUT		SECOND CUT	
Color	No. of Pieces	Dimensions	No. of Pieces	Dimensions
Black print	**Lattice corner squares**			
	4	4½ × 42-inch strips	25	4½-inch squares
Tan floral print	**Border**		Cut *1* strip into the following:	
	9	7½ × 42-inch strips	2	7½ × 11-inch strips
Black print	**Border corner squares**			
	1	7½ × 42-inch strip	4	7½-inch squares

Block Borders

Refer to "Block Borders" on page 156 for instructions. Follow the directions in Steps 1 and 2 to make 16 background blocks with borders.

Appliqué

Refer to "Appliqué" on page 156 for instructions. Follow the directions in Steps 1 through 3 to add topiaries with bows to eight of the background blocks and to add topiaries with vines to the remaining eight background blocks. Use the appliqué patterns on pages 162–164.

Piecing the Lattice

Follow the instructions under "Piecing the Lattice" on page 157. You will be making 140 lattice blocks. The lattice blocks will be sewn together to make 20 lattice units of three squares each and 20 lattice units of four squares each.

Assembling the Top

Refer to Steps 1 through 5 under "Assembling the Top" on page 157. Referring to the **King-Size**

Duvet Cover Layout on page 159 for placement, arrange the topiary blocks and lattice units in their proper positions. You will have four rows of four topiary blocks with lattice units between each block. Keep track of your layout while sewing the blocks and lattice together.

Adding Borders

Refer to "Adding Borders" on page 157 for instructions. You will be sewing an additional 11-inch green print outer border strip to just two of the 84-inch strips. The shorter strips will be sewn to the top and bottom of the duvet cover.

For the tan floral print border, the outer measurements will be different for the top and bottom and the sides. Trim the strips to match the dimensions of the pieced top.

Adding the Backing

STEP 1. Cut the backing fabric into three equal lengths, approximately 96 inches each. Trim the selvage edges off all three pieces.

STEP 2. With right sides together, sew two backing pieces together

lengthwise to make one piece, approximately 80 × 96 inches. Press. Fold and press ¼ inch to the wrong side along one long edge. Fold again 1 inch to the wrong side. Press. Topstitch along the folded edge to make a hem.

STEP 3. Fold and press ¼ inch to the wrong side along one long edge of the remaining backing piece. Fold again 3 inches to the wrong side. Press. Topstitch along the folded edge to make a hem. Mark placement and make ten buttonholes on the hemmed edge. The first and last buttonholes are spaced 12 inches from the sides, and the remaining eight buttonholes are spaced approximately 7½ inches apart.

STEP 4. Follow Steps 4 through 6 under "Adding the Backing" on page 158 to complete the duvet cover.

APPLIQUÉ PATTERN KEY

———— Tracing line

- - - - - Tracing line
(will be hidden behind
other fabric)

Match
with
Topiary
Circle
Pattern

TOPIARY WITH VINE PATTERN

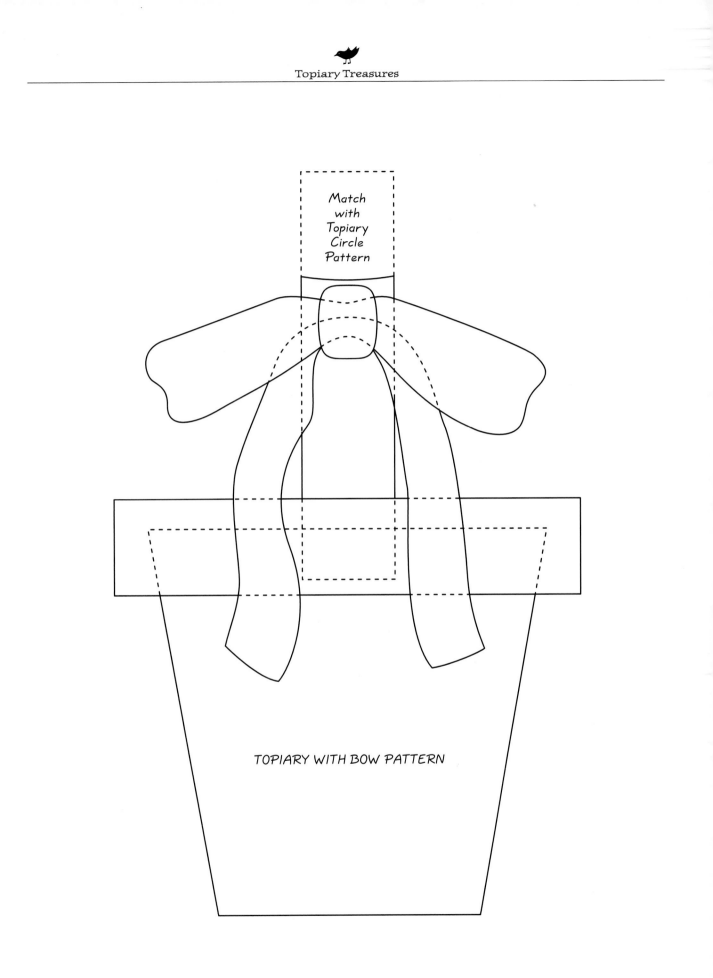

TOPIARY WITH BOW PATTERN

Match
with
Topiary
Circle
Pattern

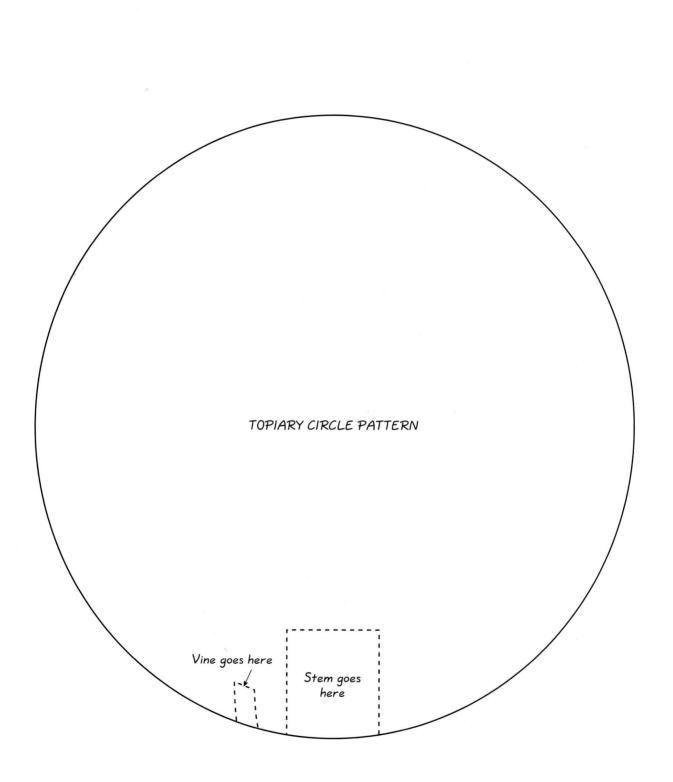

TOPIARY CIRCLE PATTERN

Vine goes here

Stem goes
here

CHECKS AND RUFFLES PILLOW SHAMS

Echoing the square-in-square blocks in the lattice of the

Topiary Treasures duvet cover, the ruffled pillow shams on the following page

are the perfect complement to the coordinated ensemble (directions on page

167). You'll be stylishly ready for quiet bedtime reading or a morning

breakfast in bed. These instructions are written to make three

pillow shams to fit on a king-size bed.

Finished Size: 40 × 32 inches (including ruffle)

MATERIALS

(Obvious directional prints are not recommended.)

To make 3 pillow shams:

■ ¼ yard gold print for center

■ ½ yard dark tan print for small triangles

■ ⅞ yard green print for small diamonds and accent border

■ 1 yard tan print for large triangles

■ ⅞ yard red-and-black check for large diamonds

■ ⅛ yard red print for small corner squares

■ ½ yard tan floral print for border

■ ⅓ yard black print for large corner squares

■ 4¾ yards black-and-tan check for ruffle

2¾ yards fabric for backing

Strong crochet thread or #5 pearl cotton

165

CUTTING

Prewash and press all of your fabrics. Using a rotary cutter, see-through ruler, and cutting mat, prepare the pieces as described below. Measurements for all pieces include ¼-inch seam allowances.

FABRIC	FIRST CUT		SECOND CUT	
Color	No. of Pieces	Dimensions	No. of Pieces	Dimensions
Gold print	**Center**			
	1	4½ × 42-inch strip	3	4½ × 12½-inch pieces
Dark tan print	**Small triangles**			
	8	1½ × 42-inch strips	192	1½-inch squares
Green print	**Small diamonds**			
	3	2½ × 42-inch strips	48	2½-inch squares
	Accent border			
	12	1½ × 42-inch strips	No second cut	
Tan print	**Large triangles**			
	12	2½ × 42-inch strips	192	2½-inch squares
Red-and-black check	**Large diamonds**			
	6	4½ × 42-inch strips	48	4½-inch squares
Red print	**Small corner squares**			
	1	2½ × 42-inch strip	12	2½-inch squares
Tan floral print	**Border**			
	5	2½ × 42-inch strips	6	2½ × 16½-inch strips
			6	2½ × 12½-inch strips
Black print	**Large corner squares**			
	2	4½ × 42-inch strips	12	4½-inch squares
Black-and-tan check	**Ruffle**			
	15	11 × 42-inch strips	No second cut	
Backing fabric	6	15 × 32-inch pieces	No second cut	

Quick Corner Triangles

You will be making three pillow shams. Refer to "Making Quick Corner Triangles" on page 269 and "Assembly Line Piecing" on page 268. Press the seams toward the triangle just added.

STEP 1. Sew two 1½-inch dark tan print squares to each of the forty-eight 2½-inch green print squares. See **Diagram 1**. Press.

DIAGRAM 1

STEP 2. Sew two additional 1½-inch dark tan print squares to the units from Step 1. See **Diagram 2**. Press.

DIAGRAM 2

STEP 3. Sew two 2½-inch tan print squares to each of the forty-eight 4½-inch red-and-black check squares. Refer to **Diagram 3**. Press.

DIAGRAM 3

STEP 4. Sew two additional 2½-inch tan print squares to the units from Step 3, as shown in **Diagram 4**. Press.

DIAGRAM 4

Assembly

Use ¼-inch seams and press after each sewing step. Follow the arrows in the diagrams for pressing directions.

STEP 1. Sew thirty-six 2½-inch dark tan/green corner triangle units together, as shown in **Diagram 5**, to make six units of six squares each. Press. Each unit will now measure 2½ × 12½ inches.

DIAGRAM 5

STEP 2. Compare the units from Step 1 to the tops and bottoms of the 4½ × 12½-inch gold print center pieces. You may need to take in or let out a few seams (¹⁄₁₆ inch or less) to make them fit.

Sew the three 4½ × 12½-inch gold print center pieces between the six units from Step 1. See **Diagram 6**. Press.

DIAGRAM 6

STEP 3. Sew the remaining twelve 2½-inch dark tan/green corner triangle units together in pairs to make six 2½ × 4½-inch units of two squares each. See **Diagram 7**. Press.

Make 6
DIAGRAM 7

STEP 4. Sew the six units from Step 3 between the twelve 2½-inch red print corner squares, as shown in **Diagram 8**. Press.

Make 6
DIAGRAM 8

STEP 5. Sew the three units from Step 2 between the six units from Step 4. See **Diagram 9**. Press.

DIAGRAM 9

STEP 6. Sew the three units from Step 5 between the six 2½ × 16½-inch tan floral border strips. See **Diagram 10**. Press.

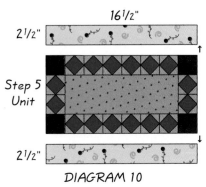

DIAGRAM 10

STEP 7. Sew the three units from Step 6 between the six 2½ × 12½-inch tan floral border strips. See **Diagram 11** on the following page. Press.

STEP 8. Sew thirty 4½-inch tan/red-and-black corner triangle units together, as shown in **Diagram 12** on the following page, to make six units of five squares each. Press. Each unit will now measure 4½ × 20½ inches.

STEP 9. Fit, pin, and sew the three units from Step 7 between the six units from Step 8. See **Diagram 13** on the following page. Press.

STEP 10. Sew the remaining eighteen 4½-inch tan/red-and-black corner triangle units together, as shown in **Diagram 14** on the following page, to make six units of three squares each. Press. Each unit will now measure 4½ × 12½ inches.

STEP 11. Sew the six units from Step 10 between the twelve 4½-inch black print corner squares. See **Diagram 15** on the following page. Press.

DIAGRAM 11

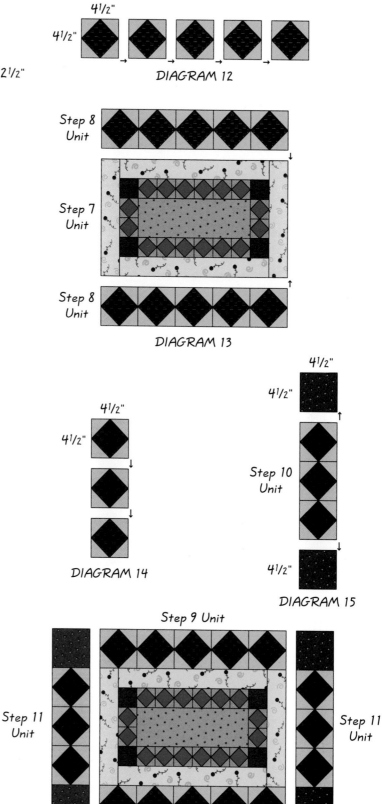

DIAGRAM 12

DIAGRAM 13

DIAGRAM 14

DIAGRAM 15

DIAGRAM 16

STEP 12. Sew the three units from Step 9 between the six units from Step 11. See **Diagram 16**. Press. The pillow tops will now measure 28½ × 20½ inches.

STEP 13. Sew one 1½ × 42-inch accent border strip each to the top and bottom of each unit from Step 12. Trim the excess length of the accent border, and press the seams toward the accent border.

STEP 14. Sew the remaining 1½ × 42-inch accent border strips to the sides of each unit from Step 13. Trim the excess length and press.

Ruffles and Backings

STEP 1. With right sides together, sew the short edges of five 11 × 42-inch black-and-tan check ruffle strips together to make a continuous loop. Press the ruffle in half lengthwise with wrong sides together. Repeat with the remaining ten strips to make two more ruffles.

STEP 2. Sew a gathering stitch along the raw edge of each ruffle by zigzag stitching over the crochet thread or pearl cotton. Divide each ruffle into quarters, and mark.

STEP 3. Measure the pillow sham, and mark the center on the raw edge of each of the four sides.

STEP 4. With right sides together and matching the marks, position and pin a ruffle on each pillow sham top. Gather each ruffle by pulling the gathering cord. Evenly distribute the gathers as you pin the ruffles to the sham tops. Hand baste the ruffles to the sham tops. The ruffles will be sewn in place when the backings are added.

STEP 5. Narrow hem one long edge of each 15 × 32-inch backing piece by folding under ¼ inch to the wrong side. Press. Fold again ¼ inch to the wrong side. Press. Topstitch along the folded edge.

STEP 6. With right sides up, lay one backing piece over the second piece so that the hemmed edges overlap 3 inches. Baste the pieces together at the sides where they overlap. See **Diagram 17**.

DIAGRAM 17

Repeat with the remaining four backing pieces to make two more backings.

STEP 7. With the ruffle in the middle, position the pillow sham top and backing with right sides together, and pin them in place. The backing will extend 1 to 1½ inches beyond the edges of the sham top. Using ¼-inch seams, sew around the edges of the pillow sham. Trim the backing to the same size as the sham top. Trim the corners, turn the pillow

Whiten Up!

Try making the pillow shams in white, cream, beige, and ecru for an elegant, more formal look.

sham right side out, and press. Repeat to finish the remaining two pillow shams.

PILLOW SHAM LAYOUT

TOPIARIES-TO-GO WALL QUILT

Turn the page to see some cute little potted topiaries that look as if they could have come from a garden show, where small and portable sculpted plants are a hot trend. Working with fabrics, instead of with branches and leaves, you have the freedom to shape these garden whimsies and know they'll stay this way forever—with no more pruning needed!

The three-dimensional cardinal, bow, buttons, and yo-yos add to the character and charm of this wall quilt.

Finished Size: 32 × 20 inches

MATERIALS AND CUTTING

Prewash and press all of your fabrics. Using a rotary cutter, see-through ruler, and cutting mat, prepare the pieces as described below. Measurements for all pieces include ¼-inch seam allowances.

FABRIC	YARDAGE	NO. OF PIECES	DIMENSIONS
Gold print for background and checkerboard	⅝ yard	1	16½ × 24½-inch piece (background)
		2	1½ × 30-inch strips (checkerboard)
		1	1½-inch square (checkerboard)
Black print for accent border, binding, and optional tabs	⅝ yard	2	1 × 24½-inch strips (accent border)
		2	1 × 17½-inch strips (accent border)
		4	2¾ × 42-inch strips (binding)
		1	2½ × 40-inch strip (tabs)
Green print for checkerboard	⅛ yard	2	1½ × 30-inch strips
		1	1½-inch square

(continued)

MATERIALS AND CUTTING —CONTINUED

FABRIC	YARDAGE	NO. OF PIECES	DIMENSIONS
Red print for side border	⅛ yard (cut into one 3½ × 42-inch strip)	2	3½ × 19½-inch strips
Backing fabric	¾ yard	—	—
Lightweight batting	¾ yard	—	—
Green print for large appliqué topiary circle and cone	¼ yard	—	—
Several coordinated fabrics for appliqué pieces and yo-yos	Scraps, or ⅛-yard pieces	—	—

Lightweight, sewable fusible web; green decorative cording (optional); embroidery floss; assorted buttons; Rit dye (optional); organdy ribbon; 6-inch square of red felt for dimensional bird; polyester fiberfill stuffing

Assembling the Background

Assemble the quilt top before adding the appliqué pieces. Be sure to use ¼-inch seams and to press after each sewing step.

STEP 1. Sew the 1 × 24½-inch accent border strips to the top and bottom of the 24½ × 16½-inch gold print background piece. Press the seams toward the accent border.

STEP 2. Sew the 1 × 17½-inch accent border strips to the sides. Press.

STEP 3. Alternating the two colors, sew the four 1½ × 30-inch checkerboard strips together to make a 4½ × 30-inch strip set. Change sewing direction with each strip sewn, and press the seams toward the darker fabric as you go. Cut this strip set into

thirds, approximately 10 inches each. See **Diagram 1**.

STEP 4. Resew the thirds together to make a 12½ × 10-inch strip set. Cut this strip set into halves, approximately 5 inches each. See **Diagram 2**.

STEP 5. Resew the halves together to make a 24½ × 5-inch strip set. Using a rotary cutter and ruler, cut two 1½ × 24½-inch strips from this strip set. There should be 24 squares in each strip. See **Diagram 3** on the following page.

STEP 6. Sew the 1½-inch gold print square to the end of one checkerboard strip. Sew the 1½-inch green print square to the end of the second checkerboard strip. See **Diagram 4** on the following page. Press. There should be 25 squares in each strip.

DIAGRAM 1

DIAGRAM 2

24½"

5"

1½"

DIAGRAM 3

24½"

1½"

1½"

DIAGRAM 4

STEP 7. Compare the checkerboard strips to the bottom of the quilt. You may need to take in or let out a few seams (1/16 inch or less) to make them fit. Make adjustments before you sew the checkerboard strips together. If you do make adjustments, make them in the same place on each strip so that the strips will still match up. Refer to "Fitting Pieced Borders" on page 274 for further instructions. Sew the checkerboard strips together and press. Pin and sew the checkerboard to the bottom of the quilt. Press the seam toward the accent border.

STEP 8. Sew the 3½ × 19½-inch side border strips to the sides. Press the seams toward the side border.

Appliqué

The appliqué pieces were added to the background using the technique described in "Blanket Stitch Appliqué" on page 272. You can machine appliqué with either a satin stitch or blanket stitch if you prefer. Refer to "Machine Appliqué" on pages 271–272 for instructions on either technique. Be sure to use a lightweight, sewable fusible web.

STEP 1. Refer to "Quick-Fuse Appliqué" on pages 270–271. Trace the three potted topiaries from the appliqué patterns on pages 176–181. Choosing one leaf from Topiary #3, trace 20 leaves for the side border.

STEP 2. Position and fuse the appliqué pieces to the background, referring to the **Wall Quilt Layout** for placement. Before fusing Topiary #3 on the right, place the decorative cording under the edges of the circles and the pot. Hand stitch the cording in place. You can also use a machine satin stitch if you prefer. Position and fuse 10 leaves in each side border strip.

STEP 3. Use two strands of embroidery floss to blanket stitch around the edges of the appliqué pieces and stem stitch the curved lines on the rim of the pot. Refer to "Decorative Stitches" on page 272 for instructions. Mark the vines in the side border.

Layering the Quilt

Arrange and baste the backing, batting, and top together, following the directions in "Layering the Quilt" on page 275. Trim the batting and backing to ¼ inch from the raw edges of the quilt top.

Binding the Quilt

Using the four 2¾ × 42-inch binding strips, follow the directions for "Binding the Quilt" on pages 275–276.

Finishing Stitches

STEP 1. Machine or hand quilt in the seam lines of the background and accent border and between

32"

20"

WALL QUILT LAYOUT

the squares of the checkerboard. Outline the appliqué designs by quilting ¹⁄₁₆ inch from the edges. Quilt a 1¼-inch diagonal grid in the background. Use six strands of embroidery floss to quilt the vines in the side border.

STEP 2. Refer to "Making Yo-yos" on pages 272–273. Make five small and nine large yo-yos from the patterns below. Sew the yo-yos to the middle topiary, referring to the **Wall Quilt Layout** for placement.

STEP 3. Sew assorted buttons to the left and right topiaries, Topiary #1 and Topiary #3. You can dye your own buttons with Rit dye. See "How to Dye Buttons" on page 139 for instructions. Tie the organdy ribbon into a bow, and hand sew it to the left topiary.

STEP 4. Make a dimensional bird, following the directions in "How to Make a Dimensional Bird" at right. Hand sew the bird onto the left topiary.

STEP 5. If you want to add hanging tabs, fold the 2½ × 40-inch black print tab strip in half lengthwise with right sides together. Sew a ¼-inch seam along the edge opposite the fold, turn the strip right side out, and press. Topstitch along the edges of both sides. Cut the strip into five 7½-inch pieces. Fold each piece in half, and stitch a ¼-inch seam along the cut edge. Turn each tab right side out, and press with the seam at the bottom of the tab. Space the tabs evenly across the top of the quilt back. Hand stitch the tabs in place.

How to Make a Dimensional Bird

STEP 1. Make a template for the bird body, including the beak from the pattern on page 177. Cut the 6-inch red felt square in half, and draw around the template on one half. Pin the felt with the traced shape to the second felt piece. Cut out the bird on the drawn line, cutting through both layers.

STEP 2. Trace the bird beak from the pattern on page 177 onto a fusible web. Use a scrap of gold fabric and quick-fuse the beak to the bird.

STEP 3. Use two strands of embroidery floss to blanket stitch around the edges of the bird. Leave a small opening for stuffing. Lightly stuff the bird with polyester fiberfill, and continue the blanket stitch to close the opening. Use embroidery floss to add a French-knot eye to the bird. See "Decorative Stitches" on page 272.

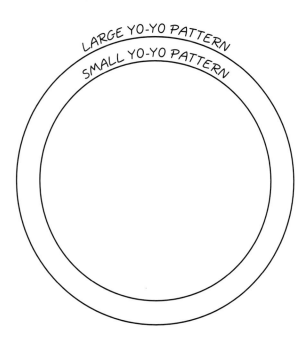

LARGE YO-YO PATTERN

SMALL YO-YO PATTERN

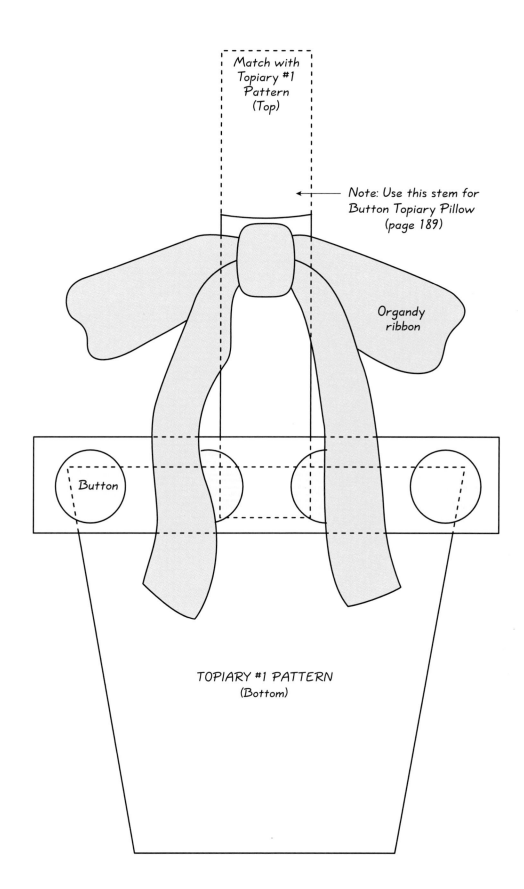

Match with
Topiary #1
Pattern
(Top)

Note: Use this stem for
Button Topiary Pillow
(page 189)

Organdy
ribbon

Button

TOPIARY #1 PATTERN
(Bottom)

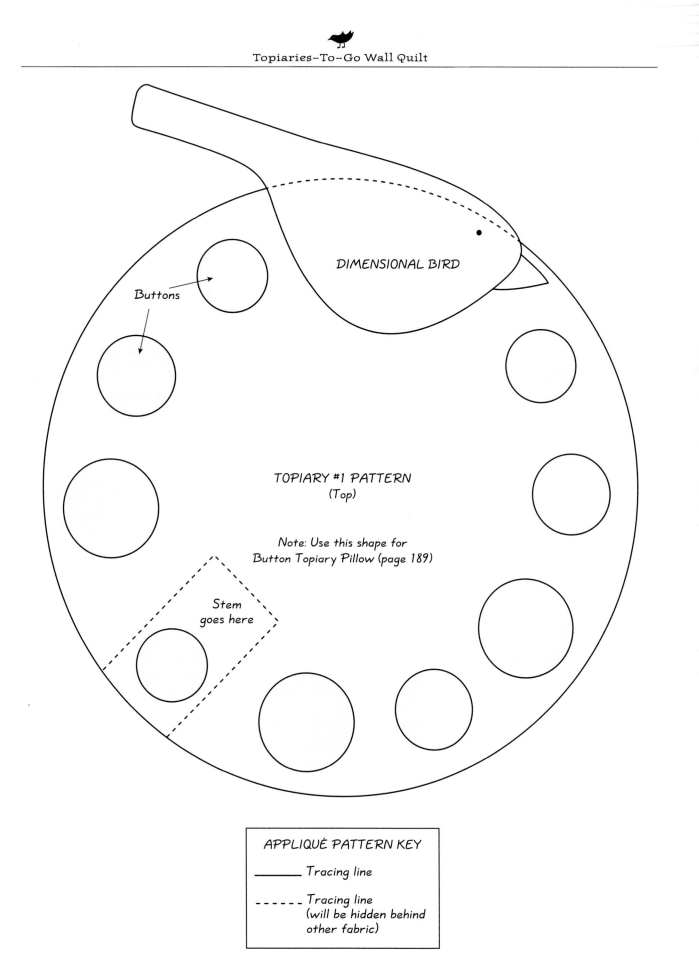

DIMENSIONAL BIRD

Buttons

TOPIARY #1 PATTERN
(Top)

Note: Use this shape for
Button Topiary Pillow (page 189)

Stem
goes here

APPLIQUÉ PATTERN KEY

_____ Tracing line

- - - - - Tracing line
(will be hidden behind
other fabric)

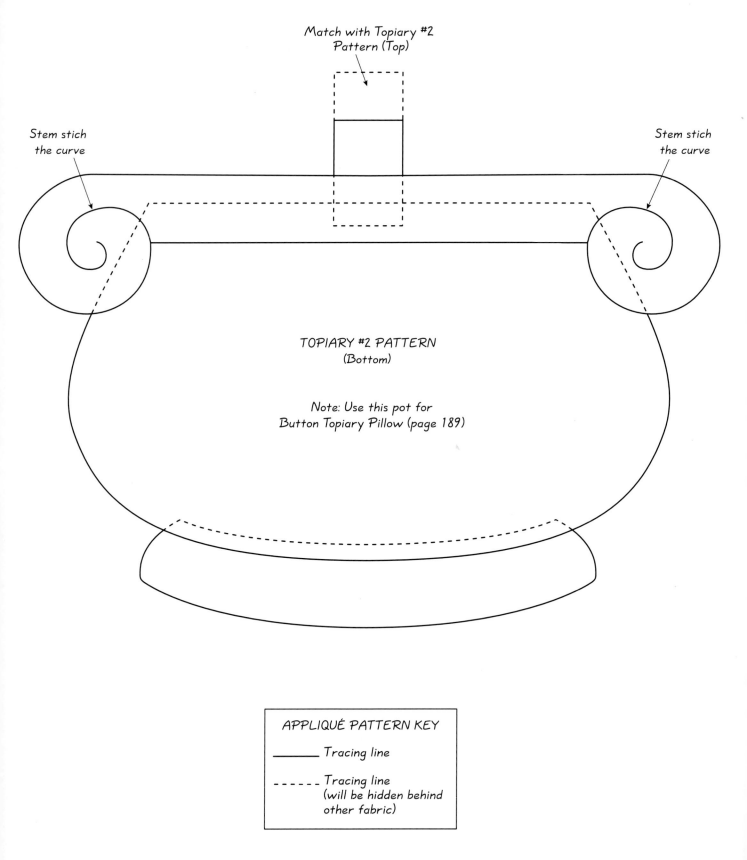

Match with Topiary #2
Pattern (Top)

Stem stich
the curve

Stem stich
the curve

TOPIARY #2 PATTERN
(Bottom)

Note: Use this pot for
Button Topiary Pillow (page 189)

APPLIQUÉ PATTERN KEY

——————— Tracing line

- - - - - - - Tracing line
(will be hidden behind
other fabric)

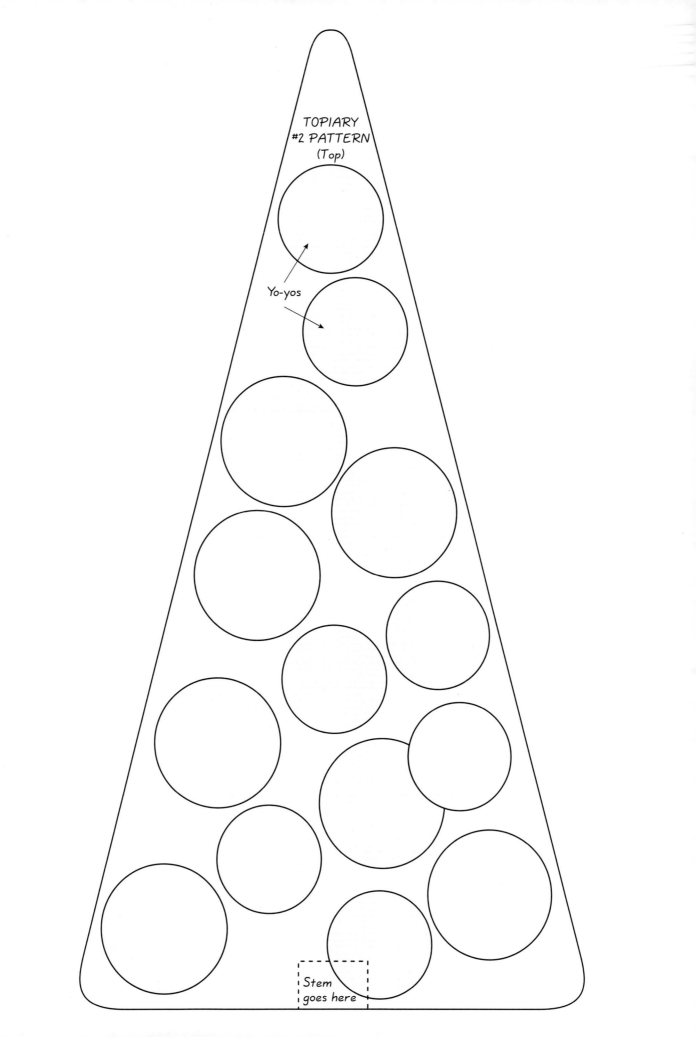

TOPIARY
#2 PATTERN
(Top)

Yo-yos

Stem
goes here

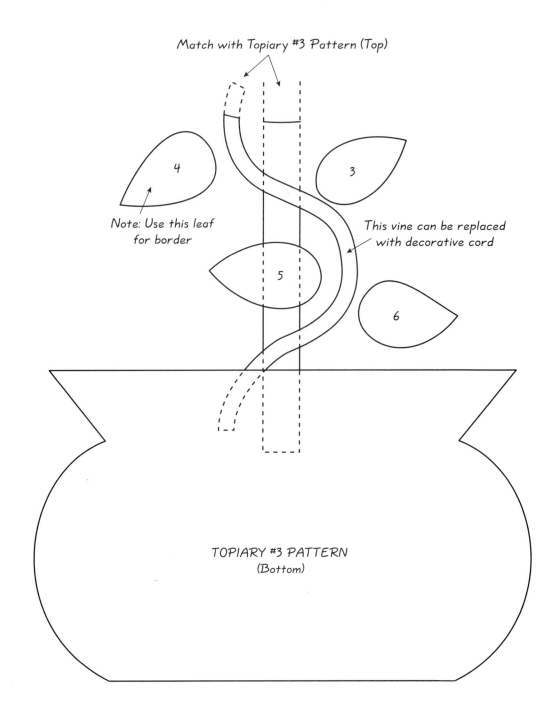

Match with Topiary #3 Pattern (Top)

4

Note: Use this leaf
for border

3

This vine can be replaced
with decorative cord

5

6

TOPIARY #3 PATTERN
(Bottom)

APPLIQUÉ PATTERN KEY

———— Tracing line

- - - - - - Tracing line
(will be hidden behind
other fabric)

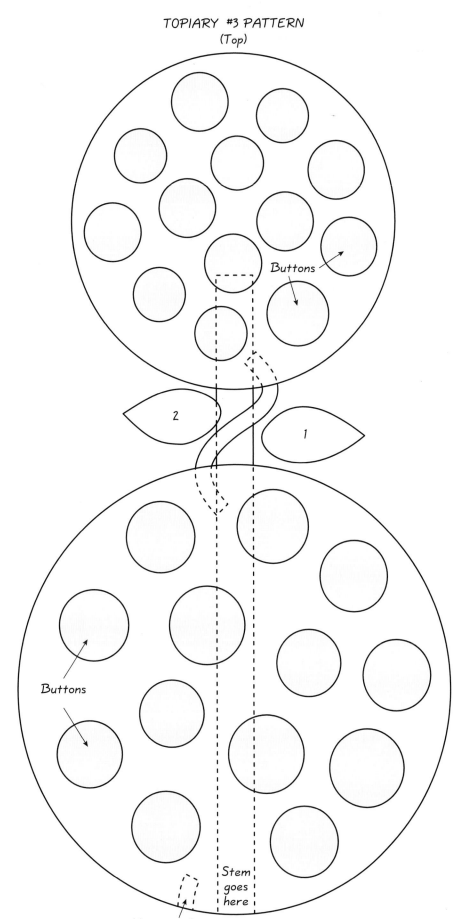

Buttons

2

1

Buttons

Stem
goes
here

Vine goes here

181

TABLE TOPPER

Add a decorator touch to your room with this boldly graphic

Table Topper. The center square carries over the square-in-square theme

set by the lattice of the Topiary Treasures Duvet Cover (directions on page

155). I used home-decorator fabrics in my table topper, left out the batting,

and skipped the quilting. These shortcuts make it especially quick and easy.

Finished Size: 34 inches square

MATERIALS

(Obvious directional prints are not recommended.)

■ ⅓ yard green-and-black check for center square and border diamonds

■ ¾ yard red print for triangles and outer border

■ ⅝ yard tan print for small and large triangles

■ ¼ yard black print for 1-inch borders

■ ⅛ yard gold print for corner squares

1⅛ yards fabric for backing

4 decorative tassels

CUTTING

Prewash and press all of your fabrics. Using a rotary cutter, see-through ruler, and cutting mat, prepare the pieces as described below. Measurements for all pieces include ¼-inch seam allowances.

FABRIC	FIRST CUT		SECOND CUT	
Color	No. of Pieces	Dimensions	No. of Pieces	Dimensions
Green-and-black check	**Center square** (Cut this square first.)			
	1	8½-inch square	No second cut	
	Border diamonds			
	4	2½ × 30-inch strips	40	2½-inch squares

(continued)

CUTTING—CONTINUED				
FABRIC	**FIRST CUT**		**SECOND CUT**	
Color	**No. of Pieces**	**Dimensions**	**No. of Pieces**	**Dimensions**
Red print	**Triangles** (Cut these squares first.)			
	2	6⅝-inch squares	No second cut	
	Outer border			
	2	5½ × 34½-inch strips	No second cut	
	2	5½ × 24½-inch strips	No second cut	
Tan print	**Small triangles** (Cut these strips first.)			
	7	1½ × 42-inch strips	160	1½-inch squares
	Large triangles			
	2	8⅞-inch squares	No second cut	
Black print	**1-inch borders**			
	4	1½ × 42-inch strips	4	1½ × 22 ½-inch strips
			4	1½ × 16½-inch strips
Gold print	**Corner squares**			
	1	1½ × 42-inch strip	8	1½-inch squares

Quick Corner Triangles

Refer to "Making Quick Corner Triangles" on page 269 for instructions on making the corner triangle units. Press the seams toward the triangle just added.

STEP 1. Sew two 1½-inch tan print squares to each of the forty 2½-inch green-and-black check squares. See **Diagram 1**. Press.

DIAGRAM 1

STEP 2. Sew two additional 1½-inch tan print squares to the units from Step 1. See **Diagram 2**. Press.

2½"

2½"

DIAGRAM 2

Assembly

STEP 1. Using a rotary cutter and ruler, cut the two 6⅝-inch red print squares in half diagonally to make four triangles. See **Diagram 3**.

Cut 6⅝"

6⅝"

Arrow indicates straight of grain
DIAGRAM 3

STEP 2. Using a ¼-inch seam, sew the 8½-inch green-and-black

check square between two red print triangles. Press the seams toward the triangles. Trim the points off the triangles, as shown in **Diagram 4**.

Trim off points after sewing→

6⅝"   6⅝"

6⅝"   6⅝"

DIAGRAM 4

STEP 3. Sew the unit from Step 2 between the two remaining red print triangles. Press. Using a rotary cutter and ruler, trim the square to measure 11¾ inches square. See **Diagram 5** on the following page.

11³/₄ "   11³/₄ "

DIAGRAM 5

Cut   8⁷/₈"

8⁷/₈"

Arrow indicates straight of grain
DIAGRAM 6

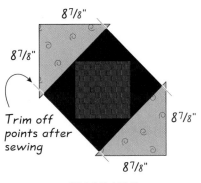

8⁷/₈"

8⁷/₈"

8⁷/₈"

Trim off points after sewing

8⁷/₈"

DIAGRAM 7

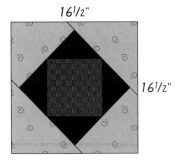

16¹/₂"

16¹/₂"

DIAGRAM 8

STEP 4. Using a rotary cutter and ruler, cut the two 8⅞-inch tan print squares in half diagonally to make four triangles. See **Diagram 6**.

STEP 5. Sew the unit from Step 3 between two tan print triangles. Press the seams toward the triangles. Trim the points off the triangles, as shown in **Diagram 7**.

STEP 6. Sew the unit from Step 5 between the two remaining tan print triangles. See **Diagram 8**. Press. Using a rotary cutter and ruler, trim the square to measure 16½ inches square.

Adding the Borders

STEP 1. Sew one 1½ × 16½-inch black print border strip to the top and one to the bottom of the table topper. Press the seams toward the border.

STEP 2. Sew one 1½-inch gold print corner square to each end of the remaining 1½ × 16½-inch black print border strips. Press the seams toward the border. Pin and sew the border strips to the sides. Press.

STEP 3. Sew eighteen 2½-inch tan/green-and-black corner triangle units together, as shown in **Diagram 9**, to make two pieced border strips with 9 squares each. Press the seams in one direction. Each border strip will now measure 2½ × 18½ inches.

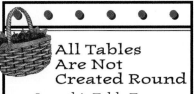

All Tables Are Not Created Round

I use this Table Topper over a table skirt on a round table. Don't hesitate to put it on a square or rectangular table. Make the topper in a color scheme to pair with any favorite table—cherry, pine, or a painted flea-market find.

STEP 4. Compare the pieced border strips to the top and bottom of the table topper. You may need to take in or let out a few seams (¹⁄₁₆ inch or less) to make them fit. Pin and sew the border strips to the top and bottom of the table topper. Press the seams toward the black print border.

STEP 5. Sew the remaining twenty-two 2½-inch tan/green-and-black corner triangle units together, as shown in **Diagram 10**, to make two pieced border strips with 11 squares each. Press. Each border strip will now measure 2½ × 22½ inches.

2¹/₂"

2¹/₂"

2¹/₂"

2¹/₂"

DIAGRAM 9

DIAGRAM 10

STEP 6. Fit, pin, and sew the pieced border strips to the sides. Press.

STEP 7. Sew one 1½ × 22½-inch black print border strip to the top and one to the bottom of the table topper. Press the seams toward the black print border.

STEP 8. Sew one 1½-inch gold print corner square to each end of the remaining 1½ × 22½-inch black print border strips. Press the seams toward the border. Pin and sew the border strips to the sides. Press.

STEP 9. Sew the 5½ × 24½-inch red print outer border strips to the top and bottom of the table topper. Press the seams toward the outer border.

STEP 10. Sew the 5½ × 34½-inch red print outer border strips to the sides. Press.

Finishing

Position the top and backing with right sides together, and pin them in place. Using ¼-inch seams, sew around the edges, leaving an 8- to 10-inch opening for turning. Trim the backing to the same size as the top. Trim the corners, turn the table topper right side out, hand stitch the opening closed, and press. Topstitch along the outer edges. Hand sew a decorative tassel to each corner.

TABLE TOPPER LAYOUT

COLOR OPTION

If you've fallen in love with pastels, make the table topper for a special room in pale blue, violet, sea green, and peach.

COZY COUNTRY PILLOWS

QUICK AND EASY ● COUNTRY ACCENTS

uddle up with these pillows and a good book for a quiet, relaxing evening. This pillow set can be the final polishing touch to complete a bedroom ensemble or a stylish grouping for a living room or family room. The Yo-yo Topiary Pillow is shown in the drawer in the photo. On the chair are the Button Topiary Pillow, *middle* (directions on page 189), the Yo-yo Vine Pillow, *left* (page 191), and the Sunflower Pillow, *right* (page 192).

YO-YO TOPIARY PILLOW

Finished Size:
20 × 14½ inches

Assembly

See "Materials and Cutting" on page 188. Assemble the pillow top before adding the appliqué pieces. Be sure to use ¼-inch seams and to press after each sewing step.

STEP 1. Sew the three 4½ × 7-inch gold print background pieces together. See **Diagram 1** on page 188. Press the seams, following the arrows in the diagram.

20"

14½"

MATERIALS AND CUTTING *(for Yo-yo Topiary Pillow)*

Prewash and press all of your fabrics. Using a rotary cutter, see-through ruler, and cutting mat, prepare the pieces as described below. Measurements for all pieces include ¼-inch seam allowances.

FABRIC	YARDAGE	NO. OF PIECES	DIMENSIONS
Gold prints for background	⅛ yard *each* of 3 fabrics	1	4½ × 7-inch piece each
Black solid for accent border and binding	¼ yard (cut into two 1× 42-inch strips and two 1½ ×42-inch strips)	2	1 × 12½-inch strips (accent border)
		2	1 × 8-inch strips (accent border)
		2	1½ × 18½-inch strips (binding)
		2	1½ × 15-inch strips (binding)
Green print for wide border	¼ yard (cut into two 3 × 42-inch strips)	2	3 × 13½-inch strips
		2	3 × 13-inch strips
Lining fabric	½ yard	—	—
Lightweight batting	1 yard (includes enough to make a custom-fit pillow form)	2	13 × 18½-inch pieces (custom-fit pillow form)
Backing fabric	½ yard	2	12½ × 15-inch pieces
Several coordinated fabrics for appliqué pieces and yo-yos	Scraps, or ⅛-yard pieces	—	—

Lightweight, sewable fusible web; embroidery floss; 4 decorative tassels; polyester fiberfill stuffing

DIAGRAM 1

STEP 2. Sew the 1 × 12½-inch accent border strips to the top and bottom of the unit from Step 1. Press the seams toward the accent border.

STEP 3. Sew the 1 × 8-inch accent border strips to the sides. Press.

STEP 4. Sew the 3 × 13½-inch wide border strips to the top and bottom. Press the seams toward the wide border.

STEP 5. Sew the 3 × 13-inch wide border strips to the sides. Press.

STEP 6. Sew the 1½ × 18½-inch binding strips to the top and bottom. Press the seams toward the binding.

STEP 7. Sew the 1½ × 15-inch binding strips to the sides. Press.

Appliqué

The appliqué pieces were added to the background using the technique described in "Blanket Stitch Appliqué" on page 272. You can machine appliqué with either a satin stitch or blanket stitch if you prefer. Refer to "Machine Appliqué" on pages 271–272. Use a lightweight, sewable fusible web.

STEP 1. Refer to "Quick-Fuse Appliqué" on pages 270–271. Trace three topiary pots and stems and two sets of leaves from the appliqué pattern on page 195.

STEP 2. Position and fuse the appliqué pieces to the background, referring to the Yo-yo Topiary Pillow layout on page 187 for placement.

STEP 3. Use two strands of embroidery floss to blanket stitch around the edges of the appliqué pieces. The yo-yos will be added later.

Layering the Pillow Front

Arrange and baste the lining, batting, and top together, following the directions in "Layering the Quilt" on page 275.

Finishing Stitches

STEP 1. Machine or hand quilt in the seam lines of the background pieces and accent border. Outline the appliqué designs by quilting $\frac{1}{16}$ inch from the edges. Quilt a $1\frac{1}{2}$-inch diagonal grid in the wide border. Do not quilt in the seam lines next to the binding.

STEP 2. Trim the batting and lining to the same size as the top.

STEP 3. Refer to "Making Yo-yos" on pages 272–273. Make one small, one medium, and two large yo-yos from the patterns on page 195. Sew the small and medium yo-yos to the center topiary. Sew the large yo-yos to the left and right topiaries.

Making the Pillow Back

STEP 1. Narrow hem one 15-inch edge of each $12\frac{1}{2} \times 15$-inch

backing piece by folding $\frac{1}{4}$ inch to the wrong side. Press. Fold again $\frac{1}{4}$ inch to the wrong side. Press. Topstitch along the folded edge.

STEP 2. With right sides up, lay one backing piece over the second piece so that the hemmed edges overlap $3\frac{1}{2}$ inches. See **Diagram 2.** Baste the pieces together at the top and bottom where they overlap. The pillow back will now measure $20\frac{1}{2} \times 15$ inches.

20½"

15"

3½" overlap

DIAGRAM 2

Finishing the Pillow

STEP 1. With right sides together, sew the quilted pillow front to the back, using $\frac{1}{4}$-inch seams. Trim the corners, turn the pillow right side out, and press.

STEP 2. Machine stitch in the seam lines between the binding and the border. Hand sew one tassel to each corner of the pillow.

STEP 3. Refer to "Making Custom-Fit Pillow Forms" on page 194 and follow all directions. Insert the pillow form through the opening in the back of the pillow.

14"

20"

BUTTON TOPIARY PILLOW

Finished Size: 14 × 20 inches
(See the pillow on the chair, middle, in the photo on page 187.)

Assembly

See "Materials and Cutting" on page 190. Assemble the pillow top before adding the appliqué pieces. Be sure to use $\frac{1}{4}$-inch seams and to press after each sewing step.

STEP 1. Sew the $1 \times 8\frac{1}{2}$-inch accent border strips to the top and bottom of the $8\frac{1}{2} \times 14\frac{1}{2}$-inch gold print background piece. Press the seams toward the accent border.

STEP 2. Sew the $1 \times 15\frac{1}{2}$-inch accent border strips to the sides. Press.

STEP 3. Sew the $2 \times 9\frac{1}{2}$-inch wide border strips to the top and bottom. Press the seams toward the wide border.

STEP 4. Sew the $2 \times 18\frac{1}{2}$-inch wide border strips to the sides. Press.

MATERIALS AND CUTTING *(for Button Topiary Pillow)*

Prewash and press all of your fabrics. Using a rotary cutter, see-through ruler, and cutting mat, prepare the pieces as described below. Measurements for all pieces include ¼-inch seam allowances.

FABRIC	YARDAGE	NO. OF PIECES	DIMENSIONS
Gold print for background	⅓ yard	1	8½ × 14½-inch piece
Black solid for accent border and binding	¼ yard (cut into two 1 × 42-inch strips and two 1½ × 42-inch strips)	2	1 × 15½-inch strips (accent border)
		2	1 × 8½-inch strips (accent border)
		2	1½ × 20½-inch strips (binding)
		2	1½ × 12½-inch strips (binding)
Red print for wide border	⅙ yard (cut into two 2 × 42-inch strips)	2	2 × 18½-inch strips
		2	2 × 9½-inch strips
Lining fabric	½ yard	—	—
Lightweight batting	1 yard (includes enough to make a custom-fit pillow form)	2	12½ × 18½-inch pieces (custom-fit pillow form)
Backing fabric	½ yard	2	12½ × 14½-inch pieces
Several coordinated fabrics for appliqué pieces	Scraps, or ⅛- to ¼-yard pieces	—	—

Lightweight, sewable fusible web; embroidery floss; assorted buttons; organdy ribbon; 4 decorative tassels; polyester fiberfill stuffing

STEP 5. Sew the 1½ × 12½-inch binding strips to the top and bottom. Press the seams toward the binding.

STEP 6. Sew the 1½ × 20½-inch binding strips to the sides. Press.

Appliqué

The appliqué pieces were added to the background using the technique described in "Blanket Stitch Appliqué" on page 272. You can machine appliqué with either a satin stitch or blanket stitch if you prefer. Refer to "Machine Appliqué" on pages 271–272. Use a lightweight, sewable fusible web for all of these techniques.

STEP 1. Refer to "Quick-Fuse Appliqué" on pages 270–271. Using the appliqué patterns on pages 177–178 from the Topiaries-to-Go Wall Quilt, trace the circle and stem from Topiary #1 and the pot from Topiary #2.

STEP 2. Position and fuse the appliqué pieces to the background, referring to the Button Topiary Pillow layout on page 189 for placement.

STEP 3. Use two strands of embroidery floss to blanket stitch around the edges of the appliqué pieces. Use two strands of embroidery floss to stem stitch the curved lines on the rim of the pot, referring to "Decorative Stitches" on page 272 for instructions.

Layering the Pillow Front

Arrange and baste the lining, batting, and top together, following the directions in "Layering the Quilt" on page 275.

Finishing Stitches

STEP 1. Machine or hand quilt in the seam lines of the background and accent border. Outline the appliqué design by quilting 1⁄16 inch from the edges. Quilt a 1-inch diagonal grid in the background and wide border. Do not quilt in the seam lines next to the binding.

STEP 2. Trim the batting and lining to the same size as the top.

STEP 3. Sew assorted buttons to the topiary.

Making the Pillow Back

STEP 1. Narrow hem one 14½-inch edge of each 12½ × 14½-inch backing piece by folding ¼ inch to the wrong side. Press. Fold again ¼ inch to the wrong side. Press. Topstitch along the folded edge.

STEP 2. With right sides up, lay one backing piece over the second piece so that the hemmed edges overlap 3 inches. See **Diagram 3**. Baste the pieces together at the sides where they overlap. The pillow back will now measure 14½ × 20½ inches.

Finishing the Pillow

STEP 1. With right sides together, sew the quilted pillow front to the

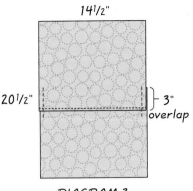

14½"

20½"

3" overlap

DIAGRAM 3

back, using ¼-inch seams. Trim the corners, turn the pillow right side out, and press.

STEP 2. Machine stitch in the seam lines between the binding and the border. Tie the organdy ribbon into a bow, and hand sew it to the topiary. Hand sew one tassel to each corner of the pillow.

STEP 3. Refer to "Making Custom-Fit Pillow Forms" on page 194 and follow all directions. Insert the pillow form through the opening in the back of the pillow.

14"

14"

YO-YO VINE PILLOW

Finished Size: 14 inches square

(See the pillow on the chair, left, in the photo on page 187.)

Assembly

See "Materials and Cutting" on the following page. Be sure to use ¼-inch seams and to press after each sewing step.

STEP 1. Sew the 1 × 9½-inch accent border strips to the top and bottom of the 9½-inch gold print background square. Press the seams toward the accent border.

STEP 2. Sew the 1 × 10½-inch accent border strips to the sides. Press.

STEP 3. Sew the 2½ × 10½-inch wide border strips to the top and bottom. Press the seams toward the wide border.

STEP 4. Sew the 2½ × 14½-inch wide border strips to the sides. Press.

Decorating the Pillow Top

STEP 1. Using the Yo-yo Vine Pillow patterns on pages 196–197, lightly mark vines on the background. Use six strands of embroidery floss and a running stitch to make the vines.

STEP 2. Refer to "Quick-Fuse Appliqué" on pages 270–271 and "Blanket Stitch Appliqué" on page 272. Trace 24 leaves from the appliqué pattern on page 195. Be sure to use a lightweight, sewable fusible web. Position and fuse the leaves to the background, referring to the Yo-yo Vine Pillow patterns on pages 196–197 for placement. Use two strands of embroidery floss to blanket stitch around the edges of the leaves.

MATERIALS AND CUTTING *(for Yo-yo Vine Pillow)*

Prewash and press all of your fabrics. Using a rotary cutter, see-through ruler, and cutting mat, prepare the pieces as described below. Measurements for all pieces include ¼-inch seam allowances.

FABRIC	YARDAGE	NO. OF PIECES	DIMENSIONS
Gold print for background	⅓ yard	1	9½-inch square
Red print for accent border	⅛ yard (cut into two 1 × 42-inch strips)	2 / 2	1 × 10½-inch strips / 1 × 9½-inch strips
Black print for wide border	¼ yard (cut into two 2½ × 42-inch strips)	2 / 2	2½ × 14½-inch strips / 2½ × 10½-inch strips
Backing fabric	⅓ yard	2	14½ × 9½-inch pieces
Several coordinated fabrics for appliqué leaves and yo-yos	Scraps	—	—

Embroidery floss; lightweight, sewable fusible web; assorted buttons (approximately 18); purchased 14-inch pillow form

STEP 3. Refer to "Making Yo-yos" on pages 272–273. Make four small and five medium yo-yos from the patterns on page 195. Sew the yo-yos to the vines, referring to the Yo-yo Vine Pillow patterns on pages 196–197 for placement.

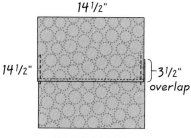

14½"

14½"

3½" overlap

DIAGRAM 4

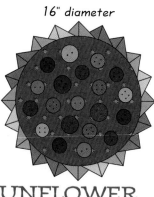

16" diameter

Making the Pillow Back

STEP 1. Narrow hem one 14½-inch edge of each 14½ × 9½-inch backing piece by folding ¼ inch to the wrong side. Press. Fold again ¼ inch to the wrong side. Press. Topstitch along the folded edge.

STEP 2. With right sides up, lay one backing piece over the second piece so that the hemmed edges overlap 3½ inches. See **Diagram 4**. Baste the pieces together at the sides where they overlap. The pillow back will now measure 14½ inches square.

Finishing the Pillow

STEP 1. With right sides together, sew the pillow top to the back, using ¼-inch seams. Trim the corners, turn the pillow right side out, and press.

STEP 2. Hand sew assorted buttons to the border, referring to the Yo-yo Vine Pillow layout on page 191 for placement. Insert the 14-inch pillow form through the opening in the back of the pillow.

SUNFLOWER PILLOW

**Finished Size:
16 inches in diameter**

(See the pillow on the chair, right, in the photo on page 187.)

Assembly

STEP 1. See "Materials and Cutting," on the opposite page. To make the prairie points, fold each 4-inch gold print square in half with wrong sides together. Fold again as shown in **Diagram 5** on the opposite page. Press.

DIAGRAM 5

STEP 2. To divide the black print center circle into fourths, fold it in half, and then fold it in half again as shown in **Diagram 6**. Mark the edges at each fold.

DIAGRAM 6

STEP 3. With right sides together and raw edges even, position and pin one prairie point centered on each mark around the circle. See **Diagram 7**.

DIAGRAM 7

Easy Circles

To draw a circle for the Sunflower Pillow, try one of these easy options:

- Use a pencil tied to a string. Anchor the end of the string with a pin.
- Trace around a plate or bowl that is the right size for the circle.
- Purchase a yardstick compass. These are available in most quilt shops and art supply stores.

STEP 4. Position four additional prairie points in each quarter of the circle, overlapping and spacing them evenly. Pin and baste the prairie points in position.

Making the Pillow Back

STEP 1. Narrow hem one 16-inch edge of each 10 × 16-inch backing piece by folding ¼ inch to the wrong side. Press. Fold again ¼ inch to the wrong side. Press. Topstitch along the folded edge.

STEP 2. With right sides up, lay one backing piece over the second piece so that the hemmed edges overlap 3 inches. See **Diagram 8** on the following page. Baste the pieces together at the sides where they overlap. The pillow back will now measure 16 inches square.

MATERIALS AND CUTTING (for Sunflower Pillow)

Prewash and press all of your fabrics. Using a rotary cutter, see-through ruler, and cutting mat, prepare the pieces as described below. Measurements for all pieces include ¼-inch seam allowances.

FABRIC	YARDAGE	NO. OF PIECES	DIMENSIONS
Black print for center	½ yard	1	14½-inch circle
Gold prints for prairie points	⅛ yard *each* of 5 fabrics	4	4-inch squares each
Backing fabric	⅓ yard	2	10 × 16-inch pieces
Batting for custom-fit pillow form	½ yard	2	14½-inch circles
Assorted buttons; polyester fiberfill stuffing			

16"

16"

} 3"
overlap

DIAGRAM 8

Finishing the Pillow

STEP 1. With the prairie points in the middle, position the pillow top and back with right sides together and pin them in place. Using ¼-inch seam allowances, sew around the pillow. Trim the back and prairie points to the same size as the top. Clip the seam every ½ inch, and turn the pillow right side out.

STEP 2. Hand sew assorted buttons to the pillow.

STEP 3. Refer to "Making Custom-Fit Pillow Forms," at right, and follow all directions. Use two 14½-inch circles. Insert the pillow form through the opening in the back of the pillow.

Making Custom-Fit Pillow Forms

The secret to an attractive finished pillow is a pillow form that fits perfectly inside the pillow. This cannot always be achieved with standard-size pillow forms, but you can easily make your own. All you need is some batting and polyester fiberfill stuffing.

For Pillows without Binding

STEP 1. Add ½ inch to the finished size of the pillow. Cut two pieces of batting to those dimensions. For example, the Yo-yo Vine Pillow finishes 14 inches square, so you will need to cut two pieces of batting, each 14½ inches square.

STEP 2. Using ¼-inch seams, sew the two pieces of batting together, leaving a 3- to 4-inch opening for turning. Turn the batting so that the seam allowances are on the inside.

STEP 3. Stuff the pillow form with the polyester fiberfill until it reaches the desired firmness. Hand stitch the opening closed.

For Pillows with Binding

Determine the finished size of the binding. Double it and subtract that amount from the finished size of the pillow. Add ½ inch and cut two pieces of batting to those dimensions. For example, the Yo-yo Topiary Pillow finishes 20 × 14½ inches and has a 1-inch finished binding. You will need to cut two pieces of batting, each 18½ × 13 inches. Follow Steps 2 and 3 above to finish the pillow form.

LARGE YO-YO

MEDIUM YO-YO

SMALL YO-YO

YO-YO PATTERNS

LEAF PATTERN FOR
YO-YO VINE PILLOW

APPLIQUÉ PATTERN KEY

———— Tracing line

- - - - - Tracing line
(will be hidden behind
other fabric)

TOPIARY POT PATTERN

195

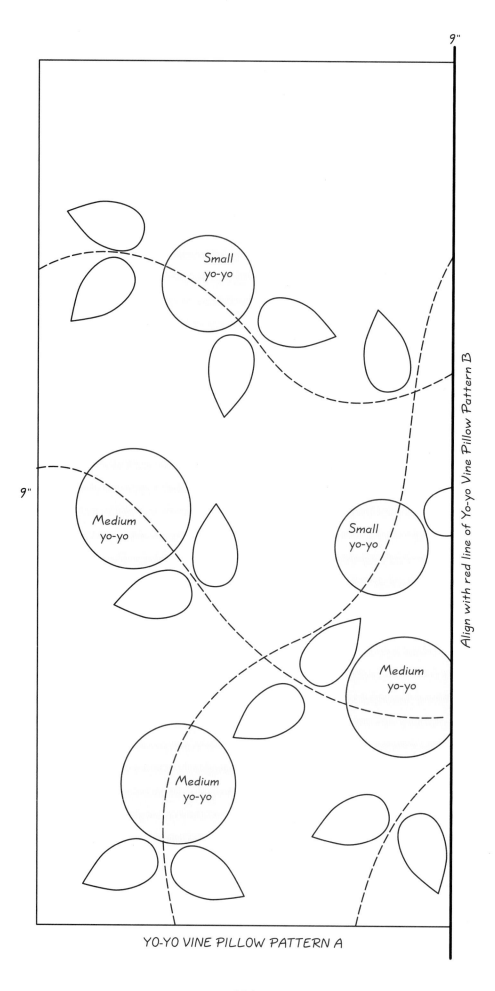

9"

9"

Small
yo-yo

Small
yo-yo

Medium
yo-yo

Medium
yo-yo

Medium
yo-yo

Align with red line of Yo-yo Vine Pillow Pattern B

YO-YO VINE PILLOW PATTERN A

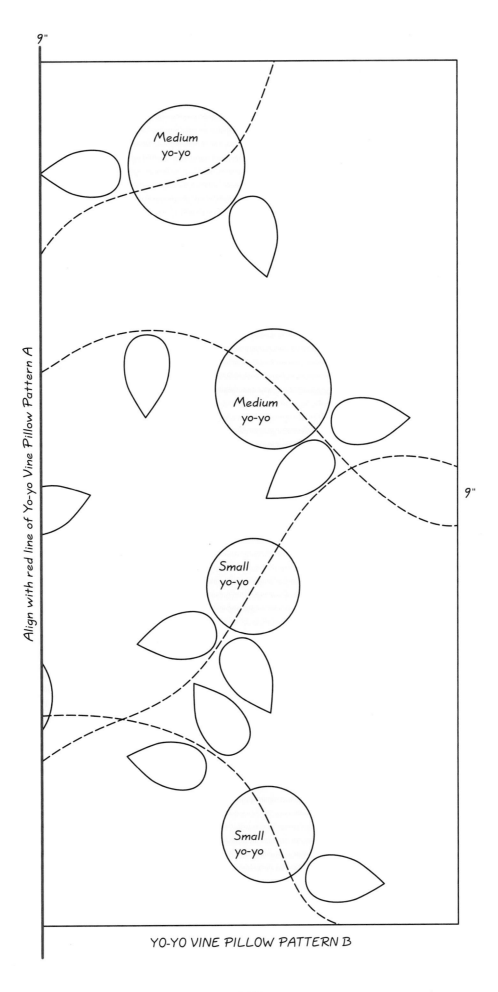

9"

9"

Align with red line of Yo-yo Vine Pillow Pattern A

Medium yo-yo

Medium yo-yo

Small yo-yo

Small yo-yo

YO-YO VINE PILLOW PATTERN B

SPORTS FEVER KID'S BEDROOM

My nine-year-old son, Murphy, has a serious case of sports fever! He's constantly on the move, playing soccer and baseball, skateboarding, roller blading, or shooting baskets. I had lots of fun playing with the sports theme to design these projects especially for his bedroom. (And I scored lots of points with Murphy in the process!) For a bedroom of hearts and flowers, see page 228.

GO, TEAM!

"Totally awesome" is one way a child might describe this Sports Quilt

and the coordinating Sports Pillowcase (directions on page 205). Just about

every sport is represented in easy machine-appliquéd designs. Pennants,

jerseys, stars, balls, and other sports equipment adorn the quilt, while

skateboards accent the pillowcases. This is the place to be after the game!

Sports Quilt

Finished Size: 75 × 87 inches

MATERIALS

(Obvious directional prints are not recommended.)

■ 4⅛ yards blue solid for background, corner squares, and striped patchwork border. (See Note below.)

■ ⅜ yard red print for inner accent border

⅜ yard *each* of 8 assorted fabrics for patchwork borders

■ 1⅛ yards dark blue print for outer accent border and binding

5½ yards fabric for backing

5½ yards lightweight batting

■ ⅝ yard red print for appliqué background squares

Scraps, or ⅛- to ¼-yard pieces, of several coordinated fabrics for appliqué pieces

4 yards lightweight, sewable fusible web

Permanent fine-point felt pen

Thread to match appliqué pieces

4 yards Tear-Away fabric stabilizer

Note: Sixty-inch-wide lightweight denim was used to avoid piecing the background in the quilt shown in the photo. You will need 3 yards of 60-inch-wide fabric.

CUTTING

Prewash and press all of your fabrics. Using a rotary cutter, see-through ruler, and cutting mat, prepare the pieces as described below. Measurements for all pieces include ¼-inch seam allowances.

FABRIC	FIRST CUT		SECOND CUT	
Color	No. of Pieces	Dimensions	No. of Pieces	Dimensions
Blue solid	**Background** (See Note below.)			
	2	49 × 31-inch pieces	No second cut	
	Large corner squares (Cut these squares from the excess width of the background piece.)			
	4	8½-inch squares	No second cut	
	Small corner squares (Cut these squares from the excess width of the background piece.)			
	4	4½-inch squares	No second cut	
	Striped patchwork border			
	16	2½ × 42-inch strips	No second cut	
Red print	**Inner accent border**		Cut *1* strip into the following:	
	7	1½ × 42-inch strips	2	1½ × 21-inch strips
Assorted fabrics	**Inner patchwork border**—from *each* of the 8 fabrics, cut the following:			
	1	4½ × 42-inch strip	No second cut	
	Striped patchwork border—from *each* of the 8 fabrics, cut the following:			
	2	2½ × 42-inch strips	No second cut	
Dark blue print	**Outer accent border**		Cut *1* strip into the following:	
	7	1½ × 42-inch strips	2	1½ × 21-inch strips
	Binding		Cut *1* strip into the following:	
	9	2¾ × 42-inch strips	2	2¾ × 21-inch strips

Note: If you are using 60-inch-wide fabric for the background, cut one 46½ × 58½-inch piece from the 3 yards of fabric.

Assembling the Background

With right sides together, sew the two 49 × 31-inch blue solid background pieces together with ¼-inch seams to make one piece approximately 49 × 62 inches. Press the seams to one side. Recut this piece into one 46½ × 58½-inch piece. Note: If you are using 60-inch-wide fabric, skip this step.

Appliqué

The appliqué pieces were added to the background using the technique described in "Machine Appliqué" on pages 271–272. Use a small zigzag stitch. Be sure to use a lightweight, sewable fusible web.

STEP 1. Refer to "Quick-Fuse Appliqué" on pages 270–271. Draw five 9-inch squares on the paper side of the fusible web, leaving at least ½ inch between squares. Fuse the drawn squares to the wrong side of the red print appliqué background fabric. Cut out the squares on the drawn lines.

STEP 2. Trace an assortment of 25 sports designs and 15 stars for the background from the appliqué patterns on pages 208–215. Trace 4 soccer balls from the appliqué pattern on page 213 for the large corner squares. See the **Quilt Layout** on page 204 for guidance.

STEP 3. Choose 5 of the appliqué designs from Step 2, and fuse them to the red print appliqué background squares. Refer to "Try an Appliqué Pressing Sheet," at right.

STEP 4. Allowing for ¼-inch seams on the raw edges, position and fuse the appliqué designs to the 46½ × 58½-inch blue solid background piece, referring to the **Quilt Layout** on the following page for placement. Position and fuse the soccer balls to the 8½-inch blue solid corner squares. Use the permanent felt pen to draw stitching lines on the baseballs and seam lines on the basketballs.

STEP 5. Machine appliqué around the edges of the appliqué pieces. Use the Tear-Away fabric stabilizer on the wrong side of the background piece for an even machine stitch. Remove the stabilizer after stitching.

Adding the Borders

STEP 1. Sew one 1½ × 21-inch inner accent border strip to each of two 1½ × 42-inch inner accent border strips to make two strips approximately 1½ × 63 inches each. Press. Sew the border strips to the top and bottom of the background piece. Trim the excess length, and press the seams toward the accent border.

STEP 2. Sew the four remaining 1½ × 42-inch inner accent border strips together in pairs to make two strips approximately 1½ × 84 inches each. Press. Sew the border strips to the sides. Trim the excess length and press.

Try an Appliqué Pressing Sheet

The Appliqué Pressing Sheet by Bear Thread Designs makes positioning appliqué designs a snap. To use the pressing sheet, trace the appliqué designs on a plain sheet of paper, then retrace them onto the back of that paper. Use this reversed image as a guide for positioning and fusing. See "Quilting by Mail" on page 280 for ordering information.

STEP 3. Arrange the eight 4½ × 42-inch inner patchwork border strips in a pleasing order. Sew the strips together to make a 32½ × 42-inch strip set. Change sewing direction with each strip sewn, and press the seams in one direction as you go. Using a rotary cutter and ruler, cut seven 4½ × 32½ strips from this strip set. There should be 8 squares in each strip. See **Diagram 1**.

32½"

4½"

42"

DIAGRAM 1

STEP 4. Sew three 4½ × 32½-inch inner patchwork border strips together to make one 4½ × 96½-inch strip with 24 squares. Use a seam ripper to separate this strip into two 4½ × 48½-inch strips

with 12 squares each. Compare the strips to the top and bottom of the quilt. You may need to take in or let out a few seams (⅟₁₆ inch or less) to make them fit. Pin and sew the border strips to the top and bottom. Press the seams toward the accent border.

STEP 5. Sew the four remaining 4½ × 32½-inch inner patchwork border strips together in pairs to make two 4½ × 64½-inch strips with 16 squares each. Use a seam ripper to remove 1 square from each strip to make two 4½ × 60½-inch strips with 15 squares each.

STEP 6. Sew one 4½-inch blue solid corner square to each end of the patchwork border strips from Step 5. Press the seams toward the border. Fit, pin, and sew the border strips to the sides. Press.

STEP 7. Sew one 1½ × 21-inch outer accent border strip to each of two 1½ × 42-inch outer accent border strips to make two strips approximately 1½ × 63 inches each. Press. Sew the border strips to the top and bottom. Trim the excess length, and press the seams toward the outer accent border.

STEP 8. Sew the four remaining 1½ × 42-inch outer accent border strips together in pairs to make two strips approximately 1½ × 84 inches each. Press. Sew the border strips to the sides. Trim the excess length and press.

STEP 9. Alternate eight 2½ × 42-inch blue solid patchwork border strips and eight 2½ × 42-inch patchwork border strips of contrasting colors. Sew the strips together to make a 32½ × 42-inch strip set. Change sewing direction with each strip sewn, and press the seams in one direction as you go. Repeat with the remaining patchwork border strips to make a second strip set. Using a rotary cutter and ruler, cut four 8½ × 32½-inch strips from each strip set. There should be 16 pieces in each strip. See **Diagram 2**.

DIAGRAM 2

STEP 10. Sew four 8½ × 32½-inch striped patchwork border strips together in pairs to make two 8½ × 64½-inch strips with 32 pieces each. Use a seam ripper to remove one 3-piece unit from each strip to make two 8½ × 58½-inch strips with 29 pieces each. Set the 3-piece units aside for use in the next step. Fit, pin, and sew the border strips to the top and bottom. Press the seams toward the accent border.

STEP 11. Sew the remaining four 8½ × 32½-inch striped patchwork border strips together in pairs to make two 8½ × 64½-inch strips with 32 pieces each. Sew one 3-piece unit from Step 10 to one end of each strip to make two 8½ × 70½-inch strips with 35 pieces each.

STEP 12. Sew one 8½-inch blue solid corner square to each end of the striped patchwork border

strips from Step 11. Press the seams toward the border. Fit, pin, and sew the border strips to the sides. Press.

Layering the Quilt

STEP 1. Cut the backing fabric in half crosswise, and trim the selvage edges off both pieces. With right sides together, sew the two backing pieces together to make one piece approximately 80 × 99 inches. Press.

STEP 2. Arrange and baste the backing, batting, and top together, following the directions in "Layering the Quilt" on page 275.

Finishing Stitches

Machine or hand quilt as desired. Murphy's quilt was machine quilted around the appliqué designs. A large stipple pattern was quilted in the background, along with freehand stars that were scattered about randomly.

QUILT LAYOUT

Binding the Quilt

STEP 1. Trim the batting and backing to ¼ inch from the raw edges of the quilt top.

STEP 2. Sew the eight 2¾ × 42-inch binding strips together in pairs to make four strips approximately 2¾ × 84 inches each. Sew one 2¾ × 21-inch binding strip to each of two 2¾ × 84-inch binding strips to make two strips approximately 2¾ × 105 inches each.

STEP 3. Using the two 2¾ × 84-inch binding strips for the top and bottom and the two 2¾ × 105-inch binding strips for the sides, follow the directions for "Binding the Quilt" on pages 275–276.

Sports Pillowcase

Finished Size: 30 × 19 inches

(See the pillowcase in the photo on page 200.)

MATERIALS AND CUTTING

Prewash and press all of your fabrics. Using a rotary cutter, see-through ruler, and cutting mat, prepare the pieces as described below. Measurements for all pieces include ¼-inch seams (to make 1 pillowcase).

FABRIC	YARDAGE	NO. OF PIECES	DIMENSIONS
▦ Red plaid for pillowcase	⅞ yard	1	25½ × 39½-inch piece
▪ Blue print for border	⅜ yard	1	10½ × 39½-inch piece
▪ Red print for accent border	⅛ yard	1	1 × 39½-inch strip
Several coordinated fabrics for appliqué pieces	Scraps, or ⅛-yard pieces	—	—
Lightweight, sewable fusible web; Tear-Away fabric stabilizer			

Assembly

STEP 1. Fold the 10½ × 39½-inch border strip in half lengthwise with wrong sides together and press.

STEP 2. Sew the 1 × 39½-inch accent border strip between the 25½ × 39½-inch red plaid pillowcase piece and the 5¼ × 39½-inch folded border strip. See **Diagram 3.** Press the seams toward the accent border. Fold the pillowcase in half crosswise and press.

STEP 3. Refer to "Quick-Fuse Appliqué" on pages 270–271. Be sure to use a lightweight, sewable fusible web. Trace one skateboard from the appliqué pattern on page 215 and two small and two large stars from the appliqué patterns on page 212. Referring to the **Pillowcase Layout** on the following page for placement, position and fuse the appliqué pieces to the border, centering them between the fold and the raw edge.

DIAGRAM 3

STEP 4. Refer to "Machine Appliqué" on pages 271–272. Use a small zigzag stitch to machine appliqué around the edges of the appliqué pieces. Use the Tear-Away fabric stabilizer on the wrong side of the border for an even machine stitch. Remove the stabilizer after stitching.

STEP 5. Fold the pillowcase in half crosswise with right sides together. Using ¼-inch seams, pin and sew the end opposite the border and edge opposite the fold. See **Diagram 4.** Turn the pillowcase right side out and press.

Fold

DIAGRAM 4

PILLOWCASE LAYOUT

Sports Jacket

Turn a simple denim jacket into something awesome with easy machine-appliquéd designs.

Materials
Child's denim jacket
Scraps, or ⅛- to ¼-yard pieces, of several coordinated fabrics for appliqué pieces
Lightweight, sewable fusible web
Tear-Away fabric stabilizer

Assembly
STEP 1. Refer to "Quick-Fuse Appliqué" on pages 270–271. Be sure to use a lightweight, sewable fusible web. Trace one skateboard and four lightning bolts from the appliqué pattern on page 215, three large stars from page 212, and one set of in-line skates from page 214.

STEP 2. Position and fuse the appliqué pieces to the back of the jacket, referring to the photo below for placement.

STEP 3. Refer to "Machine Appliqué" on pages 271–272. Use a small zigzag stitch to machine appliqué around the edges of the appliqué pieces. Use the Tear-Away fabric stabilizer on the wrong side of the jacket for an even machine stitch. Remove the stabilizer after stitching.

BASKETBALL AND HOOP PATTERNS

Draw lines on basketball
with felt pen

APPLIQUÉ PATTERN KEY

——————— Tracing line

- - - - - - - Tracing line
(will be hidden behind
other fabric)

BASEBALL MITT PATTERN

FOOTBALL PATTERN

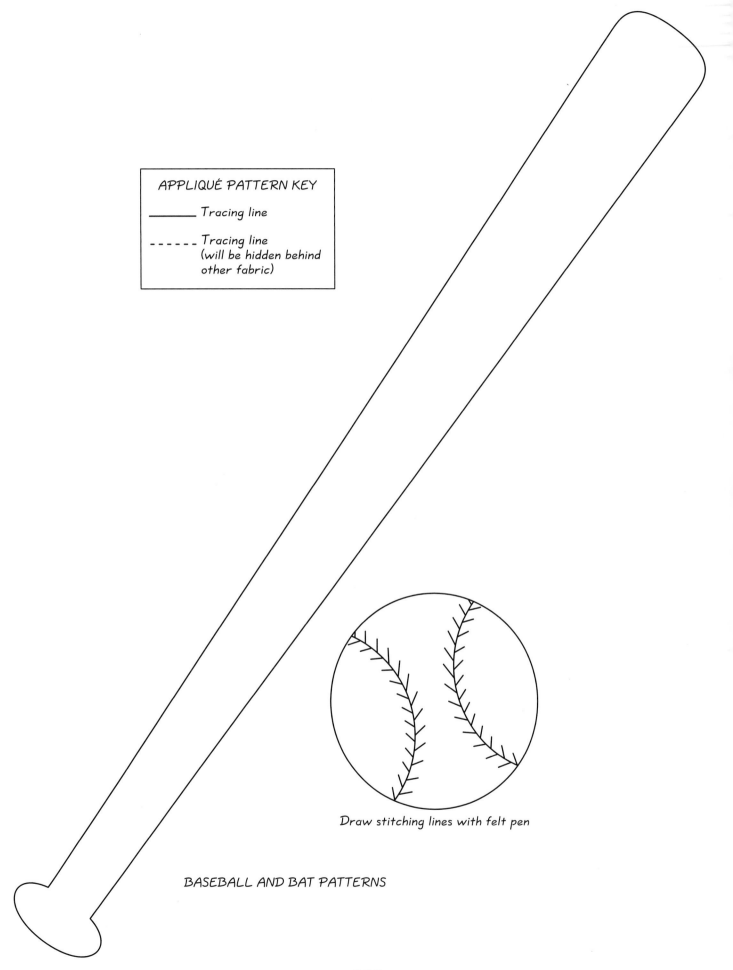

APPLIQUÉ PATTERN KEY

———— Tracing line

- - - - - Tracing line
(will be hidden behind
other fabric)

Draw stitching lines with felt pen

BASEBALL AND BAT PATTERNS

209

HOCKEY PATTERNS

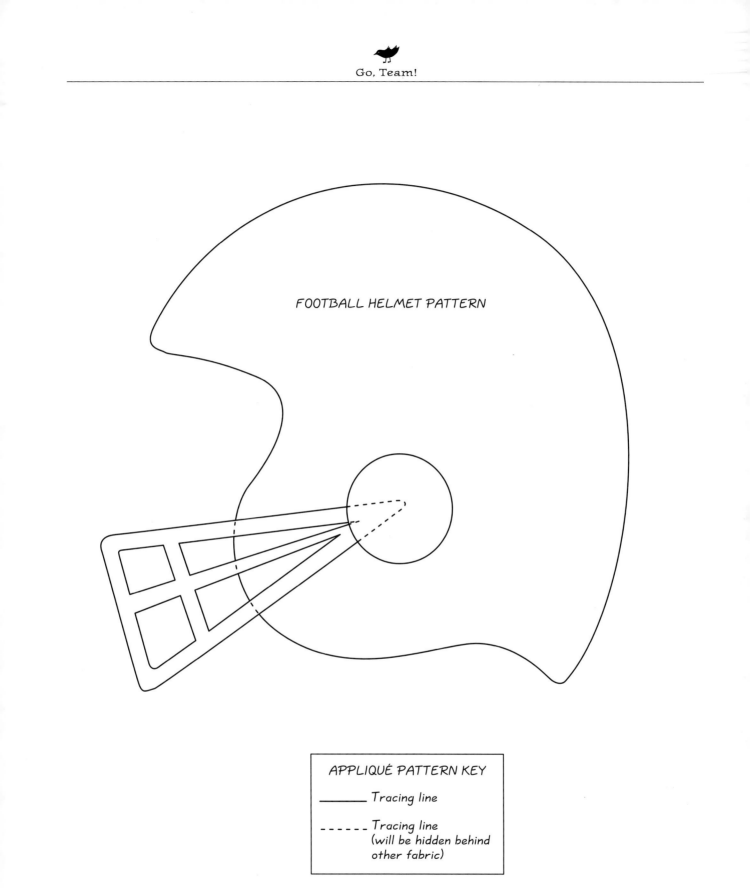

FOOTBALL HELMET PATTERN

APPLIQUÉ PATTERN KEY

_____ Tracing line

- - - - - Tracing line
(will be hidden behind
other fabric)

JERSEY PATTERN

LARGE STAR
PATTERN

SMALL STAR
PATTERN

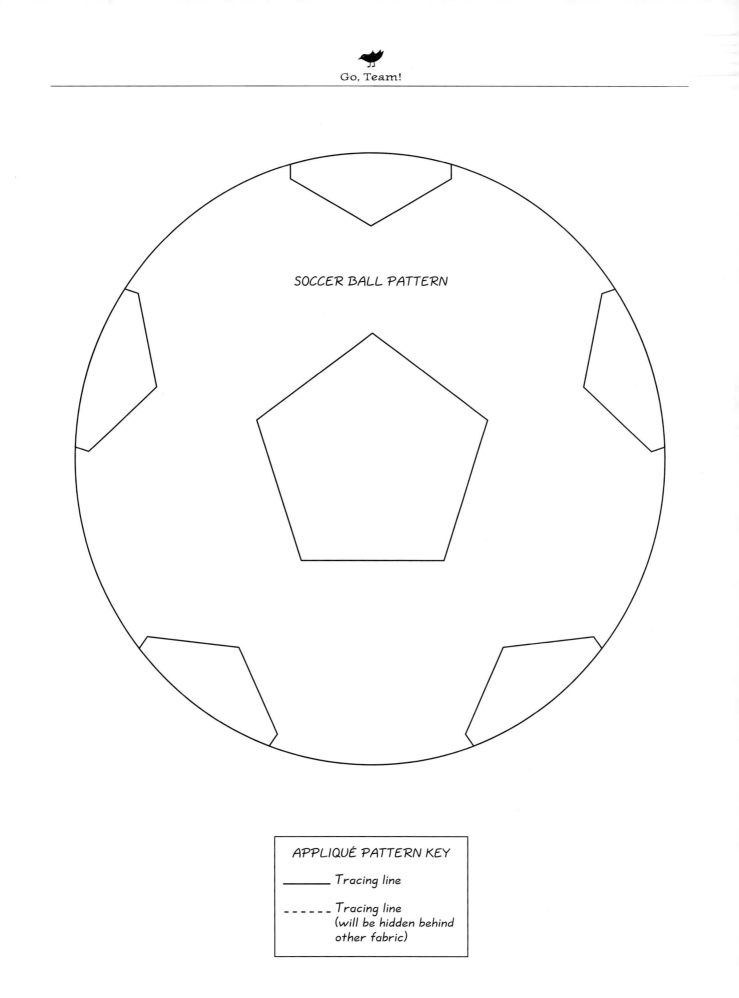

SOCCER BALL PATTERN

APPLIQUÉ PATTERN KEY

_____ Tracing line

- - - - - - Tracing line
(will be hidden behind
other fabric)

APPLIQUÉ PATTERN KEY

———— Tracing line

- - - - - Tracing line
(will be hidden behind
other fabric)

Trace this skate for poster quilt

IN-LINE SKATES PATTERN

SKATEBOARD PATTERN

PENNANT PATTERN

215

WEEKENDER

POSTER QUILT

Posters are a staple decorating item for kids. Make a fabric version that

will thrill any sports-minded youngster. Easy piecing and quick-fuse appliqué

guarantee that this project will go together quickly and successfully. In one

weekend you'll have a perfect gift for a special young athlete.

Finished Size: 28 × 38 inches

MATERIALS AND CUTTING

Prewash and press all of your fabrics. Using a rotary cutter, see-through ruler, and cutting mat, prepare the pieces as described below. Measurements for all pieces include ¼-inch seam allowances.

FABRIC	YARDAGE	NO. OF PIECES	DIMENSIONS
Blue solid for background and border	⅞ yard	5	9½-inch squares (background)
		2	4½ × 27½-inch strips (border)
Red check for background	⅓ yard	4	9½-inch squares
Black print for accent border	⅛ yard	2	1½ × 27½-inch strips
Black print for binding	⅜ yard	4	2¾ × 42-inch strips
Backing fabric	1 yard	—	—
Flannel for batting	1 yard	—	—
Several coordinated fabrics for appliqué pieces	Scraps, or ⅛- to ¼-yard pieces	—	—
Fusible web; permanent fine-point felt pen			

Assembling the Background

Assemble the quilt top before adding the appliqué pieces. Be sure to use ¼-inch seams and to press the seams after each sewing step.

STEP 1. Sew one 9½-inch red check background square between two 9½-inch blue solid background squares, as shown in **Diagram 1**. Press the seams, following the direction of the arrows in the diagram. Repeat to make a second unit.

DIAGRAM 1

STEP 2. Sew the one remaining 9½-inch blue solid background square between the two remaining 9½-inch red check background squares. Press the seams toward the red check squares.

STEP 3. Sew the unit from Step 2 between the two units from Step 1. See **Diagram 2**. Press.

27½"

Step 1 Unit — 9½"

Step 2 Unit — 9½"

Step 1 Unit — 9½"

DIAGRAM 2

STEP 4. Sew the 1½ × 27½-inch accent border strips to the top and bottom. Press the seams toward the accent border.

STEP 5. Sew the 4½ × 27½-inch border strips to the top and bottom. Press the seams toward the accent border.

Appliqué

STEP 1. Refer to "Quick-Fuse Appliqué" on pages 270–271. Referring to the **Quilt Layout**, trace one of each sports design (but just one of the in-line skates) for the background squares and ten additional large stars for the border from the appliqué patterns on pages 207–215.

STEP 2. Quick-fuse each sports design to the center of its corresponding background square.

Soccer Fans

For kids whose favorite sport is soccer, use the soccer ball in all the squares of the Poster Quilt. Or appliqué the child's name, number, and team name in some of the squares. Each background square can be a different fabric, if you want to use up your scraps.

Position and fuse one design at a time, referring to the photo on page 216 for placement. Quick-fuse five large stars to each border strip, allowing for ¼-inch seams.

STEP 3. Use a permanent felt pen to draw stitching lines on the baseball and seam lines on the basketballs.

Layering the Quilt

Arrange and baste the backing, flannel, and top together, following the directions in "Layering the

28"

38"

QUILT LAYOUT

Quilt" on page 275. Trim the flannel and backing to ¼ inch from the raw edges of the quilt top.

Binding the Quilt

Using the four 2¾ × 42-inch binding strips, follow the direc-

tions for "Binding the Quilt" on pages 275–276.

Finishing Stitches

Machine or hand quilt in the seam lines of the background squares, accent border, and

border. Outline the appliqué designs by quilting around the edges. Quilt vertical lines between the stars in the border.

TEAM PILLOWS

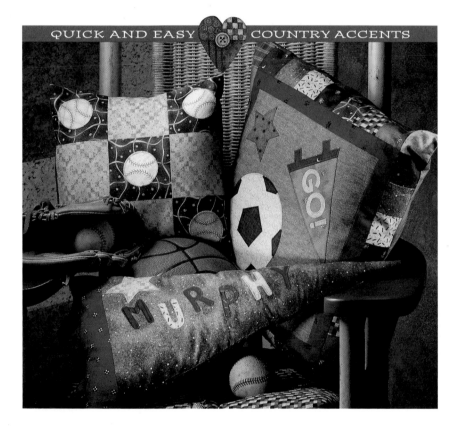

Whether the sport is baseball, soccer, or anything in between, these sportive pillows will be welcome in any team player's bedroom. Soften a chair with them, or add them to a bed for lounging and reading. Shown on the chair are the Personalized Pennant Pillow, *bottom*, the Home Run Nine-Patch Pillow, *top left* (directions on page 221), and the Soccer Ball Pillow, *top right* (page 222).

12" 20"

PERSONALIZED PENNANT PILLOW

Finished Size: 20 × 12 inches

Assembly and Appliqué

STEP 1. See "Materials and Cutting" on the following page. Using a ¼-inch seam, sew the 3 × 14-inch border strip to the 21 × 14-inch green print pennant piece. Press the seam toward the border.

MATERIALS AND CUTTING (for Personalized Pennant Pillow)

Prewash and press all of your fabrics. Using a rotary cutter, see-through ruler, and cutting mat, prepare the pieces as described below. Measurements for all pieces include ¼-inch seam allowances.

FABRIC	YARDAGE	NO. OF PIECES	DIMENSIONS
▪ Green print for pennant and backing	¾ yard	1 1	21 × 14-inch piece (pennant) 24 × 14-inch piece (backing)
▪ Red print for border and tabs	⅛ yard	1 1	3 × 14-inch strip (border) 3 × 12-inch strip (tabs)
Several coordinated fabrics for appliqué pieces	Scraps, or ⅛-yard pieces	—	—
Lightweight, sewable fusible web; Tear-Away fabric stabilizer; polyester fiberfill stuffing			

STEP 2. Cut the pillow top from the unit from Step 1, as shown in **Diagram 1**. Cut the pillow back to the same size as the front from the 24 × 14-inch green print backing piece.

DIAGRAM 1

STEP 3. Refer to "Quick-Fuse Appliqué" on pages 270–271. Be sure to use a lightweight, sewable fusible web. Trace the large star from the appliqué pattern on page 212. To add a name, draw letters to fit the pennant. The size of the letters will vary depending on the length of the name you are using. Trace the letters in reverse onto the paper side of the fusible web.

STEP 4. Allowing for ¼-inch seams on the raw edges, position

and fuse the appliqué pieces to the pennant.

STEP 5. Refer to "Machine Appliqué" on pages 271–272. Use a small zigzag stitch to machine appliqué around the edges of the appliqué pieces. Use the Tear-Away fabric stabilizer on the underside of the pennant for an even machine stitch. Remove the stabilizer after stitching.

A Signature Idea

Have your child print his or her own name to use as a basis for drawing your letters.

Finishing the Pillow

STEP 1. To make the tabs, fold the 3 × 12-inch red print tab strip in half lengthwise with right sides together. Sew a ¼-inch seam along the edge opposite the fold, turn

the strip right side out, and press. Topstitch along the edges of both sides. Cut the strip into two 6-inch pieces and fold each piece in half. Position the tabs keeping the raw edges even with the raw edge of the border. Pin and baste the tabs in place. They will be sewn into the seam when the pillow is finished. See **Diagram 2**.

STEP 2. Position the pillow top and backing with right sides together and pin them in place. Using ¼-inch seams, sew around the edges, leaving a 3- to 4-inch opening for turning. Trim the corners and point, turn the pillow right side out, and press. Stuff the pillow with the polyester fiberfill and hand stitch the opening closed.

DIAGRAM 2

12"

12"

HOME RUN NINE-PATCH PILLOW

Finished Size: 12 inches square

(See the pillow on the chair, upper left, in the photo on page 219.)

Assembly and Appliqué

See "Materials and Cutting" below. Assemble the pillow top before adding the appliqué pieces. Be sure to use ¼-inch seams and to press after each sewing step.

STEP 1. Sew the 4½-inch blue print squares and gold print squares together in rows, as shown in **Diagram 3**. Press the

seams toward the blue squares. Sew the rows together and press, following the arrows in the diagram, to complete the pillow top.

12½"

4½"

4½"

4½"

DIAGRAM 3

STEP 2. Refer to "Quick-Fuse Appliqué" on pages 270–271. Be sure to use a lightweight, sewable fusible web. Trace five baseballs from the appliqué pattern on page 209.

STEP 3. Allowing for ¼-inch seams on the raw edges, position and fuse one baseball to the center of each blue print background square.

STEP 4. Refer to "Machine Appliqué" on pages 271–272. Use a small zigzag stitch to machine appliqué around the edges of the baseballs. Use the Tear-Away fabric stabilizer on the underside for an even machine stitch. Remove the stabilizer after stitching. Use the permanent felt pen to draw stitching lines on the baseballs.

Making the Pillow Back

STEP 1. Narrow hem one 12½-inch edge of each 8½ × 12½-inch backing piece by folding ¼ inch to the wrong side. Press. Fold again ¼ inch to the wrong side. Press. Topstitch along the folded edge.

STEP 2. With right sides up, lay one backing piece over the second piece so that the hemmed edges overlap 3½ inches. See **Diagram 4** on the following page. Baste the pieces together at the sides where

---

MATERIALS AND CUTTING *(for Home Run Nine-Patch Pillow)*

Prewash and press all of your fabrics. Using a rotary cutter, see-through ruler, and cutting mat, prepare the pieces as described below. Measurements for all pieces include ¼-inch seam allowances.

FABRIC	YARDAGE	NO. OF PIECES	DIMENSIONS
▪ Blue print for background	⅛ yard	5	4½-inch squares
▫ Gold print for background	⅛ yard	4	4½-inch squares
Backing fabric	⅓ yard	2	8½ × 12½-inch pieces
Several coordinated fabrics for appliqué baseballs	Scraps, or ⅛-yard pieces	—	—

Lightweight, sewable fusible web; Tear-Away fabric stabilizer; permanent, fine-point felt pen; purchased 12-inch pillow form they overlap. The pillow back will now measure 12½ inches square.

12½"

12½"

} 3½" overlap

DIAGRAM 4

Finishing the Pillow

STEP 1. With right sides together, sew the pillow front to the back, using ¼-inch seam allowances. Trim the corners, turn the pillow right side out, and press.

STEP 2. Insert the 12-inch pillow form through the opening in the back of the pillow. To make your own pillow form, refer to "Making Custom-Fit Pillow Forms" on page 194.

18"

18"

SOCCER BALL PILLOW

Finished Size: 18 inches square

(See the pillow on the chair, upper right, in the photo on page 219.)

Assembly and Appliqué

See "Materials and Cutting" on the opposite page. Assemble the pillow top before adding the appliqué pieces. Be sure to use ¼-inch seams and to press after each sewing step.

STEP 1. Sew the 1½ × 12½-inch accent border strips to the top and bottom of the 12½-inch blue solid background square. Press the seams toward the accent border.

STEP 2. Sew the 1½ × 14½-inch accent border strips to the sides. Press.

STEP 3. For the patchwork border, arrange the nine 2½ × 12-inch patchwork border strips in a pleasing order. Sew the strips together to make an 18½ × 12-inch strip set. Using a rotary cutter and ruler, cut four 2½ × 18½-inch strips from this strip set. There should be nine squares in each strip. See **Diagram 5**.

18½"

12"

2½"

DIAGRAM 5

STEP 4. For the top and bottom, use a seam ripper to remove two squares from each of two 2½ × 18½-inch patchwork border strips to make two 2½ × 14½-inch strips with seven squares each. Compare the strips to the top and bottom of the pillow top. You may need to take in or let out a few seams

(⅟₁₆ inch or less) to make them fit. Pin and sew the patchwork border strips to the top and bottom. Press the seams toward the accent border.

STEP 5. Fit, pin, and sew the remaining two 2½ × 18½-inch patchwork border strips to the sides. Press.

STEP 6. Refer to "Quick-Fuse Appliqué" on pages 270–271. Be sure to use a lightweight, sewable fusible web. Trace two large stars from the appliqué pattern on page 212, one soccer ball from page 213, and one pennant from page 210.

STEP 7. Position and fuse the appliqué pieces to the background square, referring to the Soccer Ball Pillow layout for placement.

STEP 8. Refer to "Machine Appliqué" on pages 271–272. Use a small zigzag stitch to machine appliqué around the edges of the appliqué pieces. Use the Tear-Away fabric stabilizer on the underside for an even machine stitch. Remove the stabilizer after stitching.

Making the Pillow Back

STEP 1. Narrow hem one 18½-inch edge of each 11½ × 18½-inch backing piece by folding ¼ inch to the wrong side. Press. Fold again ¼ inch to the wrong side. Press. Topstitch along the folded edge.

MATERIALS AND CUTTING *(for Soccer Ball Pillow)*

Prewash and press all of your fabrics. Using a rotary cutter, see-through ruler, and cutting mat, prepare the pieces as described below. Measurements for all pieces include ¼-inch seam allowances.

FABRIC	YARDAGE	NO. OF PIECES	DIMENSIONS
■ Blue solid for background	⅜ yard	1	12½-inch square
■ Red print for accent border	⅛ yard (cut into two 1½ × 42-inch strips)	2 2	1½ × 14½-inch strips 1½ × 12½-inch strips
Assorted fabrics for patchwork border	⅛ yard, or 2½ × 12-inch strip, *each* of 9 fabrics	1	2½ × 12-inch strip *each*
Backing fabric	⅜ yard	2	11½ × 18½-inch pieces
Several coordinated fabrics for appliqué pieces	Scraps, or ⅛- to ¼-yard pieces	—	—
Lightweight, sewable fusible web; Tear-Away fabric stabilizer; purchased 18-inch pillow form			

STEP 2. With right sides up, lay one backing piece over the second piece so that the hemmed edges overlap 3½ inches. See **Diagram 6.** Baste the pieces together at the sides where they overlap. The pillow back will now measure 18½ inches square.

18½"

18½"

3½" overlap

DIAGRAM 6

Finishing the Pillow

STEP 1. With right sides together, sew the pillow front to the back, using ¼-inch seams. Trim the corners, turn the pillow right side out, and press.

STEP 2. Insert the 18-inch pillow form through the opening in the back of the pillow. To make your own pillow form, refer to "Making Custom-Fit Pillow Forms" on page 194.

Debbie's Decorating Diary

I came up with four possible themes for my son, Murphy's, room. I let him choose from Sports, Undersea World, On Safari, or Bugs, Frogs, and Nature. It was a slam dunk choice—Sports!

SPORTING GOODS

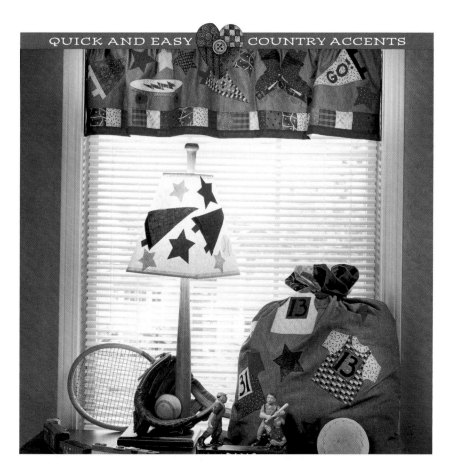

QUICK AND EASY COUNTRY ACCENTS

Reward good sportsmanship by making these fun accessories that will add just the right finishing touches to a sports-theme bedroom. Both the Patchwork Sports Valance and the Sports Laundry Bag (directions on page 226) are easy to make with minimal patchwork and machine appliqué.

50"

12"

PATCHWORK SPORTS VALANCE

Finished Size: 50 × 12 inches

These instructions are written for a valance that fits a 33-inch-wide window. You can customize the valance to fit any window. To determine the finished width of the valance, measure your window and multiply the width by 1½. Round up to the nearest even number. Adjust the fabric requirements and cutting dimensions on the following Materials and Cutting list accordingly. Read the first paragraph under each subsequent section for additional directions on customizing your valance.

Appliqué

For a custom valance, cut the background piece 8½ inches long by the width of the valance. It may be necessary to cut two or more pieces. If so, add ¼ inch to each piece for the seam allowance. Choose an appropriate number of sports designs from the appliqué patterns on pages 207–215 to fit the width of the valance. See "Materials and Cutting" on the opposite page.

STEP 1. Using a ¼-inch seam, sew the two 8½ × 25½-inch blue solid background pieces together to make one 8½ × 50½-inch background piece. Press the seam open.

MATERIALS AND CUTTING

Prewash and press all of your fabrics. Using a rotary cutter, see-through ruler, and cutting mat, prepare the pieces as described below. Measurements for all pieces include ¼-inch seam allowances (to make 1 valance).

FABRIC	YARDAGE	NO. OF PIECES	DIMENSIONS
Blue solid for background	⅝ yard	2	8½ × 25½-inch pieces
Assorted fabrics for patchwork border	Scrap, or ⅛-yard piece, *each* of 8 fabrics	25	2½-inch squares *total*
Red print for border	⅙ yard (cut into three 1½ × 42-inch strips)	2	1½ × 38½-inch strips
		2	1½ × 12½-inch strips
Backing fabric	¾ yard	2	12½ × 25½-inch pieces
Several coordinated fabrics for appliqué pieces	Scraps, or ⅛- to ¼-yard pieces	—	—
Lightweight, sewable fusible web; Tear-Away fabric stabilizer			

STEP 2. Refer to "Quick-Fuse Appliqué" on pages 270–271. Be sure to use a lightweight, sewable fusible web. Trace six large stars from the appliqué pattern on page 212, three pennants from page 210, one skateboard from page 215, and one pair of in-line skates from page 214.

STEP 3. Allowing for ¼-inch seams on the raw edges, position and fuse the appliqué pieces to the background, referring to the valance layout on page 224 for placement. It may be helpful to use the Appliqué Pressing Sheet as described on page 203.

STEP 4. Refer to "Machine Appliqué" on pages 271–272. Use a small zigzag stitch to machine appliqué around the edges of the appliqué pieces. Use the Tear-Away fabric stabilizer on the underside of the background. Remove the stabilizer after stitching.

Borders and Backing

For a custom valance, determine how many 2½-inch patchwork border squares you need. Divide the finished width of the valance by 2 and cut that many squares from an assortment of fabrics. Cut each red print border strip 1½ inches by the width of the valance. Cut the backing 12½ inches by the width of the valance. It may be necessary to piece the red border strips and backing. If so, add ¼ inch to each piece for the seam allowance.

STEP 1. Arrange the twenty-five 2½-inch patchwork border squares in a pleasing order. Using ¼-inch seams, sew the squares together to make a 2½ × 50½-inch strip.

STEP 2. Compare the patchwork border strip to the bottom of the blue solid background. You may need to take in or let out a few seams (¹⁄₁₆ inch or less) to make it fit. Pin and sew the strip to the bottom of the background. Press the seam toward the background.

STEP 3. Sew one 1½ × 38½-inch red print border strip to each of the 1½ × 12½-inch red border strips to make two 1½ × 50½-inch strips. Press.

STEP 4. Sew the border strips from Step 3 to the top and bottom of the valance front. Press the seams toward the red print border.

STEP 5. Sew the two 12½ × 25½-inch backing pieces together to make one 12½ × 50½-inch backing piece. Press the seam open.

STEP 6. With right sides together, pin the sides of the valance front and backing together. Sew the sides together, beginning at the seam line of the top red print border and the blue solid background. See **Diagram 1**.

DIAGRAM 1

STEP 7. Turn the valance right side out and press the side seams. Press under and topstitch the edges of the unsewn side seams as shown in **Diagram 2**.

DIAGRAM 2

STEP 8. Turn the valance inside out so that right sides are together. Pin and sew the top and bottom of the valance, leaving a 3- to 4-inch opening for turning. Turn the valance right side out, hand stitch the opening closed, and press.

STEP 9. To complete the casing for the rod, pin and stitch in the seam line between the top red print border and blue solid background.

24"

28"

SPORTS LAUNDRY BAG

Finished Size: 24 × 28 inches

(See the laundry bag in the photo on page 224.)

Appliqué

STEP 1. See "Materials and Cutting" on the opposite page. Refer to "Quick-Fuse Appliqué"

on pages 270–271. Be sure to use a lightweight, sewable fusible web. Trace three jerseys and five large stars from the appliqué patterns on page 212.

STEP 2. Fold the 48½ × 23½-inch blue solid background piece in half crosswise with wrong sides together, and press. Allowing for ¼-inch seams on the raw edges, position and fuse the appliqué pieces to the background between the fold and raw edge, referring to the Laundry Bag layout at left for placement.

STEP 3. Refer to "Machine Appliqué" on pages 271–272. Use a small zigzag stitch to machine appliqué around the edges of the appliqué pieces. Use the Tear-

---

Polarfleece Throw

(See the throw on the top bunk in the photo on page 198.)

Materials

1 purchased Polarfleece throw
Scraps, or ⅛- to ¼-yard pieces, of several coordinated fabrics for appliqué pieces
Lightweight, sewable fusible web
Tear-Away fabric stabilizer
#5 perle cotton

Assembly

STEP 1. See "Quick-Fuse Appliqué" on pages 270–271. Trace an assortment of sports designs from the patterns on pages 207–215.

STEP 2. Position and fuse the designs to the throw.

STEP 3. Refer to "Machine Appliqué" on pages 271–272. Use a small zigzag stitch to machine appliqué around the edges of the appliqué pieces. Use the Tear-Away fabric stabilizer on the underside of the throw for an even machine stitch. Remove the stabilizer after stitching.

STEP 4. If your Polarfleece throw is finished with a large blanket stitch, use two strands of a contrasting color of pearl cotton to hand stitch over every other stitch.

MATERIALS AND CUTTING

Prewash and press all of your fabrics. Using a rotary cutter, see-through ruler, and cutting mat, prepare the pieces as described below. Measurements for all pieces include ¼-inch seam allowances.

FABRIC	YARDAGE	NO. OF PIECES	DIMENSIONS
Blue solid for background	1½ yards	1	48½ × 23½-inch piece
Red print for accent border	⅛ yard	2	1½ × 42-inch strips
Assorted fabrics for patchwork border	⅙ yard *each* of 6 fabrics	2	4½-inch squares *each*
Lining fabric	1½ yards	1	48½ × 28½-inch piece
Several coordinated fabrics for appliqué pieces	Scraps, or ⅛- to ¼-yard pieces	—	—
Lightweight, sewable fusible web; Tear-Away fabric stabilizer; 1⅔ yards cording for drawstring			

Away fabric stabilizer on the wrong side of the background for an even machine stitch. Remove the stabilizer after stitching.

Assembly

STEP 1. Using ¼-inch seams, sew the twelve 4½-inch patchwork border squares together to make a 4½ × 48½-inch strip.

STEP 2. Sew the two 1½ × 42-inch accent border strips together to make one strip approximately 1½ × 84 inches. Press. Trim the strip to 1½ × 48½ inches.

STEP 3. Sew the lining, patchwork border, accent border, and background together in the order shown in **Diagram 3**. Press the seams, following the arrows in the diagram.

STEP 4. Fold the laundry bag in half with right sides together. Using ¼-inch seams, sew along the ends

and the edge opposite the fold. Leave an opening in the lining for turning and in the accent border for the drawstring. Backstitch on both sides of the accent border to reinforce the drawstring opening. See **Diagram 4**.

STEP 5. Turn the laundry bag right side out, hand stitch the opening closed, and press. Tuck the lining inside and press along the top edge.

STEP 6. To make the drawstring casing, stitch in the seam line on both sides of the accent border. Thread the cording through the casing, and tie a knot in each end.

DIAGRAM 3

DIAGRAM 4

HEARTS AND FLOWERS BEDROOM

Take one girl's bedroom, add these sweet and sentimental projects,

and you'll have an enchanting decorator look. All the projects are based on the

directions for the Sports Fever Kid's Bedroom projects (directions begin on page

201), including the bed quilt, pillowcase, throw pillows, valance, laundry bag,

and jacket. I've changed the motifs and the fabric colors, but the materials,

yardages, cutting, and assembling are basically the same.

Hearts and Flowers Quilt

Finished Size: 75 × 87 inches

Make this sweet girl's quilt following the directions for the Sports Quilt on page 201. Use pinks, yellows, and pale blues and greens rather than bright primary colors. Simply replace the sports designs with the hearts and flowers designs, using the appliqué patterns on page 232. Fuse hearts to the small corner squares and flowers to the large corner squares.

Machine or hand quilt as desired. The quilt in the photo on the opposite page was machine quilted around the appliqué designs. A large stipple and heart pattern was quilted in the background. Make one yo-yo for each flower from the large yo-yo pattern on page 195. Sew a yo-yo to each flower center.

Refer to "Making Yo-yos" on pages 272–273.

Note: The Hearts and Flowers Quilt made from the Sports Quilt directions will be slightly larger than the quilt shown in the photo on the opposite page. There will be more of a drop on the sides of the quilt.

Ruffled Posy Pillow

Finished Size: 18 inches in diameter

(See the pillow on the bed, middle, in the photo on page 228.)

MATERIALS AND CUTTING

Prewash and press all of your fabrics. Using a rotary cutter, see-through ruler, and cutting mat, prepare the pieces as described below. Measurements for all pieces include ¼-inch seam allowances.

FABRIC	YARDAGE	NO. OF PIECES	DIMENSIONS
☐ Green print for pillow top and backing	½ yard	2	12½-inch circles
◼ Blue print for ruffle	⅝ yard	2 1	6½ × 40-inch strips 6½ × 20-inch strip
Several coordinated fabrics for appliqué pieces and yo-yos	Scraps, or ⅛- to ¼-yard pieces	—	—

¼ yard lightweight, sewable fusible web; Tear-Away fabric stabilizer;
1¼ yards strong crochet thread or #5 perle cotton; polyester fiberfill stuffing

Appliqué

STEP 1. Refer to "Quick-Fuse Appliqué" on pages 270–271. Use a lightweight, sewable fusible web. Trace one flower and six leaves from the appliqué patterns on page 232.

STEP 2. Position and fuse the design to the center of the pillow top.

STEP 3. Refer to "Machine Appliqué" on pages 271–272. Use a small zigzag stitch to machine appliqué around the edges of the appliqué pieces. Use the Tear-Away fabric stabilizer on the underside of the pillow top. Remove the stabilizer after stitching.

Finishing the Pillow

STEP 1. Refer to "Making Yo-yos" on pages 272–273. Make one large yo-yo from the pattern on page 232. Sew the yo-yo to the center of the flower.

STEP 2. Using ¼-inch seams, sew the two 6½ × 40-inch and one 6½ × 20-inch ruffle strips together to make a continuous loop. Press the ruffle in half lengthwise with wrong sides together.

STEP 3. Sew a gathering stitch along the raw edge of the ruffle by zigzag stitching over the crochet thread or pearl cotton. Divide the ruffle into quarters and mark.

STEP 4. Divide the pillow top in quarters by gently folding it in half two times. Mark the folds. Matching the marks and keeping the raw edges together, position and pin the ruffle onto the pillow top. Gather the ruffle by pulling the gathering cord. Evenly distribute the gathers as you pin the ruffle to the pillow top. See **Diagram 1**. Baste the ruffle to the pillow top.

DIAGRAM 1

STEP 5. With the ruffle in the middle, position the pillow top and backing with right sides together, and pin them in place. Using ¼-inch seam allowances, sew around the pillow, leaving a 3- to 4-inch opening for turning. Turn the pillow right side out and press. Stuff the pillow with the polyester fiberfill, and hand stitch the opening closed.

HEARTS PILLOW

To create the pillow shown on the bed, left, in the photo on page 228, follow the directions for the Soccer Ball Pillow on page 222. To make the circle of hearts, draw an 8-inch circle on the center of the background square. Using the circle as a positioning guide, fuse nine hearts traced from the appliqué pattern on the following page. Refer to "Making Yo-yos" on pages 272–273. Make five large yo-yos from the pattern on page 195. Sew one yo-yo to each corner of the accent border and one to the center of the pillow.

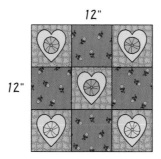

NINE-PATCH PILLOW

To make the nine-patch pillow shown on the bed, right, in the photo on page 228, choose some pretty pastel fabrics. Follow the directions for the Home Run Nine-Patch Pillow on page 221, replacing the baseballs with five hearts traced from the appliqué pattern on page 232. Refer to "Making Yo-yos" on pages 272–273. Make five small yo-yos from the pattern on page 232. Sew one yo-yo to the center of each heart.

PILLOWCASE

Make a soft and feminine pillowcase by adding hearts and yo-yos to the border. Follow the directions for the Sports Pillowcase on page 205.

Trace four hearts from the appliqué pattern on page 232 and fuse them to the pillowcase border. Refer to "Making Yo-yos" on pages 272–273. Make four small yo-yos from the pattern on page 232. Sew one yo-yo to the center of each heart.

LAUNDRY BAG

Follow the directions for the Sports Laundry Bag on page 226. Replace the jerseys and stars on the bag with hearts and flowers. Trace four hearts, three flowers with round centers, and nine leaves from the appliqué patterns on page 232. Position and fuse the appliqué pieces to the bag, referring to the illustration above for placement.

VALANCE

Follow the directions for the Patchwork Sports Valance on page 224. Replace the sports designs with hearts and flowers, using the appliqué patterns on page 232. Refer to "Making Yo-yos" on pages 272–273. Make one large yo-yo for each flower from the pattern on page 232. Sew a yo-yo to each flower center.

JACKET

Turn a plain denim jacket into a wardrobe favorite for a young girl. Follow the directions for the Sports Jacket on page 206. Trace three hearts, one flower, and three leaves from the appliqué patterns below. Sew assorted buttons to the back of the jacket.

LEAF PATTERN

FLOWER PATTERN

LARGE YO-YO PATTERN

SMALL YO-YO PATTERN

FLOWER CENTER PATTERN

(Can be used in place of yo-yo)

HEART PATTERN

CHARMING NOOKS, CRANNIES, AND DOORS

Nearly every house has wonderful little out-of-the-way areas that I like to call nooks and crannies. They are perfect for showcasing different decorating themes. In this section, I've included projects for a Gardening Nook (page 234) and a Christmas Nook (page 243), along with a Holiday Front Door (page 252).

GARDENING NOOK

Whether you're a gardener or not, the sweet Garden Gatherings

Angel hanging on the wall will win you over. The framed Garden Bouquet

(directions on page 237) on the left side of the table is a freshly gathered

bouquet of yo-yos and quick-fused three-dimensional flowers—a great gift

idea! The Tulip Pot (page 238) hanging on the wall is cute

as a button with a button-embellished frame.

Garden Gatherings Angel

Finished Picture Size: 20 ×16 inches   **Finished Framed Size: 24 × 20 inches**

MATERIALS AND CUTTING

Prewash and press all of your fabrics. Using a rotary cutter, see-through ruler, and cutting mat, prepare the pieces as described below. Measurements for all pieces include ¼-inch seam allowances.

FABRIC	YARDAGE	NO. OF PIECES	DIMENSIONS
Blue prints for sky background	Scrap, or ⅛-yard piece, *each* of 8 to 12 fabrics	40	2½-inch squares *total*
Green prints for grass background	Scrap, or ⅛-yard piece, *each* of 8 to 12 fabrics	40	2½-inch squares *total*
Muslin for framing strips	⅛ yard (cut into two 1¾ × 42-inch strips)	2 / 2	1¾ × 20½-inch strips / 1¾ × 19-inch strips
Several coordinated fabrics for appliqué pieces, dimensional flowers and leaves, and yo-yos	Scraps, or ⅛- to ¼-yard pieces	—	—

Fusible web; embroidery floss; assorted buttons; 16 × 20-inch piece of cotton batting; 16 × 20-inch frame; tacky glue or masking tape

Assembly

Assemble the background before adding the appliqué pieces. Be sure to use ¼-inch seams and press seams after each sewing step.

STEP 1. Lay out the 2½-inch blue print background squares in a pleasing arrangement of four rows with ten squares each. Keep track of your layout while sewing the sky background together. Press the seams in Rows #1 and #3 to the left and in Rows #2 and #4 to the right. Join the rows and press.

STEP 2. Repeat Step 1 for the 2½-inch green print squares.

STEP 3. Sew the unit from Step 1 to the unit from Step 2. Press.

STEP 4. Sew the 1¾ × 20½-inch muslin framing strips to the top and bottom. Press the seams toward the framing strips. Sew the 1¾ × 19-inch framing strips to the sides. Press.

Appliqué

STEP 1. Refer to "Quick-Fuse Appliqué" on pages 270–271. Trace the angel from the appliqué patterns on pages 240–241. To make dimensional wings, fuse the wings to the selected wing fabric and cut them out. Instead of fusing the wings to the background, fuse them to the wrong side of a second piece of wing fabric. Trim even with the edges of the fused wings.

STEP 2. Position the wings behind the angel and fuse the angel to the background, referring to the **Angel Layout** for placement. Sew the wings to the background by

stitching along the center of each wing. Use two strands of embroidery floss and a running stitch.

STEP 3. Trace a total of 10 to 15 flowers and a total of 35 to 42 leaves from the patterns on page 239. To make dimensional flowers and leaves, fuse the flowers and leaves to the selected fabrics, and cut them out. Instead of fusing the flowers and leaves to the background, fuse each to the wrong side of a second piece of flower or leaf fabric. Trim even with the edges of the fused flowers and leaves. For the bell-shaped flowers, fringe the fluted edge by cutting ½-inch slits approximately 1/16 to 1/8 inch apart.

STEP 4. Refer to "Making Yo-yos" on pages 272–273. Make 25 to 30 yo-yo flowers of assorted sizes from the patterns on page 241.

STEP 5. Position the flowers on the background, referring to the **Garden Gatherings Angel**

Layout below for placement. Hand sew the flowers in place with a blind stitch, a button center, or French knots. See "Decorative Stitches" on page 272 for instructions on making French knots.

STEP 6. Mark the bucket handle and flower stems on the background. Use three strands of embroidery floss and a stem stitch to make the handle and stems, referring to "Decorative Stitches" on page 272 for instructions. Hand sew one leaf to each stem. Use two strands of embroidery floss to make a French-knot eye on the angel.

STEP 7. Place the batting on top of the cardboard backing from the picture frame. With the batting in the middle, center and stretch the picture over the cardboard. Secure the edges on the back of the cardboard with the tacky glue or masking tape. Insert the picture in the back of the frame, and secure it.

20½"

16½"

GARDEN GATHERINGS ANGEL LAYOUT

Garden Bouquet

Finished Picture Size: 8 × 10 inches
Finished Framed Size: 10 × 12 inches

(See the bouquet picture on the left side of the table in the photo on page 234.)

MATERIALS AND CUTTING

Prewash and press all of your fabrics. Using a rotary cutter, see-through ruler, and cutting mat, prepare the pieces as described below. Measurements for all pieces include ¼-inch seam allowances.

FABRIC	YARDAGE	NO. OF PIECES	DIMENSIONS
Blue prints for background	Scrap, or ⅛-yard piece, *each* of 5 to 9 fabrics	20	2½-inch squares *total*
Muslin for framing strips	⅛ yard (cut into two 1¾ × 42-inch strips)	2	1¾ × 13-inch strips
		2	1¾ × 8½-inch strips
Several coordinated fabrics for dimensional flowers and leaves and for yo-yos	Scraps, or ⅛-yard pieces	—	—
Fusible web; assorted buttons; embroidery floss; silk ribbon; 8 × 10-inch piece of cotton batting; 8 × 10-inch frame; tacky glue or masking tape			

Assembly

Assemble the background before adding the bouquet. Be sure to use ¼-inch seams and to press seams after each sewing step.

STEP 1. Lay out the 2½-inch blue print background squares in a pleasing arrangement of five rows with four squares each. Keep track of your layout while sewing the background together. Press the seams in Rows #1, #3, and #5 to the left and in Rows #2 and #4 to the right. Join the rows and press the seams in one direction.

STEP 2. Sew 1¾ × 8½-inch framing strips to the top and bottom. Press seams toward the framing strips. Sew 1¾ × 13-inch framing strips to the sides. Press.

Appliqué

STEP 1. Refer to "Quick-Fuse Appliqué" on pages 270–271. Trace a total of 4 to 6 flowers and 10 to 12 leaves from the patterns on page 239. To make dimensional flowers and leaves, fuse the flowers and leaves to the selected fabrics, and cut them out. Fuse each to the wrong side of a second piece of flower or leaf fabric. Trim even with the edges of the fused flowers and leaves. For the bell-shaped flowers, fringe the

fluted edge by cutting ½-inch slits approximately ⅟₁₆ to ⅛ inch apart. Cut slits in the circular flowers as shown on the pattern.

STEP 2. Refer to "Making Yo-yos" on pages 272–273. Make 8 to 12 yo-yo flowers of assorted sizes from the patterns on page 241.

STEP 3. Referring to the **Garden Bouquet Layout** on the following page, arrange your floral bouquet. Hand sew the flowers in place with a blind stitch, a button center, or French knots. Use two strands of embroidery floss and a backstitch to make the flower stems. See "Decorative Stitches" on page 272 for instructions on backstitching and making French knots. Hand sew the leaves to the stems.

STEP 4. Tie a bow with the silk ribbon and hand sew the bow to the bouquet stems. Drape and tack the ends in place.

STEP 5. Place the batting on top of the cardboard backing from the picture frame. With the batting in the middle, center and stretch the picture over the cardboard. Secure

the edges on the back of the cardboard with the tacky glue or masking tape. Insert the picture in the back of the frame and secure it.

GARDEN BOUQUET LAYOUT

Add a Ribbon

Hang your picture frame from a decorative ribbon. Cut two pieces of ribbon. Attach the ends of one ribbon to the back of the frame for a hanging ribbon. Tie a bow around the hanging ribbon with the other piece.

Tulip Pot

Finished Picture Size: 4 × 6 inches
Finished Framed Size: 7 × 9 inches

(See the tulip picture on the wall in the photo on page 234.)

Materials

7 × 9-inch piece of green print for background
Scraps, or ⅛-yard pieces, of several coordinated fabrics for appliqué pieces
Fusible web
Embroidery floss
Silk ribbon
4 × 6-inch piece of cotton batting
4 × 6-inch frame
Tacky glue or masking tape
Assorted buttons

Assembly

STEP 1. Refer to "Quick-Fuse Appliqué" on pages 270–271. Trace the tulip pot from the

appliqué pattern on the opposite page. Quick-fuse the design to the center of the 7 × 9-inch green print background piece.

STEP 2. Mark the tulip stems on the background. Use two strands of embroidery floss and a stem stitch to make the stems, referring to "Decorative Stitches" on page 272 for instructions.

STEP 3. Tie a bow with the silk ribbon and hand sew the bow to the vase.

STEP 4. Place the batting on top of the cardboard backing from the picture frame. With the batting in the middle, center and stretch the

picture over the cardboard. Secure the edges on the back of the cardboard with the tacky glue or masking tape. Insert the picture in the back of the frame and secure it. Glue assorted buttons to the frame.

4"

6"

TULIP LAYOUT

Painting Tip

Paint your picture frame to coordinate with your pot of tulips. Add a miniature checkerboard around the opening. Instead of gluing buttons to the frame, paint small clusters of tulips!

APPLIQUÉ PATTERN KEY

——————— Tracing line

- - - - - Tracing line (will be hidden behind other fabric)

TULIP POT PATTERN

LEAF PATTERNS

GARDEN GATHERINGS ANGEL FLOWER PATTERNS

Cut slits

GARDEN BOUQUET FLOWER PATTERNS

ANGEL PATTERN
ASSEMBLY DIAGRAM

Match with
Angel Pattern
B

Match with
Angel Pattern
D

ANGEL PATTERN
A

Match with Angel Pattern C

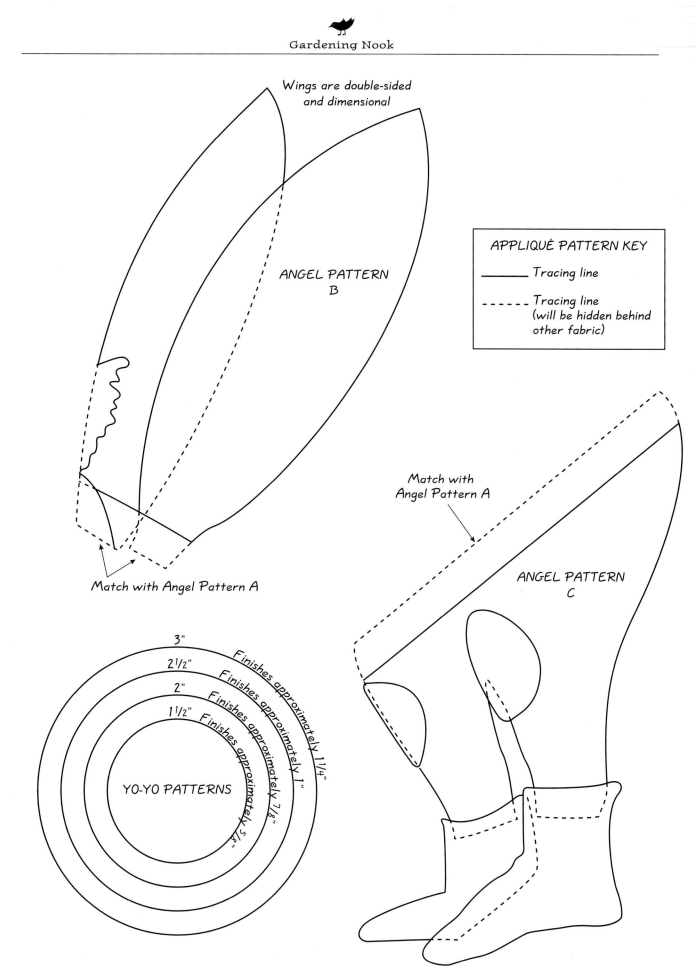

Wings are double-sided
and dimensional

ANGEL PATTERN
B

APPLIQUÉ PATTERN KEY

——— Tracing line

– – – Tracing line
(will be hidden behind
other fabric)

Match with
Angel Pattern A

ANGEL PATTERN
C

Match with Angel Pattern A

3"
2¹⁄₂"
2"
1¹⁄₂"

Finishes approximately 1¹⁄₄"
Finishes approximately 1"
Finishes approximately ⁷⁄₈"
Finishes approximately ⁵⁄₈"

YO-YO PATTERNS

Match with
Angel Pattern
E

ANGEL PATTERN
E

Match with
Angel Pattern D

APPLIQUÉ PATTERN KEY

———— Tracing line

- - - - Tracing line
(will be hidden behind
other fabric)

Match with
Angel Pattern
A

Stem stitch handle

Every other shape is green

Black

Black rim

Gray

ANGEL PATTERN D

CHRISTMAS NOOK

Decorate a nook for Christmas with six quick and easy framed wallhangings, and enjoy it all winter. As seen on the next page, the delightful Merry Snowman and Birdhouse hanging on the wall has a pieced background that adds to its charm. The Embroidered Tree (directions on page 245), resting on the shelf against the wall, is hand stitched—you get a handmade look with minimal effort. The Birdhouse and Candle pictures (page 246) on the wall, along with the Star and Moon fabric pieces (page 247) on the shelves, are great fun to make from your scraps. They make wonderful gifts, as well!

Merry Snowman and Birdhouse

Finished Picture Size: 12 × 14 inches   **Finished Framed Size: 15 × 18 inches**

MATERIALS AND CUTTING

Prewash and press all of your fabrics. Using a rotary cutter, see-through ruler, and cutting mat, prepare the pieces as described below. Measurements for all pieces include ¼-inch seam allowances.

FABRIC	YARDAGE	NO. OF PIECES	DIMENSIONS
Gray prints for sky background	Scrap, or ⅛-yard piece, *each* of 6 to 8 fabrics	30	2½-inch squares *total*
Tan prints for snow background	Scrap, or ⅛-yard piece, *each* of 6 to 8 fabrics	12	2½-inch squares *total*
Muslin for framing strips	⅛ yard (cut into two 1¾ × 42-inch strips)	2	1¾ × 12½-inch strips
		2	1¾ × 17-inch strips
Several coordinated fabrics for appliqué pieces	Scraps, or ⅛- to ¼-yard pieces	—	—

Fusible web; embroidery floss; assorted buttons; 11 × 14-inch piece of cotton batting; 11 × 14-inch frame; tacky glue or masking tape

Assembly

Assemble the background before adding the appliqué pieces. Be sure to use ¼-inch seams and to press after each sewing step.

STEP 1. Lay out the 2½-inch gray print background squares in a pleasing arrangement of five rows with six squares each. Keep track of your layout while sewing the sky background together. Press the seams in Rows #1, #3, and #5 to the left and in Rows #2 and #4 to the right. Join the rows and press.

STEP 2. Lay out the 2½-inch tan print background squares in a pleasing arrangement of two rows with six squares each. Keep track of your layout while sewing the snow background together. Press the seams in Row #1 to the right and in Row #2 to the left. Join the rows and press.

STEP 3. Sew the unit from Step 1 to the unit from Step 2. Press.

STEP 4. Sew the 1¾ × 12½-inch framing strips to the top and bottom. Press the seams toward the framing strips. Sew the 1¾ × 17-inch framing strips to the sides. Press.

Appliqué

STEP 1. Refer to "Quick-Fuse Appliqué" on pages 270–271. Trace the snowman and birdhouse from the appliqué patterns on pages 249–250. Quick-fuse the design to the background, referring to the photo on the opposite page for placement.

STEP 2. Mark the holly stem and bird legs on the background. Use two strands of embroidery floss and a backstitch to make the stem and legs. Use three strands of embroidery floss to make French knots for the snowman face and bird

eyes. See "Decorative Stitches" on page 272 for instructions on backstitching and making French knots. If desired, sew assorted buttons to the birdhouse and holly stem.

STEP 3. Place the batting on top of the cardboard backing from the picture frame. With the batting in the middle, center and stretch the picture over the cardboard. Secure the edges on the back of the cardboard with the tacky glue or masking tape. Insert the picture in the back of the frame and secure it.

MERRY SNOWMAN
AND BIRDHOUSE LAYOUT

Embroidered Tree

Finished Picture Size: 11 × 14 inches
Finished Framed Size: 13 × 16 inches

(See the tree picture on the wall in the photo on the opposite page.)

Materials

15 × 18-inch piece of brown solid wool for background
Scraps of several coordinated fabrics for appliqué stars
Fusible web
Embroidery floss

Assorted ceramic buttons
11 × 14-inch piece of cotton batting
11 × 14-inch frame
Tacky glue or masking tape
11 × 14-inch mat with 8 × 11-inch opening

Assembly

STEP 1. Transfer the embroidery design from the pattern on page 251 to the center of the 15 × 18-inch brown solid background piece.

Ceramic Buttons

The charming ceramic buttons featured in the Embroidered Tree are by Debbie Mumm designs for Mill Hill. Look for these and many other delightful designs in your local quilt shop. If you are unable to find them, see "Quilting by Mail" on page 280.

STEP 2. Refer to "Quick-Fuse Appliqué" on pages 270–271. Trace the stars from the appliqué pattern on page 251. Quick-fuse the stars to the background, referring to the pattern on page 251 for placement.

STEP 3. Use three strands of embroidery floss and a backstitch to make the tree and snow. Use two strands of embroidery floss to make French knots for the falling snow. See "Decorative Stitches" on page 272 for instructions.

STEP 4. Sew assorted ceramic buttons to the background, referring to the pattern on page 251 for placement.

STEP 5. Place the batting on top of the cardboard backing from the picture frame. With the batting in the middle, center and stretch the picture over the cardboard. Secure the edges on the back of the cardboard with the tacky glue or masking tape. Insert the mat and picture in the back of the frame and secure them.

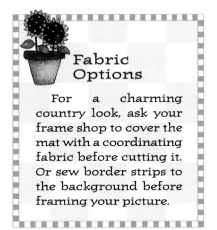

Fabric Options

For a charming country look, ask your frame shop to cover the mat with a coordinating fabric before cutting it. Or sew border strips to the background before framing your picture.

Birdhouse or Candle

Finished Picture Size: 5 × 7 inches
Finished Framed Size: 8 × 10 inches

(See the birdhouse and candle pictures on the wall in the photo on page 244.)

Materials

To make 1 picture:

5 × 7-inch piece of tan print for background
Scraps of several coordinated fabrics for appliqué pieces
Fusible web
Embroidery floss
Assorted buttons
5 × 7-inch piece of cotton batting
5 × 7-inch frame
Tacky glue

Assembly

STEP 1. Refer to "Quick-Fuse Appliqué" on pages 270–271. Trace the birdhouse from the appliqué pattern on page 250 or the candle from page 248. Quick-fuse the design to the center of the 5 × 7-inch tan print background piece, referring to the photo on page 244 for placement.

STEP 2. For the birdhouse picture, use two strands of embroidery floss to make a French-knot eye on the bird, referring to "Decorative Stitches" on page 272 for instructions. Sew buttons to the birdhouse to make the "holes." For the candle picture, mark the lines for the "glow" on the background.

Take Brush in Hand

Paint your frame with coordinating colors to complement your design.

Use two strands of embroidery floss and a running stitch to outline the glow. Sew buttons to the holly leaves to make berries.

5½"

5½"

Star or Moon

Finished Picture Size: 3 inches square
Finished Framed Size: 5½ inches square

(See the star and moon pictures on the shelves in the photo on page 244.)

Materials

To make 1 picture:

3-inch square of red wool or felt for background
Scraps of coordinated fabrics for star or moon appliqués
⅛ yard, or 4-inch piece, fusible web
Embroidery floss
Button
3-inch square of cotton batting
3 × 3-inch frame
Tacky glue

Assembly

STEP 1. Refer to "Quick-Fuse Appliqué" on pages 270–271. Trace the star or moon from the appliqué patterns on page 250. Quick-fuse the design to the center of the red background square, referring to the photo on page 244 for placement.

STEP 2. Use two strands of embroidery floss to sew a running stitch around the star. Sew a button to the center of the star. For the moon picture, use two strands of embroidery floss and a backstitch to make the eyebrow. Use two strands of embroidery floss to sew a running stitch around the moon and to make a French-knot eye. See "Decorative Stitches" on page 272 for instructions on backstitching and making French knots.

STEP 3. Place the batting on top of the cardboard backing from the picture frame. With the batting in

STEP 3. Place the batting on top of the cardboard backing from the picture frame. With the batting in the middle, center the picture on the cardboard. Secure the edges of the batting and background with tacky glue. Insert the picture in the back of the frame and secure it.

the middle, center the picture on the cardboard. Secure the edges of the batting and background with the tacky glue. Insert the picture in the back of the frame and secure it.

Add a Checkerboard

Paint a miniature checkerboard around the opening of the frame.

APPLIQUÉ PATTERN KEY

———— Tracing line

- - - - - Tracing line
(will be hidden behind
other fabric)

CANDLE PATTERN

Align bird legs here

BIRD PATTERN

MERRY SNOWMAN PATTERN

APPLIQUÉ PATTERN KEY

——————— Tracing line

- - - - - - - Tracing line
(will be hidden behind
other fabric)

BIRDHOUSE PATTERN

STAR PATTERN

MOON
PATTERN

← Cut off branch
here for
framed birdhouse

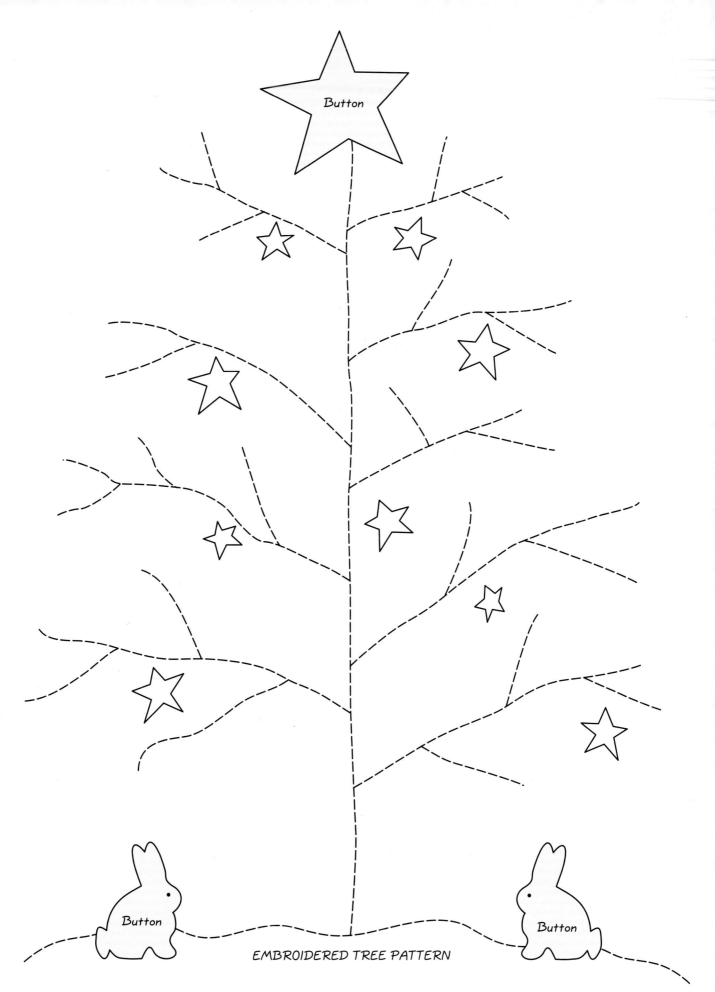

Button

Button

Button

Button

EMBROIDERED TREE PATTERN

HOLIDAY FRONT DOOR

Welcome guests to your home with this personalized Christmas

Stocking Door Banner. Add a tree decorated with handmade Felt Ornaments

(directions on page 257), a Christmas Garland (page 257), and a Rustic

Holiday Swag (page 258) above the door, and you'll have an entryway

dressed for the warmest of entrances. It may be just enough to tempt

Santa to climb down from the roof and use the front door.

Christmas Stocking Door Banner

Finished Size: 21 × 25 inches

MATERIALS AND CUTTING

Prewash and press all of your fabrics. Using a rotary cutter, see-through ruler, and cutting mat, prepare the pieces as described below. Measurements for all pieces include ¼-inch seam allowances.

FABRIC	YARDAGE	NO. OF PIECES	DIMENSIONS
Tan print for background	½ yard	1	13½ × 17½-inch piece
Black solid for accent border and binding	½ yard	2	1 × 18½-inch strips (accent border)
		2	1 × 13½-inch strips (accent border)
		4	2¾ × 42-inch strips (binding)
Red print for checkerboard	⅛ yard	2	1½ × 42-inch strips
Green print for checkerboard	⅛ yard	2	1½ × 42-inch strips

(continued)

MATERIALS AND CUTTING — CONTINUED

FABRIC	YARDAGE	NO. OF PIECES	DIMENSIONS
Gold print for patchwork points border	¼ yard (cut into three 2½ × 42-inch strips)	40	2½-inch squares
Black print for patchwork points border	¼ yard (cut into three 2½ × 42-inch strips)	18 4	2½ × 4½-inch pieces 2½-inch squares
Gold print for tabs	⅛ yard	1	2½ × 32-inch strip
Backing fabric	¾ yard		
Lightweight batting	¾ yard		
Red solid wool for stocking top	⅙ yard	1	4 × 7¾-inch piece
Red plaid wool for stocking bottom	⅜ yard	—	—
Lining fabric for stocking	⅜ yard	—	—
Several coordinated felt or overdyed wool fabrics for holly leaves, appliqué pieces, and yo-yos	Scraps, or ⅛-yard pieces	—	—

Marking pencil; embroidery floss; lightweight, sewable fusible web; #3 pearl cotton; polyester fiberfill stuffing; ½-inch dowel, 24 inches long, stained; tacky glue

Assembly

STEP 1. Using ¼-inch seams, sew the 1 × 13½-inch accent border strips to the top and bottom of the tan print background. Press the seams toward the accent border.

STEP 2. Sew the 1 × 18½-inch accent border strips to the sides. Press.

STEP 3. To make the checkerboard, alternate the two colors and sew the four 1½ × 42-inch checkerboard strips together to make a 4½ × 42-inch strip set. Change sewing direction with

each strip sewn, and press the seams toward the darker fabric as you go. Cut this strip set into fourths, approximately 10 inches each. See **Diagram 1**.

DIAGRAM 1

STEP 4. Resew the fourths together to make a 16½ × 10-inch strip set. Using a rotary cutter and ruler, cut five 1½ × 16½-inch strips from this strip set. There should be 16 squares in each strip. See **Diagram 2**.

DIAGRAM 2

STEP 5. For the top and bottom, use a seam ripper to remove 2 squares from each of two

1½ × 16½-inch strips to make two 1½ × 14½-inch strips with 14 squares each. Compare the strips to the top and bottom. You may need to take in or let out a few seams (⅟₁₆ inch or less) to make them fit. Referring to the **Door Banner Layout** on the following page for placement of the red and green squares, pin and sew the checkerboard strips to the top and bottom.

STEP 6. For the sides, use a seam ripper to remove two units of 4 squares each from one 1½ × 16½-inch strip. Sew one unit to each of the two remaining 1½ × 16½-inch strips to make two 1½ × 20½-inch strips with 20 squares each. Fit, pin, and sew the checkerboard strips to the sides.

Quick Corner Triangles

Refer to "Making Quick Corner Triangles" on page 269. Press the seams toward the triangle just added.

STEP 1. Sew eighteen 2½-inch gold print squares to the eighteen 4½ × 2½-inch black print pieces, as shown in **Diagram 3**. Press.

4½"

2½"

DIAGRAM 3

STEP 2. Sew eighteen additional 2½-inch gold print squares to the 18 units from Step 1. See **Diagram 4**. Press.

4½"

2½"

DIAGRAM 4

STEP 3. Sew the four remaining 2½-inch gold print squares to the four 2½-inch black print squares. See **Diagram 5**. Press.

2½"

2½"

DIAGRAM 5

Patchwork Points Border

STEP 1. For the top and bottom, sew eight 4½ × 2½-inch corner triangle units together to make two strips with four triangle units each. See **Diagram 6**. Press.

STEP 2. Referring to the photo on page 252 for placement of the gold and black triangles, fit, pin, and sew the patchwork points border strips to the top and bottom. Press the seams toward the patchwork points border.

STEP 3. For the sides, sew the remaining ten 4½ × 2½-inch corner triangle units together to make two strips with five triangle units each. See **Diagram 7**. Press.

STEP 4. Referring to the photo on page 252 for placement of the gold and black triangles, sew a 2½-inch corner triangle unit to each end of the two patchwork points border strips from Step 3. See **Diagram 8**. Press.

STEP 5. Fit, pin, and sew the patchwork points border strips to the sides. Press.

Layering the Banner

Arrange and baste the backing, batting, and top together, following the directions in "Layering the Quilt" on page 275. Trim the batting and backing to ¼ inch from the raw edges of the banner top.

Binding the Banner

Using the four 2¾ × 42-inch binding strips, follow the directions for "Binding the Quilt" on page 275–276.

Finishing Stitches

Machine or hand quilt in the seam lines of the accent border, checkerboard squares, and patchwork points. Quilt a 1-inch diagonal grid in the background.

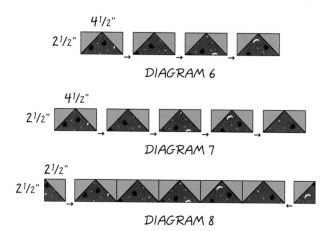

4½"

2½"

DIAGRAM 6

4½"

2½"

DIAGRAM 7

2½"

2½"

DIAGRAM 8

Making the Stocking

STEP 1. Allowing for ¼-inch seams on the raw edges, use the marking pencil to write a name on the 7¾ × 4-inch stocking top. Use two strands of embroidery floss and a running stitch to sew the name.

STEP 2. Cut out the stocking bottom and lining, using the pattern on pages 263–265. Using a ¼-inch seam, sew the stocking top to the stocking bottom. Press the seam toward the stocking top.

STEP 3. Position the stocking front and lining with right sides together, and pin them in place. Sew around the edges, leaving a 4-inch opening for turning. Trim the corners, clip the curves, turn the stocking right side out, hand stitch the opening closed, and press.

STEP 4. Refer to "Quick-Fuse Appliqué" on page 270–271. Trace the heel and toe from the appliqué patterns on page 261 and fuse them to the stocking. Be sure to use a lightweight, sewable fusible web.

STEP 5. Use two strands of embroidery floss and a running stitch to sew the center lines on the heel and toe. Use two strands of embroidery floss to blanket stitch the straight edges of the heel and toe. Leaving the top edge unstitched, use the pearl cotton to blanket stitch around the outside edges of the stocking.

STEP 6. Trace four small holly leaves (two fronts and two backs) from the pattern on page 258. For each holly leaf, position the front and back with wrong sides together. Use two strands of embroidery floss and a running stitch to sew around the edges of each leaf, leaving a small opening for stuffing. Lightly stuff each leaf with the polyester fiberfill, and continue stitching. Sew a running stitch in the center of the leaf.

STEP 7. Refer to "Making Yo-yos" on pages 272–273. Make three yo-yo berries from the pattern on page 258. When making yo-yos out of felt or wool, do not turn under the seam allowance as you gather.

STEP 8. Position and sew the two holly leaves and three yo-yo berries to the stocking, referring to the **Door Banner Layout** below for placement.

STEP 9. Position, pin, and hand sew the stocking to the banner, leaving the top edge open.

Hanging the Banner

STEP 1. To make hanging tabs, fold the 2½ × 32-inch gold print strip in half lengthwise with right sides together. Sew a ¼-inch seam on the edge opposite the fold, turn the strip right side out, and press. Topstitch along the edge of both sides. Cut the strip into four 8-inch pieces. Fold each piece in half, and stitch a ¼-inch seam along the cut edges. Turn each tab, and press it with the seam at the bottom, inside the tab. Space the tabs evenly across the top of the banner back. Hand stitch the tabs in place.

STEP 2. Make 8 holly leaves and 12 yo-yo berries, following the directions in Steps 6 and 7 under "Making the Stocking," above. Sew the holly leaves and berries to the tabs.

STEP 3. Refer to the directions for Felt Ornaments on the opposite page to make one left-facing cardinal and one right-facing cardinal. Insert the dowel through the banner tabs. Glue one cardinal to each end of the dowel.

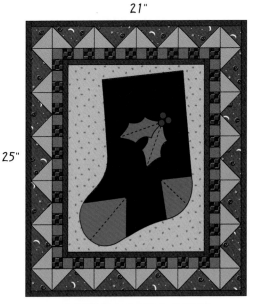

21"

25"

DOOR BANNER LAYOUT

Felt Ornaments

(See the ornaments on the tree in the photo on page 252.)

Materials

Scraps of several coordinated
   fabrics
Felt for backing
Fusible web
Pinking shears
#3 pearl cotton
Glue gun and glue sticks
Raffia
Assorted buttons

Assembly

STEP 1. Refer to "Quick-Fuse Appliqué" on pages 270–271. Trace assorted holly leaves, stars, and cardinals from the appliqué patterns on pages 258–262. Fuse each design to the wrong side of the selected fabric and cut it out. Fuse this shape to the felt background, and cut it out approximately ¼ inch from the edges with pinking shears.

STEP 2. For the holly leaf, use the pearl cotton and a running stitch to sew a vein in the center of the leaf. For the stars, glue a raffia bow and button to the front.

STEP 3. To make a hanger, cut an 8- to 10-inch length of pearl cotton. Fold it in half and knot the ends together. Glue the knotted end to the back of the ornament.

Christmas Garland

(See the garland on the tree in the photo on page 252.)

Materials

Scraps of several coordinated
   fabrics
Felt for backing
Fusible web
Pinking shears
#3 pearl cotton
Glue gun and glue sticks
Heavyweight jute
Assorted buttons

Assembly

STEP 1. Make as many holly leaves and cardinals as desired for your garland, following the directions for Felt Ornaments, above.

STEP 2. Cut the jute to the desired garland length. Position the holly leaves and cardinals on the jute, and glue them in place. Glue a button to the top of each set of holly leaves.

Rustic Holiday Swag

(See the swag above the door in the photo on page 252.)

Materials

Scraps of several coordinated
  fabrics
Felt for backing
Fusible web
Pinking shears
#3 pearl cotton
Glue gun and glue sticks
Purchased twig and vine swag
Assorted buttons

Assembly

STEP 1. Make the large star, cardinals, and small holly leaves, following the directions for Felt Ornaments on page 257.

STEP 2. Position the star, cardinals, and holly leaves on the swag, referring to the photo on page 252. Glue them in place. Glue a button to the top of the holly leaves.

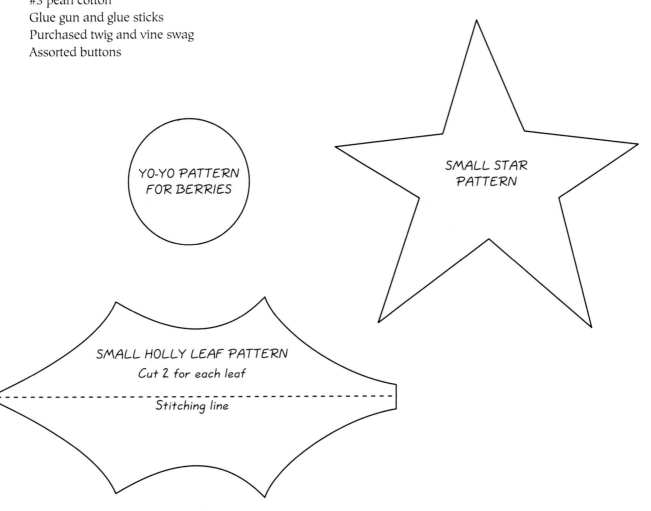

YO-YO PATTERN
FOR BERRIES

SMALL STAR
PATTERN

SMALL HOLLY LEAF PATTERN
Cut 2 for each leaf

Stitching line

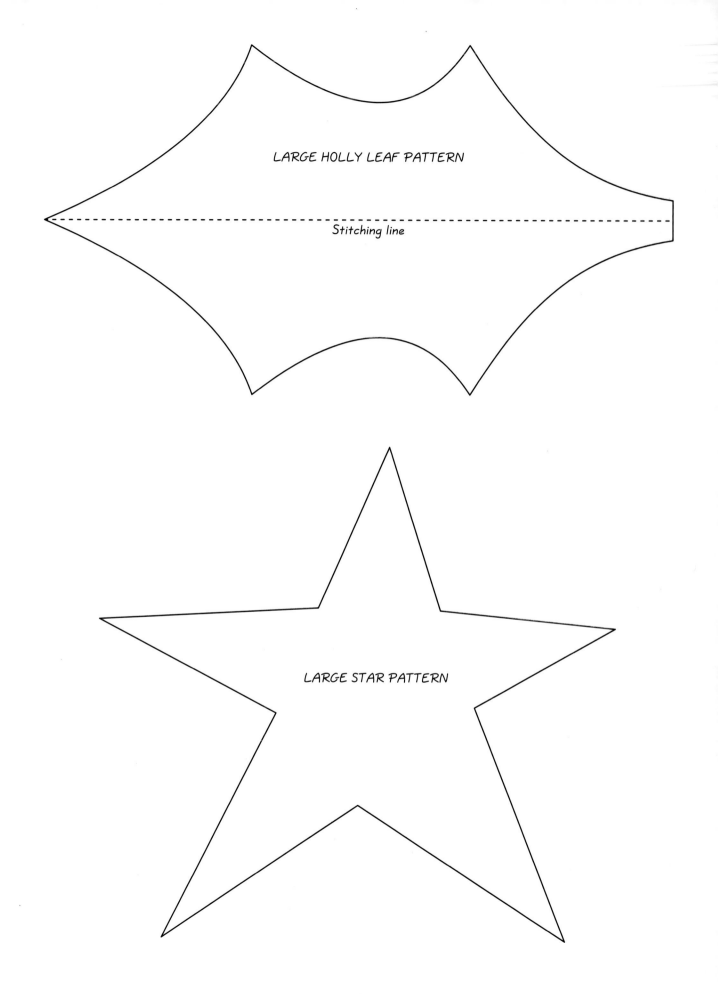

LARGE HOLLY LEAF PATTERN

Stitching line

LARGE STAR PATTERN

259

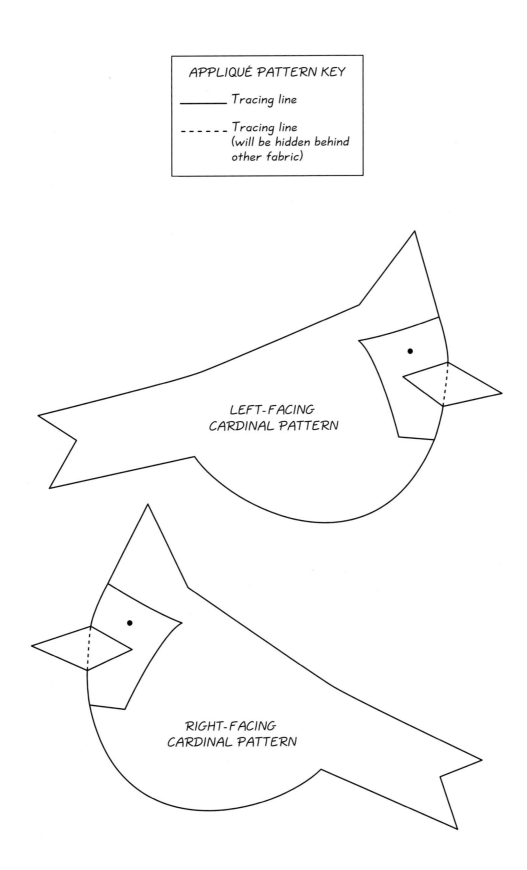

APPLIQUÉ PATTERN KEY

———— Tracing line

- - - - - Tracing line
(will be hidden behind
other fabric)

LEFT-FACING
CARDINAL PATTERN

RIGHT-FACING
CARDINAL PATTERN

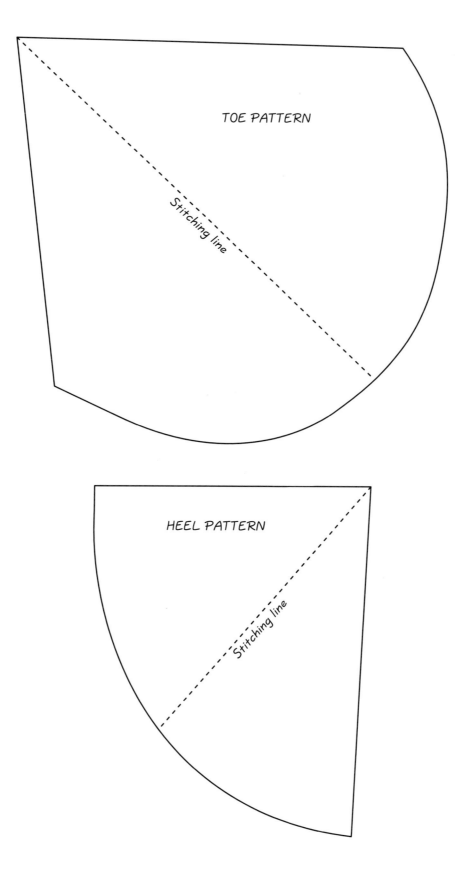

TOE PATTERN

Stitching line

HEEL PATTERN

Stitching line

TREETOP STAR PATTERN

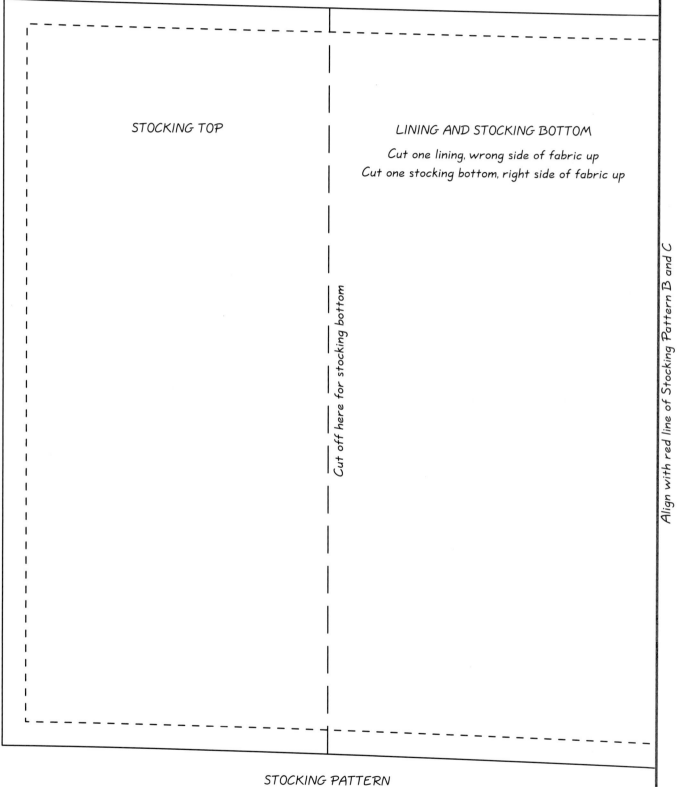

STOCKING TOP

LINING AND STOCKING BOTTOM

Cut one lining, wrong side of fabric up

Cut one stocking bottom, right side of fabric up

Cut off here for stocking bottom

Align with red line of Stocking Pattern B and C

STOCKING PATTERN
A

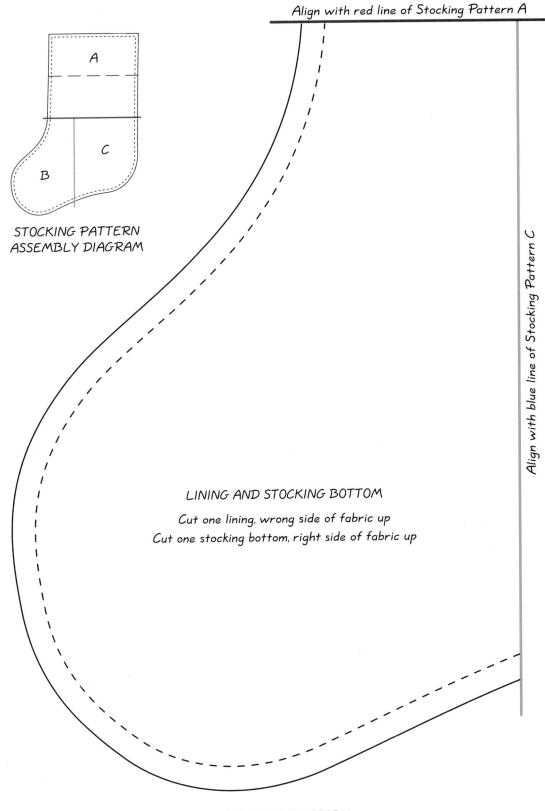

STOCKING PATTERN
ASSEMBLY DIAGRAM

Align with red line of Stocking Pattern A

Align with blue line of Stocking Pattern C

LINING AND STOCKING BOTTOM

Cut one lining, wrong side of fabric up
Cut one stocking bottom, right side of fabric up

STOCKING PATTERN
B

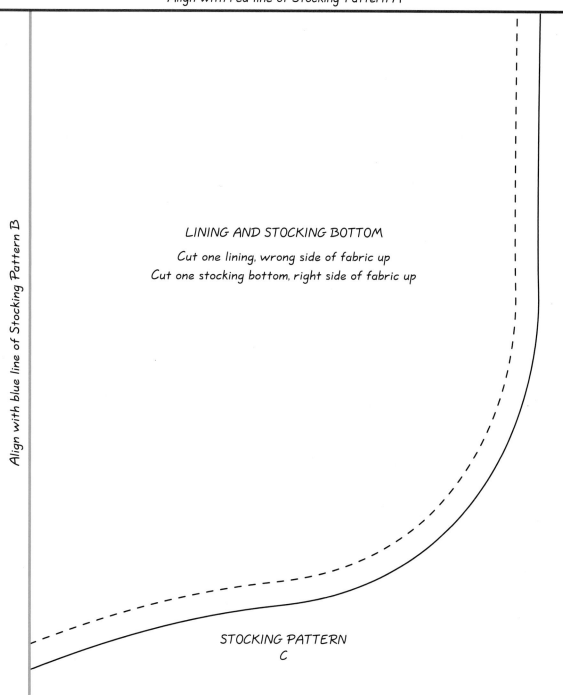

Align with red line of Stocking Pattern A

Align with blue line of Stocking Pattern B

LINING AND STOCKING BOTTOM

Cut one lining, wrong side of fabric up
Cut one stocking bottom, right side of fabric up

STOCKING PATTERN
C

QUICK COUNTRY QUILTING BASICS

Investing in the appropriate tools and learning the correct techniques will ensure that your projects go together quickly and accurately. Be sure to read and understand the techniques before you start any of the projects in this book. Refer to these pages whenever you need a refresher on any details.

CUTTING AND PIECING

In this section, I list all the tools and supplies you need to get started quilting. I also explain rotary cutting and simple sewing techniques that will help you piece your quilt together in no time at all!

What You Need for Cutting and Piecing

Sewing Machine: You need a sewing machine that has a good, reliable straight stitch for piecing. For machine appliqué, it should do a nice, even zigzag stitch.

Rotary Cutter and Cutting Mat: Rotary cutters are available in quilt shops, in fabric stores, and through mail-order catalogs. I prefer the 45 mm blade. A bigger blade gives you more control and lasts longer.

You should never use a rotary cutter without a cutting mat. The cutting mat is the surface on which you lay your fabric before cutting. The mat protects the tabletop as well as the blade of your cutter. Get the largest size mat you have room for. The 24 × 36-inch mat is an all-around good size.

See-Through Ruler: There are many shapes and sizes of these rigid plastic rulers on the market. To start out, I recommend a 6 × 24-inch ruler with a 45 degree angle line marked on it.

Sewing Thread: Select good-quality thread for piecing. Use beige or gray when piecing light fabrics, and dark gray when piecing dark fabrics.

Iron, Ironing Board, and Towel: Use your iron on the Cotton setting and keep the soleplate clean. (See "Pressing Advice" on page 269 for more details on pressing seams.)

Seam Ripper: When fitting pieced borders, a seam ripper is the perfect tool to remove extra pieces.

Scissors: Although most fabric cutting for my projects is done with a rotary cutter, you will also need a good, sharp pair of scissors.

Rotary Cutting

If this is the first time you will be using a rotary cutter, read through these directions carefully, and practice on scrap fabrics. Precise cutting is the first step in precision sewing. Take time to measure and cut your strips and pieces accurately. Begin by prewashing and pressing your fabrics. Be certain that you line your ruler up precisely with the edges of your fabric.

In the project directions, the length for a strip cut across the width is 42 inches. Variation in fabric widths has been considered in the yardage and cutting dimensions. If your fabric is less than 40 inches wide, you may need to purchase extra yardage and cut an extra strip.

STEP 1. After washing and pressing your fabric, refold selvage to selvage. Make sure the fabric is straight. Position the folded fabric so that the selvage edges are facing away from you and the folded edge is facing toward you. See **Diagram 1**.

Selvage edges

Fold

DIAGRAM 1

STEP 2. Use your see-through ruler as a cutting guide. Align one of the horizontal lines of the ruler with the folded edge of the fabric so that the ruler is square with the fabric. See **Diagram 2**. Using some pressure, hold the ruler in position, and use the rotary cutter to trim off the uneven edges on the right end of the fabric. Stop about halfway through the cut to move your hand up on the ruler. This will help to keep the ruler from slipping. You should now have a perfectly straight edge of fabric.

6" × 24" ruler

Selvage edges

Fold

Trim off uneven edges

DIAGRAM 2

STEP 3. Rotate your fabric so that the cut edges are on your left. To move your fabric, simply rotate your cutting mat. If you pick up the fabric, you risk disturbing the layers.

STEP 4. Determine the width of the first strip you want to cut. Align that line on the ruler with the cut edges of the fabric. For example, if the strip is 3 inches wide by 42 inches long, align the 3-inch line on the ruler directly over the cut edge of the fabric. A horizontal line of the ruler should also line up with the folded edge. See **Diagram 3.** When the ruler is lined up perfectly with the cut edge and the fold, hold the ruler in position, and cut.

Fold

Selvage edges

DIAGRAM 3

STEP 5. After cutting the strips, many projects require you to make a second cut from those strips. You can leave your strip folded in half so that you can cut more than one piece at a time. Lay the ruler on top of the strip. Line up one of the horizontal lines on your ruler with the long edge of your strip. Trim off the selvage end of the strip to square and straighten the edge of the fabric. See **Diagram 4.** Rotate the fabric so that this cut end is on the left. Cut the pieces as specified in the project. See **Diagram 5.**

Notes for Lefties

If you're left-handed, as I am, it may be more comfortable to measure and make your cuts from the right end of the folded fabric. Simply reverse the directions in Steps 2 and 3. Trim off the uneven edges on the left end of the fabric in Step 2. Rotate the fabric so that the trimmed edges are on your right in Step 3. Keep in mind that the diagrams are drawn for right-handers.

Fold

Trim off selvages

DIAGRAM 4

DIAGRAM 5

Assembly Line Piecing

For the quickest piecing, apply the principles of an assembly line to your sewing. By repeating the same

step over and over, you will make your piecing quick and efficient.

Let's say you are working on a quilt that has 12 blocks. The first step directs you to sew together two squares. You repeat this step of sewing the squares together 12 times (once for each block). As you proceed through the rest of the assembly steps, all of your blocks will take shape at the same time and will be completed all at once.

Continuous-Seam Technique

Any time you are using the assembly line method to piece your blocks, you can use the continuous-seam method of sewing them together.

Line up all the same pieces for the first step for each block next to your sewing machine. With right sides together, stitch the first two pieces together. Leave them where they are. Place the next set of pieces directly behind the set you have just sewn, and continue sewing. Add each set without breaking your seam until you have joined all the sets together.

You will end up with a long chain of pieces joined together by thread. See **Diagram 6.** Clip the threads between the pieces, and press.

DIAGRAM 6

Precise Piecing

To achieve precise piecing, take your time, be patient, and make sure you are sewing with an exact ¼-inch seam allowance.

Mark the throat plate on your sewing machine with masking tape exactly ¼ inch from the center of the needle. Be sure to make a test after your tape is positioned. If you adhere a few layers of tape, the tape will create a ridge to guide your fabric as you sew. Press as you sew to make sure your seams lie flat.

You may want to look for a specialty ¼-inch foot. Check with your sewing machine manufacturer to see if such a foot is made for your model. If not, there is a universal foot called the Little Foot that can be used with most machines.

In each project, block measurements are indicated after the piecing instructions. It is important that your blocks match these measurements.

Making Quick Corner Triangles

I use an easy technique to simplify the construction of pieces with triangles in one or more corners. Quick corner triangles are formed by simply sewing fabric squares to other squares and rectangles.

STEP 1. With a pencil and ruler, lightly draw a diagonal line from corner to corner on the wrong side of the fabric square that will form the triangle. This will be your sewing line. See **Diagram 7**.

Sewing line

DIAGRAM 7

STEP 2. With right sides together, place the square on the corresponding piece. Matching raw edges, pin the pieces in place, and sew on the drawn diagonal line.

STEP 3. Trim off the excess fabric, leaving a ¼-inch seam allowance. See **Diagram 8**. Press all seams toward the triangles, except when otherwise indicated. Measure each piece after adding the corner triangle. The dimensions should be the same size as the piece you started with before adding the square.

Trim ¼" away from sewing line   Finished corner triangle unit

DIAGRAM 8

Speedy Strips

With this very easy technique, you will be able to assemble checkerboards and multicolor patchwork or scrap borders in no time flat. The directions for each project will tell you the number of strips to cut and which fabrics to use to create the required strip sets.

Sew the strips together along the long edges, alternating the fabrics as directed. As you add

Pressing Advice

To prepare your ironing board for pressing, lay a terry cloth towel on the ironing board. It will provide a cushion to absorb the indentations that your seam allowances make on the front of your quilt block or top. The nap of the towel also helps prevent distortion of your fabrics when pressing.

Always press after each sewing step. First, iron the unit in the closed position (right sides together) to set the stitches. Next, open the unit and carefully finger press the seam. Then, use an iron to set the seam. With the unit right side up, bring the iron straight down on the seam. Be careful not to stretch the unit out of shape by moving the iron with too much force across your fabrics. I prefer to use a steam iron on the Cotton setting.

The arrows in the project diagrams indicate pressing direction for each step. By following these arrows, you will ensure that your seams lie flat.

each strip, always pause to press the seam. Press the seams toward the darker fabric or all in the same direction. Change sewing direction with each strip sewn. It will help avoid the warping that can occur when sewing several long strips together.

Once you have joined all the strips, you will have a large strip set. The project directions will then tell you how to cut and resew the strip set. (See "Pieced Borders" on pages 273–274 for more details on making checkerboard, patchwork, and scrap borders.)

APPLIQUÉ

Most of the appliqué projects that I've included in this book are designed for the quick-fuse technique using fusible web. A simple stroke of the iron fuses designs in place on a background. As a general guide, designs with very small pieces use the quick-fuse appliqué technique with no stitching. Designs with larger pieces can be done with machine appliqué or a hand blanket stitch.

What You Need for Appliqué

Sewing Thread: For machine appliqué, use a thread that is specifically meant for machine embroidery or a good-quality, all-purpose thread. For blanket stitch embroidery, use a good-quality embroidery floss.

Needles: Use an embroidery needle for blanket stitch embroidery.

Scissors: Use good-quality, sharp scissors for cutting designs out of fused fabric. It is nice to have two sizes of scissors, large ones for bigger pieces and smaller embroidery scissors for little pieces.

Iron: I recommend an iron without an automatic shut-off when working with quick-fuse appliqué.

Fusible Web: This paper-backed fusible adhesive is sold in precut packets or on bolts at most fabric and quilting stores. There are lightweight and heavyweight types. If you plan to do machine appliqué or a blanket stitch, use a lighter weight, *sewable fusible web*. For quick-fuse appliqué projects with edges that will not be sewn, use a heavier weight, *nonsewable fusible web*.

Tear-Away Fabric Stabilizer: Use tear-away stabilizer (sold with interfacings, under names like Stitch-N-Tear) behind the background fabric when doing machine appliqué. This keeps your fabrics from puckering and helps you achieve an even stitch.

Permanent Fine-Point Felt Pen: Use this type of pen to draw details such as eyes, noses, and mouths on various appliqué designs.

Embroidery Floss: Embroidery floss is used for the blanket stitch appliqué. Use black for an old-fashioned look, or coordinate floss color with your appliqué fabrics.

Quick-Fuse Appliqué

This is the quickest and easiest way to do appliqué. If you plan to machine stitch or do a blanket stitch, be sure to use a lightweight, sewable fusible web. For appliqué projects that will not be sewn, use a heavyweight, nonsewable fusible web.

STEP 1. Trace each of the parts of the selected appliqué design individually onto the paper side of the fusible web. Since you can see through the fusible web, you can lay it directly over the design in the book and trace the parts. The patterns are always the reverse of the finished design.

STEP 2. Using sharp paper scissors, cut loosely around the traced shapes on the fusible web, as shown in **Diagram 1**. Do not cut along the lines at this point.

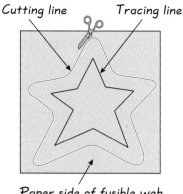

Cutting line   Tracing line

Paper side of fusible web

DIAGRAM 1

STEP 3. Check the manufacturer's instructions for the proper iron setting to use with that brand of fusible web. Fuse each piece of fusible web to the *wrong* side of your selected fabrics. Place the fusible web with the paper side up and the webbing side against your fabric.

STEP 4. When all the pieces are fused, cut out the appliqué shapes

following the tracing lines. See **Diagram 2**. Remove the paper backing from the fusible web. A thin fusing film will remain on the wrong side of the fabric.

Wrong side of fabric   Cut on tracing line

DIAGRAM 2

STEP 5. Arrange and center all the pieces of the appliqué design on the background fabric. Allow ¼ inch for the seam allowances on the edges of the background fabric if you are appliquéing before piecing. Refer to the appliqué

pattern as you position the pieces; the dotted lines indicate where certain pieces should be placed underneath others. When everything is arranged, fuse the pieces in position with your iron. If you used a heavyweight, nonsewable fusible web, you're done. See "Machine Appliqué" below or "Blanket Stitch Appliqué" on page 272 if you plan to stitch the edges of your appliqué pieces.

Machine Appliqué

This technique may be your best choice for projects you would like to launder. You can use a small, narrow zigzag stitch, a satin stitch, blanket stitch, or another decorative stitch. Use an appliqué foot if your machine has one. Always practice first to adjust your machine settings.

STEP 1. Fuse all the appliqué pieces in place on the background fabric, as directed in "Quick-Fuse Appliqué" on the opposite page.

STEP 2. To use tear-away stabilizer, cut a piece large enough to cover the area you'll be stitching. Pin the stabilizer to the wrong side of the background fabric in the stitching area. This keeps your fabrics from puckering and helps you do an even appliqué stitch.

STEP 3. Coordinate several thread colors to match the various appliqué fabric colors. Use these for the top threads, changing them as needed. If you can loosen your bobbin thread tension, you may be able to use a neutral-color bobbin thread for all of the appliqué.

Special Tips for Quick-Fuse Appliqué

- Laundering is NOT recommended for quick-fused wallhangings, ornaments, and other projects.

- When working with very small pieces, use a straight pin to move all your pieces into place.

- The Appliqué Pressing Sheet by Bear Thread Designs is helpful in positioning appliqué designs. To use the pressing sheet, trace the appliqué design onto a plain sheet of

paper; then retrace it onto the back of that paper. Use this reversed image as a guide for positioning and fusing on the pressing sheet. See "Quilting by Mail" on page 280 for ordering information.

- After fusing, check your iron for residue, and use iron cleaner as needed. Keep a towel on your ironing board to protect both the ironing surface and any clothing that may be ironed later!

Making Yo-yos

STEP 1. Make a template for the desired size yo-yo. Trace around the template on the wrong side of the fabric, and cut out along the line.

STEP 2. Thread a needle and make a double knot at one end. Turning in a ⅛- to ¼-inch seam allowance as you go, sew running stitches close to the folded edge. Your stitches should be ⅛ to 3⁄16 inch long.

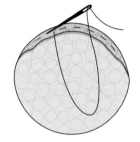

STEP 4. Stitch along the edges of each appliqué piece. When you're finished, pull away the stabilizer from the back of the fabric.

Blanket Stitch Appliqué

This hand-stitching technique is simple and gives a very traditional, old-fashioned look to your quilt. Blanket stitch is best suited to appliqué projects with relatively large, simple pieces.

After you have fused the appliqué design to the background fabric with a lightweight, sewable fusible web, use embroidery floss to outline the edges of the appliqué pieces with the blanket stitch. Use two to three strands of embroidery floss, and refer to **Diagram 3** for guidance on how to do the stitch.

DIAGRAM 3

Decorative Stitches

Backstitch

Thread the needle and knot one end. Bring the needle up at point A, one stitch length away from the beginning of the line you are stitching. Insert the needle down at point B and bring it up at point C. Repeat, inserting the needle at the end of the stitch just completed.

Backstitch

French Knot

Thread the needle and knot one end. Bring the needle up through the fabric at the point where you want the knot. Wrap the thread around the needle two times and hold the thread taut with your finger. Insert the needle back into the fabric close to where it came up. Pull the needle through to the back. The knot will remain on top.

French knot

Stem Stitch

Thread the needle and knot one end. Pull the needle up at point A, insert it down at point B, and then pull it up at point C, a point approximately halfway between points A and B.

Stem stitch

Hint: If the center hole of the yo-yo is too big, try making larger stitches.

TTING IT ALL TOGETHER

Once your blocks are pieced or appliquéd, you are ready to join them together to make the quilt. Lattice strips are the "glue" that holds the individual quilt blocks together, defining and enhancing the overall quilt design. For a smooth, flat quilt top, press all the seams toward the lattice as you sew.

Borders

In many of the projects in this book, the first border is an accent border that sets off the quilt top. The second border is usually wider and picks up one of the main colors or fabrics of the quilt. I often combine several of the quilt fabrics into pieced borders to tie it all together.

Pieced Borders

Pieced borders may look difficult and time-consuming, but looks can be deceiving! Using your rotary cutter and the technique described in "Speedy Strips" on pages 269–270, they go together in no time at all.

A checkerboard border consists of two colors, a light and a dark, and can be one or more rows. Checkerboards add a delightful touch to many quilts. Patchwork borders add a unifying look. They consist of many of the fabrics in the quilt, and each piece is the same size. A scrap border is made from many fabrics in the quilt, but the pieces are of varying widths.

The pieced borders in this book always start with a strip set. Below are some helpful guidelines for making checkerboard, patchwork, and scrap borders. In each project, you will find the necessary yardages and specific cutting and sewing instructions.

STEP 1. Arrange all the strips in a pleasing order, and sew them together side by side along the long edges to create a strip set. As you sew, press all the seams toward the darker fabric or in the same direction. The project directions may have you cut this strip set into halves, thirds, or other increments. See **Diagram 1** for an example of a strip set cut in half. **Diagram 2** shows the halves sewn together and cut again. In this example, the strip set is cut and resewn twice before the border strips are finally cut, as shown in **Diagram 3**.

DIAGRAM 1

DIAGRAM 2

DIAGRAM 3

STEP 2. Use a seam ripper to remove excess pieces as directed in the project. Fit, pin, and sew border strips to the quilt top and bottom, raw edge to raw edge. Press seams away from the pieced border. Fit, pin, and sew border strips to the sides of the quilt. Press.

Choosing a Batting

Batting is made of cotton, polyester, a blend of cotton and polyester, or wool. Cotton batting gives a very flat, traditional look. Some people find that cotton batts are harder to hand quilt but easier to machine quilt than polyester batts.

Since most of my quilts are used for wallhangings, I prefer a thin, lightweight, polyester batting. Thin batting enhances the country look of my quilts—something that thicker, puffier batting won't do.

Polyester batting is easy to hand quilt, and there is no minimum amount of quilting necessary.

Fitting Pieced Borders

Count the pieces in the border strips. With the exception of scrap borders, there should be the same number of pieces in both the top and bottom border strips. The same should be true of the side border strips.

A pieced border strip will have a fair amount of give. Depending on the length, it can be stretched to fit an extra ⅛ to ¼ inch if necessary. You can stretch your strip by gently tugging on it as you sew. Be careful not to overstretch.

If your pieced border strip needs to be adjusted more than ⅛ to ¼ inch, I suggest making your adjustments by taking in or letting out a few of the seams. For example, let's say a 16-piece patchwork border strip is ½ inch too long. Take in eight seams by ¹⁄₁₆ inch. This will not disrupt the overall look of the border.

Because pieced borders will stretch, always pin them in position before sewing them to the quilt top. Press all the seams away from the pieced border.

Marking the Quilt Top

It's easiest to mark the quilting design onto the quilt top before you layer and baste it. I prefer Quilter's Rule or Clover chalk pencils for marking.

Keep your pencil sharp to ensure neat quilting lines. Always mark lightly and do a test on scrap fabric first to make sure that you can clean away any lines that remain after quilting.

Marking a Grid

Your see-through ruler can make this marking quite easy. Using a 45 degree angle line as your reference, mark your first line at a 45 degree angle to the horizontal seam lines of the quilt. See the middle illustration in **Diagram 4** on the opposite page. Then continue to mark lines across your quilt in regular increments. Next, align the 45 degree angle on your ruler with one of the vertical seam lines of the quilt, and mark your grid lines in the other direction. These intersecting lines will form a grid that you can use to quilt nice, straight lines. See the bottom illustration in **Diagram 4** on the opposite page.

Outline Quilting

There are two options for outline quilting pieced blocks, lattice, and borders. You can quilt "in the ditch," which means you add a line of stitches directly next to a seam line. This requires no marking. Quilt along the seam line on the side that does not have the seam allowance. The other option

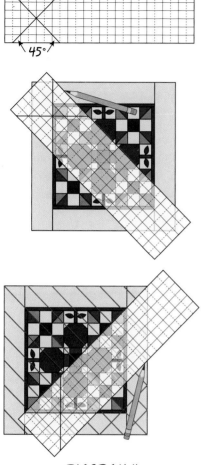

DIAGRAM 4

is to quilt ¼ inch from the seam line. If you do this, I recommend using quilter's ¼-inch masking tape rather than marking. Position the tape and use the edge as your quilting guide. Lift up the tape and reuse it until the stickiness is gone. Do not leave the tape on your quilt for long periods of time, because some sticky residue may remain on the fabric.

To outline appliqué designs, quilt ¹⁄₁₆ to ⅛ inch away from the edges of the designs.

Layering the Quilt

Your next task is to layer the quilt top, batting, and backing, and baste them all together. Refer to **Diagram 5** for all of the layering steps.

DIAGRAM 5

STEP 1. Cut the batting and backing pieces 4 to 6 inches larger than the quilt top.

STEP 2. Press the quilt top and backing. Find a large work area, such as the dining room table. Lay the backing piece down first with the right side facing down. Lay the batting on top of the backing, and smooth it out. Then place the quilt top (face up) on top. Make sure everything is centered and that the backing, batting, and quilt top are flat and smooth.

STEP 3. The backing and batting should extend 2 to 3 inches beyond the quilt top on all four sides, since some shifting may take place during basting and quilting.

STEP 4. To keep the layers in place as you baste, pin them together. Place a pin every 6 inches in vertical and horizontal rows. Begin basting in the center, and work out to the outer edges of the quilt. Baste vertically and horizontally, forming a 3- to 4-inch grid. Don't skimp on this basting. It is critical to keep the layers flat while you are quilting. Last, baste or pin completely around the outer edges of the quilt top.

Basting Hints

Here are some tips for making basting easier.

- Use longer needles than you normally use for hand stitching.
- Thread several needles with extra-long lengths of thread before you begin.
- Take long stitches, 1 to 3 inches in length.
- Divide your quilt into quarters for basting. Work in one quarter at a time, basting from the center to the outer edges.

Binding the Quilt

For the wall-size and other small projects in this book that you will be hand quilting, it's okay to add the binding to the quilt before doing the actual quilting. For larger projects and those that you will be machine quilting, quilt *before* binding.

STEP 1. Cut the binding strips as indicated in the directions for each project. Press the strips in half with wrong sides together.

STEP 2. Trim the batting and backing to ¼ inch from the raw edges of the quilt top.

STEP 3. With the raw edges even, lay the binding strips on the top and bottom edges of the quilt top. Pin the binding strips in place. Sew ¼ inch from the quilt edge. Trim the excess length of the binding, and press the seams toward the binding.

STEP 4. Align the raw edges of the binding strips with the edges of the quilt sides. Repeat the sewing and pressing directions given in Step 3. Your quilt should now look like the one shown in **Diagram 6.**

DIAGRAM 6

STEP 5. Fold the top and bottom bindings around to the back, so that the folded edge of the binding meets the seam line, as shown in **Diagram 7.** Press and pin in position.

DIAGRAM 7

STEP 6. Fold the side bindings around to the back so that the folded edges meet the seam lines. Press and pin in position. Hand stitch all the way around the binding. Stitch closed the little opening at all four corners, as shown in **Diagram 8.**

DIAGRAM 8

Helpful Hints for Attaching Binding

When sewing through several layers, the top layer is pushed forward, and that can stretch and warp your binding. To prevent this from happening, follow these tips.

- Don't skimp on pins when pinning the binding to the quilt.
- Increase the stitch length on your sewing machine.
- Sew at a slow pace.
- Use a walking foot or an even feed attachment if you have one for your machine. It feeds all the layers through at the same rate.

Finishing Small Appliqué Projects

Some of the small appliqué projects direct you to use a self-binding method. You layer the top and

Tools for Hand Quilting

These are the items that you'll need in your sewing basket if you plan to do hand quilting.

Quilting Needles: These are also called betweens. If you are a beginning quilter, I suggest starting with a package of needles with an assortment of sizes. Size 10 is a commonly used size and is the needle I prefer.

Quilting Thread: Be sure to use extrastrong thread made especially for quilting. Choose a quilting thread color that coordinates with the background fabric. If you want your quilting

stitches to show up more, use a contrasting thread color.

Thimble: Choosing a comfortable thimble may require some trial and error before you settle on one you like. I prefer a leather thimble. Look for one with elastic (it stays on your finger better), a slit for your fingernail, and extra reinforcement at the fingertip.

Quilting Hoop or Frame: Hoops or frames hold the three layers taut and smooth while you are quilting, making it less likely that the fabric will pucker or wrinkle under the stitching.

backing with right sides together on top of the batting, stitch around the edges (leaving an opening for turning), turn right side out, and hand stitch the opening closed. For these projects, consider using the same fabric for the backing that you use for the binding. That way, the backing fabric won't stand out if it sneaks around to the front.

Quilting by Hand

The quilting stitch is a series of running stitches made along the lines of the quilting design you have marked. At first, you should concentrate on even stitches; as you gain experience, your stitches will naturally become smaller. Good quilting stitches are small and even.

STEP 1. Cut a length of quilting thread (approximately 18 inches), thread the needle, and knot one end.

STEP 2. About ½ inch from the point where you want to begin stitching, insert the needle through the top layer of fabric. See **Diagram 9.** Bring it up right where you want to take the first stitch. Pull on the thread until the knot rests against the surface of the fabric. With a gentle tug, pull the thread to pop the knot through the fabric, as shown in the diagram. The knot will stay securely anchored in the batting, hidden out of sight. Whenever you need to start a new thread, repeat this procedure to bury the knot.

DIAGRAM 9

STEP 3. Push just the tip of the needle down through the three layers, using the finger with the thimble on your top hand, as shown in **Diagram 10.** As soon as your finger on the underside feels the needle come through, rock it up again toward the surface. (Simultaneously press down on the head of the needle with the thimble finger and push up against the needle tip with a finger on the underside.) See **Diagram 11.**

DIAGRAM 10

DIAGRAM 11

STEP 4. Pull the needle through the fabric using the thumb and forefinger of your top hand. Pull the thread taut, but don't pull it too tight, or the fabric will pucker.

STEP 5. To end a line of stitching, bring the needle up where you want to stop. Wrap the thread around the end of the needle two times. Pull the needle through these circles of thread to form a knot. Push the needle back down through the top of the quilt and pull it up about ½ inch away. Tug on the thread to pop the knot through the top of the fabric and bury it in the batting layer. See **Diagram 12.** Pull on the thread and clip it close to the surface of the quilt. The end should disappear back beneath the quilt top.

DIAGRAM 12

Quilting by Machine

Just like hand quilting, machine quilting takes some practice. I highly recommend using a walking foot or an even feed attachment. It can help avoid the problem of having the three layers bunch up.

Machine quilting works best on smaller projects, like the appliqué wallhangings, where you quilt in the ditch along the borders. If you are trying machine quilting for the first time, keep in mind that the smaller the project, the easier it will be to quilt.

The layering process is the same as for hand quilting. Instead of hand basting, however, use safety pins to hold the layers together while you quilt. Position them so that they won't get in the way of where you plan to quilt. Do all the quilting before you add the binding (unless it is a self-binding).

STEP 1. Coordinate the thread color with the quilt top and coordinate the bobbin thread with the backing fabric.

STEP 2. Set your machine for normal straight stitching. You may want to increase the stitch length for stitching through the three layers. Starting in the center of the quilt and working out toward the edges, machine stitch in the ditch to outline the blocks and borders.

Hanging Sleeves

To make a hanging sleeve, cut a strip approximately 5 inches wide by the width of the quilt. Hem the 5-inch edges by folding under ½ inch and stitching. With right sides together, fold the strip in half lengthwise, and sew the length of the strip. Turn the sleeve right side out and press. Hand stitch the sleeve to the back of your quilt, and run a wooden dowel through it.

Quilt Labels

Be sure to add a label to the back of your quilt. Include your name, the name of the quilt, the year you made it, and where you made it. Use a permanent fine-point felt pen. Attach the label to the back of the quilt with your preferred appliqué method.

ACKNOWLEDGMENTS

This book was created with the combined talents of many people. I would like to thank and acknowledge all the dedicated and creative people who had a hand in making this book a reality. This book was my most ambitious undertaking yet, but it was worth the effort. I am very proud of it and of all those who worked diligently to make the projects and the rooms works of art.

Special thanks go to Kelly Fisher, Senior Editor, who coordinated the efforts of the Mumm's the Word editorial and sewing team. This includes Jodi Gosse and Geri Zimmer, Creative and Editorial Assistants, and Candy Huddleston, Seamstress. Not only did they sew all the beautiful projects in the book, but they also spent many a tedious hour poring over every word and number to ensure that the instructions were clear, complete, and accurate. Thanks also for sharing ideas and creativity.

I would also like to thank Nancy Kirkland, our freelance Seamstress and Quilter, and Mairi Fischer, our freelance Hand Quilter, for their dedication and fine stitching.

Jackie Saling, Art Studio Assistant (also known as my right-hand assistant), is a tremendously hard worker and has never uttered the words, "I can't do it." She never knows what I'm going to ask her to do, but she's always willing. Even the not-so-glamorous assignments, such as coordinating and hauling props to photo locations and back again, are met with a positive attitude. Jackie is a very accomplished painter. She prepared many photo props and consulted on all the room-decorating projects.

Marcia Smith, Art Director, styled and directed many of the photos. The two-page spreads for the part openers were the most complex, and she made sure that they all worked and looked beautiful. She coordinated many of the shoots and attended to all the details. Thanks to Marcia for all her planning and vision.

A very special thank-you goes to Bob Barros of Barros & Barros for creating the beautiful photographs throughout the book. He always went the extra mile on every shoot and took the time to perfect the lighting to make the projects and rooms glow.

Lois Hansen, Mark Meyer, and Barb Chase, Photo Assistants, packed up and hauled endless supplies of lights, cords, power packs, and other equipment to all our photo locations. They helped to coordinate props and find the right locations to capture the right look. Thanks to all of them for their tireless efforts and for bringing snacks to the shoots!

Lynn Guier and Bill Mound, freelance Interior Designers, designed and remodeled the master bedroom, Murphy's bedroom, and the birdhouse bathroom in my home for this book. They are extremely inspired, resourceful, and wonderful to collaborate with. They spent many days and nights in my home! I thank them for sharing their enormous talents.

Thanks go to Nancy Eubanks, freelance Painter, for sharing her skills and artistic flair in custom painting the kitchen chairs and the sofa table in the dining room. Thanks to Retta Warehime, friend and fellow quilter, who sewed the dust ruffle and draperies for the master bedroom. Melcina Siebert deserves praise for her stellar work in reupholstering the chairs for the master bedroom. She used my home decor fabrics and added the crowning touch with double piping.

Lou McKee, Artist, and Sandy Ayers, freelance Artist, lent gifted hands in helping me paint the pages for "Country Decorating with Debbie Mumm," as well as some pen-and-ink illustrations.

I want to add a thank-you to all my other friends, family, and staff whose support and enthusiasm make it possible and fun for me to create.

Lastly, a very special thank-you to the talented Suzanne Nelson and Ellen Pahl, Editors, and Carol Angstadt, Book Designer, of Rodale Press, who lent their skills, creativity, and dedication to the book. I very much appreciate the opportunity to work with you. I thank them for supporting and encouraging me and having faith in me to create this book.

QUILTING BY MAIL

Sources for Products and Supplies Mentioned in the Book

Angel Hair

The Quilting B
224 Second Street SE
Cedar Rapids, IA 52401
(319) 363-1643

Note: Yarns #05 and #23 were used for the angel hair in the Angel Quilt on page 33. In the Angel Table Runner on page 38, yarn #26 was used for the angel hair.

Appliqué Pressing Sheet

Product #206
Bear Thread Designs
Route 1, Box 1640
Belgrade, MO 63622
(573) 766-5695

Debbie Mumm's Ceramic Buttons

Gay Bowles Sales, Inc.
Mill Hill
P.O. Box 1060
Janesville, WI 53547-1060
(800) 447-1332
Fax (608) 754-0665

Narrow Loop Turner or Bow Whip

Nancy's Notions
333 Beichl Avenue
P.O. Box 683
Beaver Dam, WI 53916-0683
(800) 833-0690

Sources for General Quilting Supplies

Keepsake Quilting
Route 25B, P.O. Box 1618
Centre Harbor, NH 03226-1618
(800) 865-9458

The Quilt Farm
P.O. Box 7877
Saint Paul, MN 55107
(800) 435-6201

Quilts and Other Comforts
P.O. Box 2500
Louisiana, MO 63353
(800) 881-6624

PHOTOGRAPHY LOCATIONS

Thank you to all the folks who generously allowed us in their homes with vanfuls of photo props and equipment.

The lovely dining room was in the home of Judy and George Orr in Spokane, Washington.

The family room was photographed in a cabin on Hayden Lake, Idaho.

The kitchen in the interior and on the cover was shot in Triber's Barn antique shop, owned by Helen and Darrell Triber, in Otis Orchards, Washington.

The bathroom, bedroom, and boy's room were in the home of Debbie Mumm in Spokane, Washington.

The girl's room was in the home of Lois Hansen in Spokane, Washington.

The nooks and crannies were in the home of Candy and Mark Weaver in Spokane, Washington.

The front door was the entryway to the home of my neighbors Lori and Joe Orr in Spokane, Washington.

INDEX

METRIC EQUIVALENCY CHART

mm=millimeters
cm=centimeters

Yards to Meters

YARDS	METERS	YARDS	METERS	YARDS	METERS	YARDS	METERS	YARDS	METERS
1/8	0.11	2 1/8	1.94	4 1/8	3.77	6 1/8	5.60	8 1/8	7.43
1/4	0.23	2 1/4	2.06	4 1/4	3.89	6 1/4	5.72	8 1/4	7.54
3/8	0.34	2 3/8	2.17	4 3/8	4.00	6 3/8	5.83	8 3/8	7.66
1/2	0.46	2 1/2	2.29	4 1/2	4.11	6 1/2	5.94	8 1/2	7.77
5/8	0.57	2 5/8	2.40	4 5/8	4.23	6 5/8	6.06	8 5/8	7.89
3/4	0.69	2 3/4	2.51	4 3/4	4.34	6 3/4	6.17	8 3/4	8.00
7/8	0.80	2 7/8	2.63	4 7/8	4.46	6 7/8	6.29	8 7/8	8.12
1	0.91	3	2.74	5	4.57	7	6.40	9	8.23
1 1/8	1.03	3 1/8	2.86	5 1/8	4.69	7 1/8	6.52	9 1/8	8.34
1 1/4	1.14	3 1/4	2.97	5 1/4	4.80	7 1/4	6.63	9 1/4	8.46
1 3/8	1.26	3 3/8	3.09	5 3/8	4.91	7 3/8	6.74	9 3/8	8.57
1 1/2	1.37	3 1/2	3.20	5 1/2	5.03	7 1/2	6.86	9 1/2	8.69
1 5/8	1.49	3 5/8	3.31	5 5/8	5.14	7 5/8	6.97	9 5/8	8.80
1 3/4	1.60	3 3/4	3.43	5 3/4	5.26	7 3/4	7.09	9 3/4	8.92
1 7/8	1.71	3 7/8	3.54	5 7/8	5.37	7 7/8	7.20	9 7/8	9.03
2	1.83	4	3.66	6	5.49	8	7.32	10	9.14

Inches to Millimeters and Centimeters

INCHES	MM	CM	INCHES	CM	INCHES	CM
1/8	3	0.3	9	22.9	30	76.2
1/4	6	0.6	10	25.4	31	78.7
3/8	10	1.0	11	27.9	32	81.3
1/2	13	1.3	12	30.5	33	83.8
5/8	16	1.6	13	33.0	34	86.4
3/4	19	1.9	14	35.6	35	88.9
7/8	22	2.2	15	38.1	36	91.4
1	25	2.5	16	40.6	37	94.0
1 1/4	32	3.2	17	43.2	38	96.5
1 1/2	38	3.8	18	45.7	39	99.1
1 3/4	44	4.4	19	48.3	40	101.6
2	51	5.1	20	50.8	41	104.1
2 1/2	64	6.4	21	53.3	42	106.7
3	76	7.6	22	55.9	43	109.2
3 1/2	89	8.9	23	58.4	44	111.8
4	102	10.2	24	61.0	45	114.3
4 1/2	114	11.4	25	63.5	46	116.8
5	127	12.7	26	66.0	47	119.4
6	152	15.2	27	68.6	48	121.9
7	178	17.8	28	71.1	49	124.5
8	203	20.3	29	73.7	50	127.0